TEACHING SECOND LANGUAGE READING FOR ACADEMIC PURPOSES

TEACHING SECOND LANGUAGE READING FOR ACADEMIC PURPOSES

FRAIDA DUBIN
DAVID E. ESKEY
University of Southern California
WILLIAM GRABE
Northern Arizona University

Editors

SANDRA SAVIGNON
Consulting Editor

ADDISON-WESLEY PUBLISHING COMPANY

Reading, Massachusetts ● Menlo Park, California
Don Mills, Ontario ● Wokingham, England ● Amsterdam
Sydney ● Singapore ● Tokyo ● Madrid ● Bogota
Santiago ● San Juan

THE ADDISON-WESLEY SECOND LANGUAGE PROFESSIONAL LIBRARY SERIES

Sandra J. Savignon
Consulting Editor

HIGGINS, John and JOHNS, Tim
Computers in Language Learning

MOHAN, Bernard A.
Language and Content

SAVIGNON, Sandra J.
Communicative Competence: Theory and Classroom Practice

SAVIGNON, Sandra J. and BERNS, Margie S.
Initiatives in Communicative Language Teaching

SMITH, Stephen M.
The Theater Arts and the Teaching of Second Languages

VENTRIGLIA, Linda
Conversations of Miguel and Maria

WALLERSTEIN, Nina
Language and Culture in Conflict

Library of Congress Cataloging-in-Publication Data
Main entry under title:

Teaching second language reading for academic purposes.

Bibliography: p.
1. Language and languages—Study and teaching (Higher)
2. Reading (Higher education) I. Dubin, Fraida.
II. Eskey, David E. III. Grabe, William.
P53.75.T43 1986   418'.007'11   85-18624
ISBN 0-201-11668-5

ISBN 0-201-11668-5
5 6 7 8 9 10 11 12 13 14-MU-96 95 94 93 92 91

To Our Families

Contents

PART III

Introduction

From a purely theoretical point of view, this volume embodies an interactive approach to the teaching of reading, but the purpose of the book is practical. The eight contributing authors were more motivated by an interest in sharing effective classroom techniques for teaching reading with their colleges in the field of second language teaching than by an interest in any theory of reading. Thus *Teaching Second Language Reading for Academic Purposes,* while firmly grounded in theory, is mainly concerned with the utilization of that theory by practicing teachers, teacher trainers, program administrators, and curriculum developers.

At the same time it is true that during the last few years research in reading has moved beyond strictly top-down models to an interest in interactive models of the process, within which the reading skill is characterized as a simultaneous interaction among a wide range of interlocking skills and processes. The implications of these models have not as yet been brought to the attention of second language reading teachers, and this book constitutes a first step in that direction.

Because reading and the teaching of reading do, however, cover such a vast area, the authors do not attempt to deal with the entire range of possible issues. Nor would it be realistic in one volume to present an encyclopedia of information from which the critical issues might be sorted. We have therefore limited the scope of this book to reading for academic purposes. While there are implications for other kinds of reading programs, we are primarily concerned with teaching reading to students who will be reading for further educational achievement. Similarly, this book is not intended to address the problem of teaching illiterate students how to read. We do not deal with reading readiness instruction, initial grapheme/phoneme correspondences, or the phonics/whole word issue — all concerns that have been dealt with extensively elsewhere.

The plan of the book moves from theory to instruction, then into wider perspectives. The first two chapters provide a theory of reading and explore the potential of that theory for instruction: David Eskey establishes a theoretical base and introduces issues of particular concern to second language teachers. William Grabe investigates the general implications of reading theory for reading curricula and instruction.

Chapters 3, 4, and 5 provide detailed descriptions of specific reading courses at different levels and for different purposes: Fredricka Stoller describes the function of a reading lab for use with students at a low intermediate level. Denise Mahon furthers the discussion by focusing on reading rate development with intermediate students. And Linda Jensen treats advanced skills in the context of a comprehensive language course.

The last three chapters are devoted to areas not usually considered in discussions of second language reading: Fraida Dubin discusses issues of textual analysis which affect the ways in which teachers select, adapt, and present reading selections to their students. Sharon Allerson and William Grabe explore the problem of assessing students' reading abilities, whether for placement, diagnostic, proficiency rating, or classroom achievement purposes. And Susan Dever draws together current opinions about the application of computer technology to the teaching of reading in a second language context; at issue is whether the computer will become a major focus of future reading instruction.

Preceding each of the three major parts of the text there are are more detailed overviews, and each of the individual chapters is followed by suggestions for further reading and questions for further study and discussion. Although we have included some references to commercially available teaching materials, we have deliberately kept these to a minimum on the grounds that such references tend to date very quickly. For anyone seeking the best material on the market, systematic and frequent review is a must.

Since it is obviously somewhat unusual for so many authors to collaborate on a single text dealing with a single issue (the book should *not* be read as a collection of readings but as a developing exploration of its subject), a few words about the origins of this book are in order. At the 1983 TESOL convention in Toronto, five of the authors (Eskey, Grabe, Jensen, Mahon, and Stoller), four of whom were colleagues in the American Language Institute of the University of Southern California, offered a two-day mini-course on the teaching of reading at university level. Afterwards a number of the participants urged us to put the content of that course into some kind of printed form, and we began work on the project. At the following year's convention in Houston, two of the remaining authors (Allerson and Dubin), also colleagues at USC, joined us for a colloquium addressing interactive approaches to the teaching of reading, and subsequently joined the project team, as did Susan Dever, a colleague whose work on computer assisted instruction struck us as potentially relevent to our book.

We hope that the result of this collaborative effort — of so many minds working from so many perspectives on one particular problem — is a more comprehensive, but no less unified, text than any single author could have hoped to produce. The logistics of imposing some kind of formal order on the work of so many disparate authors has of course proved to be something of a problem. But we like to believe that whatever we have lost in consistency of style* has been more than offset by the increase in scope and knowledge of detail that eight experienced authors — teachers, administrators, and researchers — have brought to this text. It is intended for the use of all of the above, but primarily, as noted, for teachers or for teachers-in-training, either on the job or in graduate programs leading to careers in the teaching of second languages.

The Editors

ACKNOWLEDGEMENTS

For so many of us to acknowledge our debts to all of the many scholars and teachers who have influenced our thinking in this book would be quite literally impossible. But we would like to single out for thanks Professor James Coady of Ohio University, who first suggested the project and urged us to undertake it; Professor Robert Kaplan, Professor Reynaldo Macias of USC, Professor Steven Sternfeld of the University of Utah, and Carol Chapelle and Jean Zukowski/Faust of Northern Arizona University, who read and commented on particular chapters; and especially Fredricka Stoller, who, as project coordinator, somehow cajoled and threatened the rest of us into producing the manuscript which follows.

---

*Each author speaks in his or her own voice. No attempt has been made to regularize the use of first person, the choice of pronouns for general reference, or other similar matters of linguistic etiquette.

Part I

PART I: OVERVIEW

In these first two chapters, our major concern is to establish a general theory of reading and then to explore the implications of that theory for the teaching and learning of second language reading.

Eskey's chapter addresses the fundamental question of what the second language teacher needs to know about reading—that is, what reading theory has to tell us about the nature of readers and the reading process and, more particularly, about the nature of *second* language readers and reading. This chapter's major subheadings include Reading and Motivation; The Second Language Reader; The Reading Process (including reading and memory); Three Models of the Reading Process (bottom-up, top-down, and interactive); and Reading as Means and End.

Grabe moves the discussion from theory to practice within Richards and Rogers' (1982) comprehensive framework for the description of method in second language teaching—the now familiar Approach/Design/Procedure framework. Under Approach, he deals with such issues as the nature of the process, reading in relation to different languages and cultures, development of skills in first and second languages, and reading versus writing. Under Design, he explores the importance of reading in an academic setting, reading strategies for teaching, questions of curriculum and materials, and the roles of the administrator and the teacher. And under Procedure, he addresses such concerns as implementing curricular objectives in the classroom, kinds of teaching techniques, and achieving a good balance of procedures in the total reading program.

Chapter 1

Theoretical Foundations

David E. Eskey
University of Southern California

1.1 INTRODUCTION

This chapter could just as well have been entitled (more accurately, if less formally) "what every second language teacher needs to know about reading." It does not aim to provide a comprehensive survey of current reading theory and research (for which, see Pearson 1984b) but rather a practical summary of what, in general, we know about readers and the reading process, i.e., what people actually *do* when they read, and, more specifically, what we know about *second* language readers and reading.

1.2 READING AND MOTIVATION

Before turning to the "what" of reading, however, I would like to comment briefly on the even more fundamental question—from the teacher's point of view, at least—of *why* people choose, or don't choose, to read. For any approach to teaching to succeed, no matter how true to the latest "scientific principles," it must take into account the real needs and desires of learners — that rather loosely defined cluster of goals, inclinations, and biases which we call "motivation" — and we must therefore give some thought to what motivates people to read, or not to read, anything.

In the real world — as opposed to the academic world — people who read, read for intellectual profit or pleasure. That is, they believe that the content of whatever they have chosen to read will be useful to them, or will help them to understand the world better, or will give them the special kind of pleasure that comes from the experience of reading literature. For students, of course, there are constraints, called "assignments," on this freedom of choice, but even a secondary, academic goal like "passing the course" provides something like a real-world motivation for reading. Very few students read just to practice their reading, or to build up their general knowledge of a language — both objectives worth pursuing but an unlikely basis for a good reading course. Like other language teachers, reading teachers tend to find their subject fascinating in and for itself, but students in the main do not share this fascination.

What will interest students, if they can be interested, is the *content* of the reading. For most students, no text is primarily interesting as a classic example of a discourse type, or as a context for the use of grammatical devices (although such things can be dealt with in passing), but as a body of useful or stimulating information. In practice, students, like everybody else, read for meaning. For them, the language of a text is just a means to an end. The end is comprehension. Thus the first concern of any reading teacher is to find, or create, a body of material that his particular students might find interesting to read, and then to do everything in his power to relate that material to their real concerns and, most important of all, to make it as comprehensible to them as he can (Cf. Krashen and Terrell 1983:131-142).

1.3 THE SECOND LANGUAGE
READER (1)

Since reading is merely a special case of human language behavior, there is a sense in which (at a fairly high level of generality) all readers are alike, just as all walkers and talkers are alike in relation to creatures which do not walk or talk. In the real world, however, there are different *kinds* of readers, and the differences between them—for example, the differences between first and second language readers — may be of great importance to the teacher of such readers.

Differing cultural conceptions of reading

To begin with, the literate second language reader is a product of a culture which may have very different ideas about reading from those that the unwary teacher takes for granted. Such a student may have completely different conceptions of what reading is, how it should be done, and what it normally is used for from those of the teacher in what might be called the standard American academic setting. The rapid silent reading of many different kinds of texts, some of which the reader has selected for himself, that most of us regard as normal reading behavior for the serious student may, for example, be completely (and literally) foreign to the reader from a culture where reading means reading aloud, with appropriate expression, from a limited number of preselected texts, chosen for their agreed upon religious or cultural significance. And such a reader may, similarly, be confused by our conventional notions of critical reading, in which the reader may be asked to compare conflicting texts and, by means of a questioning-while-reading strategy, to make judgments on the relative validity of those texts. (Why, such a reader may ask, should he be required to read invalid texts at all?) The first job of the teacher of second language readers may therefore be to explain what it is we mean by reading in this culture, and what will be expected of students in our classes. And this may, in turn, entail his promoting, without making invidious comparisons, a whole new point of view on the academic process. New attitudes may have to be developed, and old biases may have to be overcome. The perceptive reading teacher is therefore likely to find that the reading class is a good place to talk about reading.

A little time should be devoted to the subject of what, in this culture, is expected of a reader in an academic setting, and a little to the subject of what, in any setting, the reading process involves — a subject that the teacher should know something about, and to which I now turn.

1.4 THE READING PROCESS: GOOD NEWS AND BAD NEWS

The bad news is that: no one can *teach* anyone how to read, or even how to read more effectively — at least, not in the way that one can teach the names of the U.S. presidents or how to make a Caesar salad. Reading is a complex cognitive skill (no one fully understands it) which we cannot break down into a series of steps that a teacher can take into a classroom and teach. But the good news is that: anyone can *learn* to read, and/or to read more effectively. Human beings are preprogrammed to perform language acts, like listening, speaking, reading, and writing, and if provided with real opportunities, and a minimum of guidance, in a stimulating, non-threatening context, they can learn to do these things with relative ease. Some students will, of course, make better readers than others, but everyone can learn and everyone can improve. The teacher's job is therefore to facilitate what is essentially a natural process, and to do this most effectively, he must develop some understanding of that process — without, however, entertaining the illusion that this kind of understanding will lead to a sure-fire formula for the teaching of reading to any kind of student anywhere at any time.

Comprehension and reading comprehension

The first point to be made about the reading process is that reading comprehension is not essentially different from other kinds of comprehension. The mental tasks involved are not peculiar to reading but fundamental human cognitive acts. Comprehension of any kind depends on knowledge. Comprehension means relating what we don't know, or new information, to what we already know, which is not a random collection of facts but a "theory of the world" (Smith 1982:84) in each of our heads called "cognitive structure." To draw new information from a page of script or print, we must of course have learned to identify the categories and relationships represented in the visual forms on that page (*that* knowledge must be a part of our cognitive structure), but there is nothing especially unusual about learning to identify, and to interpret, visual forms in the world around us. As Frank Smith has observed (1975:1), reading is simply one of the many ways in which human beings go about their basic business of "making sense of the world." The point of all this for the reading teacher is that no matter how well a student may know a language, he cannot read in that language with good comprehension if the subject of the text is one he knows absolutely nothing about and therefore can have no real interest in. Comprehension is always directed and controlled by the needs and purposes of an individual and therefore crucially depends on that individual's having acquired what William Grabe calls a "critical mass" (Chapter 2) of information on the subject of his inquiry, that is, an adequate amount of what is sometimes called "background information" or, more technically, "schemata," a subject to which I will return below. Thus reading comprehension is most likely to occur when students are reading what they want to read, or at least what they see some good reason to read.

The reading process: identification/interpretation

Assuming that these basic conditions have been met — that a student does have a real interest in a subject, knows enough about it, and knows the language well enough to make sense of the text — what will he actually do when he reads it? What do any of us do? Common sense suggests that we read by steadily moving our eyes across the page, identifying clusters of letters as words, then adding word to word to form phrases, clauses, and sentences which we can, finally, decode for meaning. But common sense, as Alfred North Whitehead once observed, is also what tells us that the world is flat. The truth is that we do not read like that at any level. Instead we use our eyes to take in whole chunks of text in a series of short, jerky fixations called *saccades*, and, even more surprisingly, the better readers we are, the less we actually see of the print on the page. Reading is primarily a cognitive process, which means that the brain does most of the work. In reading, that remarkable instrument must, almost simultaneously, take in the information provided by the eyes, relate it to what it already knows about the subject, and thereby construct a full meaning for the text —

which then becomes a part of what it knows about the subject and can thus in turn be used to make sense of what comes next. In so doing the brain of the reader makes use of the *minimum* number of visual cues required to convert printed text to information, just as it does in identifying other objects of vision, like streets, or buildings, or people that it knows. In none of these cases is there any need for the observer to take in every detail that his eyes can see (anyone who tried to do so would soon be overwhelmed), but rather just enough to tell him whom or what he is observing. Thus the key to fluent reading is not a kind of visual gymnastics but, as I have already noted, knowledge. In Smith's concise little aphorism, "what the brain tells the eye" is much more important than "what the eye tells the brain" (1971), provided that the brain has acquired some skill in converting printed language into real language.

This last point is important, for it must not be supposed that there is no skill involved (as Smith and Goodman sometimes seem to imply) in converting an array of marks on a page to the meaningful language those marks represent. Confronted with people and objects that we *know*, we do recognize them instantly, but confronted with less familiar (though equally visible) faces and things, we are slower and less accurate in deciding whom or what we are looking at. Similarly, readers who know the written language well can move from marks on a page to words and phrases quickly, whereas those who do not know this language well may, no matter how clearly they "see" the marks, fail to recognize, or misidentify, the language these marks are meant to evoke. Efficient use of the eyes in reading is not a matter of seeing some quantity of forms but of seeing what is there ("in reading," not "is reading" in this sentence, for example) automatically, in a series of fast and accurate fixations.

Once we have as readers acquired a fair degree of this so-called "automaticity" (for further discussion of this concept, see Samuels and Kamil, 1984), we have most of what it takes to read an appropriate text fluently. Then given the single, nonnegotiable assumption that any text which we sit down to read will make sense, our knowledge of the language in its written form provides us with the key to the identification of the basic forms and meanings of the language of the text. Combined with our general knowledge of the world, and of the particular subject matter of the discourse, this knowledge provides us with certain expectations about both the language and the content of the text. At the level of simple identification, we expect, for example, nouns to follow articles, main clauses to follow subordinate clauses, and words to come in clusters that we call *collocations*. The phrase *court of law*, for instance, suggests such nouns as *lawyer*, *judge*, and *case*, such verbs as *argue*, *convict*, and *appeal*, and such stock phrases as *dissenting opinion* and *the whole truth and nothing but the truth*. At higher cognitive levels, we also expect supporting details to follow generalizations, paragraphing to reflect real divisions in the discourse, and conclusions to follow logically from everthing that has come before. And as we read at these levels, we make predictions based on these expectations to help us interpret the meaning of the text (as we do in constructing other kinds of meaning: imagine, for example, trying to take part in a game of some kind with no knowledge of the rules and thus no means of predicting what might happen next).

The better we are at making such predictions, the less dependent we are on the text itself. Like any sample of natural language, every printed text shows a fairly high degree of redundancy, which readers with automatic recognition skills exploit. Good readers read for meaning — they do not decode as a computer would — which means that they do not actually look at all of every sentence or of every phrase, let alone every word, or letter, or punctuation mark. In a sentence that begins "What have you been . . . ," a reader hardly has to see the *ing* on the verb or the question mark to know that this is a question in the present perfect continuous — and thus to process the meanings associated with those terms. Assuming he has acquired good recognition skills, the less visual information such a reader needs to process in order to identify language forms, the more of his limited processing time he can devote to higher-level prediction (and other "integrative comprehension processes": Stanovich 1980:64) and thus to the meaning of the text as a whole.

If, as we read, our predictions get confirmed, we continue to read and to comprehend. If they do not, if the text stops making sense, then we are forced to retrace our mental steps until it begins to make sense again. If that doesn't happen too often, however, if, for any given text, our knowledge and our skill prove equal to the task, we can successfully relate whatever new information we encounter in the text to what we already know, to our cognitive structure. That is, in the most ideal sense, we can read it.

As I have tried to suggest, this complex process includes two major subprocesses. The first is simple *identification*, determining rapidly and accurately just what the text says. Good readers know the language in its printed form and convert print to language skillfully. They recognize words and phrases on the printed page for the most part automatically, with fewer errors and more quickly than weaker readers do. Most readers can recognize words more accurately and more rapidly in context, but, as noted, even in context-free situations, good readers of (for example) English also do a better and faster job of recognizing words and phrases and even word-like units which conform to the rules of the English spelling system (Stanovich 1980). To the extent that making sense of a text depends on the information acquired by means of the simple decoding of that text at the level of formal identification, good decoding skills are crucial to good reading. Thus when Smith defines *information* as simply "the reduction of uncertainty" (1982:14), it is this level he is mainly thinking of. And it does make sense to think of reading at this level as a kind of information processing, the transferring of specific "bits" of information (Smith 1982:195) from one system to another, much as this is done in systems of artificial intelligence.

But human beings are not computers. For the rapid and accurate acquisition of the basic information contained in any text, simple decoding skills will suffice (and they are certainly important). But to make any sense of information thus acquired, the human reader must relate it to what he already knows about the subject at hand, to his cognitive structure (never quite the same, of course, for any two readers), and in combining the two, he must in fact create new structures of meaning, a process that I will call *interpretation*. At this level the reader must negotiate a meaning with the writer of the text, the text serving (well or badly) as spokesperson for the writer. This is true of any kind of reading, of course, but especially true of more advanced kinds, like reading for academic purposes, where *information* takes on its more familiar meaning as a synonym for *knowledge*, the basic stuff of various systems of thought.

The way in which the brain organizes these systems has lately been the subject of a great deal of research on text or discourse processing. Such concepts as "frames," "scenarios," "scripts," and, most frequently, "schemata" have all been advanced as labels (with slightly different emphases) for the networks of real-world (and also rhetorical) information that readers refer to in interpreting texts (Anderson and Pearson 1984). To understand a line like this, for example,

The runner was called out at the plate.

the reader must have acquired a kind of "baseball schema," i.e., an organized understanding, or model, of the game, within which words like "runner," "plate," and "out" have special meanings and relate to each other in special ways. The manner in which readers access such schemata is far from well understood, but it has been well established that they do and that schemata play a major role in reading comprehension (Carrell and Eisterhold 1983).

The informed reading teacher must therefore be concerned with two kinds of complementary reading skills — (1) simple identification skills, which mainly depend on knowledge of the language, specifically, the language in its written form, and (2) the higher-level cognitive skills required for the interpretation of texts, which mainly depend on knowledge of the subject matter of the texts, and of the way that information is organized in discourse (and, no doubt, to some extent on a certain kind of native intelligence sometimes loosely referred to as "verbal aptitude").

Reading and memory

No matter how intelligent the reader, however, he will always be effectively constrained in his reading not only by the limitations of his knowledge, but also by the limited capacity of the complex human memory system (for further discussion of this system, see Stevick 1976 and Smith 1982).

There are actually three kinds of memory — a so-called *sensory store* in which the visual image itself is held for a split second for processing, a *long-term memory* in which vast amounts of information can be stored (though not always retrieved when needed) perhaps indefinitely, and a functionally crucial *short-term memory* which mediates between the other two and in which new information must be processed, some for just a few seconds, and some for transfer into long-term memory. Because its capacity is limited, and because new information quickly pushes out old, short-term memory represents a major potential bottleneck in reading.

Two things have to happen, and happen quickly, there. The visual image must be converted into *linguistic* information, that is, into meaningful segments of language. Since short-term memory can hold only four to five units of information at one time, the only way of making this process more efficient is to increase the size of what constitutes a unit — to read in whole phrases or sentences as opposed to individual words or sequences of letters. Doing this is called "chunking" and it is clearly the key to the skills that I have been referring to as simple identification skills. Simultaneously, the language forms so identified must be converted into the kind of information — propositions or ideas — that can be stored in long-term memory. What we remember of what we read is not the language itself but the meaning of that language. If, for example, you were asked to summarize the first few pages of this chapter, you would hardly be likely to reproduce them word for word. This raises the further question, of course, of how the mind determines what *should* be remembered, that is, what should be committed to long-term memory. And the answer to this question is very closely related to what I have been calling interpretive skills, by means of which the good reader successfully relates new information from a text to what he already knows in reconstructing the meaning of that text as a whole.

Notice that in performing both of these tasks, short-term memory must make use of information stored in *long*-term memory. Converting print into linguistic forms presupposes prior knowledge of the syntax and lexis of the language of the text. Converting language into larger, propositional structures presupposes a knowledge of the subject matter of the text and its relation to the real world.

To make efficient use of short-term memory, a reader therefore must develop two kinds of skills, and a breakdown in either kind of processing may produce a bottleneck in this part of memory. The reader who tries to read in too small chunks will find that by the time he has mentally plodded to the end of a line or two of print, he has long since forgotten what the beginning was about, while the reader who tries to remember everything will find that no matter how carefully he reads, he cannot make much sense of the text as a whole. And neither reader will enjoy the experience much.

To read well, within the limits imposed by the nature of the human memory system, the good reader must therefore learn, as I have noted, to take advantage of the redundancy inherent in human languages and both his knowledge of the subject matter of the text and his knowledge of the world. The most efficient reader is the reader who acquires the maximum amount of meaning from the minimum number of visual cues. In practice, this means reading at a reasonable rate, which is, as I hope I have now made plain, not a matter of moving the eyes faster over every mark on the page, but of taking in larger, and (literally) more meaningful chunks of text. The less the reader has to look at, the more he can see if he sees it right the first time. Therefore the fluent reader soon learns to identify forms automatically, and to take in whole propositions, not forms, but the truly *good* reader takes the process one step further: he continues to increase his reading rate as he improves. For the reading teacher, the implications of this should be obvious. The teacher must be constantly concerned with how fast his students read, there being a direct relationship between reading speed and reading skill, between memory requirements and comprehension. The good reader, by definition, reads fast.

1.5 THREE MODELS OF THE READING PROCESS

Much of what I have said so far, and much of what will be said in the rest of this book, presupposes a particular model of the reading process, called an "interactive" model, which can best be understood in relation to two earlier models of the process now frequently referred to as "bottom-up" and "top-down" models of reading.

In a classic paper, Goodman (1967) characterized the bottom-up model of the reading process as "the common sense notion" that "reading is a precise process [involving] exact, detailed, sequential perception and identification of letters, words, spelling patterns and larger language units." This model assumes that a reader proceeds (as most readers think they do) by moving his eyes from left to right across the page, first taking in letters, combining these to form words, then combining the words to form the phrases, clauses, and sentences of the text.

In place of this bottom-up, common sense approach, Goodman offered a very different kind of model, the various subsequent versions of which have come to be called top-down models of the reading process. Here is Goodman's original description of the model (1967:108):

> Reading is a selective process. It involves partial use of available minimal language cues selected from perceptual input on the basis of the reader's expectation. As this partial information is processed, tentative decisions are made, to be confirmed, rejected or refined as reading progresses. More simply stated, reading is a psycholinguistic guessing game. It involves an interaction between thought and language. Efficient reading does not result from precise perception and identification of all elements, but from skill in selecting the fewest, most productive cues necessary to produce guesses which are right the first time.

Since that original paper, Goodman's "guessing game" model has flourished, partly as a result of the work of Goodman himself and numerous colleagues within his system of "miscue analysis" (see, for example, Goodman 1969; Rigg 1977), but even more, perhaps, as a result of the work of the prolific psycholinguist Frank Smith, whose *Understanding Reading* (1971; 1978; 1982), a compendium of top-down ideas about reading, has been through three editions during the past twelve years. Smith's work has attracted widespread attention and considerable praise, and has clearly been a major influence on the thinking of most language teachers with an interest in reading.

Since I am one of those who have been influenced by both Goodman and Smith, the major features of a top-down model of reading can be taken directly from what I have already said about the process. Both the general notion of reading as the reconstruction of meaning based on a skillful sampling of the text, and such specific notions as the use of linguistic redundancy, the crucial role of prior knowledge (or nonvisual information) in prediction, and the necessity for reading at a reasonable rate in larger, more meaningful chunks of text are pure Goodman/Smith and now generally accepted ideas about reading. Among second language teachers interested in reading, the top-down model has already achieved something like official status as *the* model.

Because this approach is based on a better understanding of the reading process than common sense approaches to reading can provide, its effect on current methods and materials for the teaching of second language reading has been both dramatic and mainly positive. Of the many good texts now available for the teaching of reading to, for example, students of English as a second language (see Part II for examples), all have been influenced by top-down thinking and all have been produced within the last ten years (with one or two notable exceptions, like Harris's (1966) *Reading Improvement Exercises*). Curriculum planners and methodologists now also offer much sounder, and better informed, advice on designing and teaching courses in reading for the second language student (see, for example, Mackay, Barkman and Jordan 1979; Croft 1980; Hosenfeld *et al.* 1981; Grellet 1981; Nuttall 1982; Krashen and Terrell 1983), mainly thanks to the spread of top-down ideas. Thus a good deal of the credit for a new concern in language teaching with reading as an independent skill, and for improvements in reading pedagogy and materials, must be accorded to the work of Goodman and Smith and their many supporters who have successfully promoted a top-down model of the process.

That said, I should immediately add that I do have certain reservations about the top-down model (especially in relation to second language reading), and these have recently been addressed by proponents of "interactive" models of reading (Rumelhart 1977; Stanovich 1980; Lesgold and Perfetti 1981).

The major issue at hand is the relative importance of those lower-level cognitive skills that I have categorized as simple *identification* skills — the straightforward recognition of the lexical units (the individual words and phrases) and the grammatical signals required for the simple decoding of a text — and those higher-level cognitive skills that allow for the meaningful reconstruction of a text as a unified, coherent structure of meaning which I have referred to as *interpretive* skills. Top-down theorists place a much higher value on the latter, and *seem* to regard the process of becoming a more proficient reader as essentially a process of moving from reliance on the physical text (which Smith (1982) refers to as "visual information") to an increasing reliance on prior linguistic and conceptual knowledge (or "nonvisual information") for reconstructing the meaning of the text as a whole. They tend to downplay the importance of the text itself, often, for example, quoting with approval such remarks as Koler's "reading is only incidentally visual" (Smith 1982:12). In this view, as a reader becomes a better reader, he quickly passes beyond the use of lower-level skills and learns instead to rely on his interpretive skills, which assume full control of the sampling process (hence the "top-down" metaphor) and, by ensuring consistently accurate predictions, or guesses, draw a maximum of meaning from a minimum number of visual cues.

Interactive theorists, by contrast, see certain distortions in this description of the process of becoming a more efficient reader. They do not, of course, deny that as readers improve they do make increasing use of their developing knowledge of the language itself, the conventions of discourse, and the world in general, and that they can consequently derive more meaning from a smaller visual input. But they also point out that research demonstrates that good readers are not only better at interpreting texts but also at identifying language forms, and even language-like forms, and that poor readers are as likely as good ones to depend on higher-level, predictive reading strategies (Stanovich 1980), both of which facts suggest that simple identification skills (much as they may change over time as the reader develops increasing skill at processing more and larger units of language) continue to play a crucial role in good reading in concert with the higher-level cognitive skills (hence the "interactive" metaphor) required for the accurate interpretation of texts.

The crux of the debate is perhaps implicit in Goodman's "guessing game" metaphor, which has always made me nervous (Eskey 1973:172) and which I think most interactivists would reject as misleading. Clearly the fluent reader predicts as he reads, and clearly he does not read word by word, but he *does* identify forms as he reads, a reciprocal process which is partly aided by, but also crucially contributes to, his making semantically accurate predictions. For the good reader the *domain* of prediction is not the word or phrase — language forms which he can simply identify in much less time than it would take him to predict them (fluent reading is not an endless series of cloze tests) — but the larger and more meaningful divisions of the text out of which its overall meaning develops. In fact it is just because the fluent reader can process printed language automatically, and at a reasonable rate, that his conscious mind is free to devote its attention to larger questions of meaning — in contrast to the poor decoder, whose mind is too involved in puzzling out the meaning of unfamiliar language forms to give much time to higher order kinds of prediction, unless, as Carrell suggests (1984c), he simply gives up the struggle and starts guessing on the basis of what he already knows.

It is only when a reader does *not* make accurate identifications of forms that his predictions begin to look more like guessing than like anything I would want to call fluent reading. The interactive model predicts that good readers will not become progressively less concerned with identification, but rather progressively more efficient at it as they develop their interpretive skills.

The interactive model: a summary

Figure 1 provides a rough diagram of the interactive model of the reading process which this text presupposes. Reading is here conceived of as a particular type of cognitive behavior which is based, as I have noted, on certain kinds of knowledge which form a part of the reader's cognitive structure. Figure 1 thus begins with that cognitive structure in the brain, that is, with what the reader knows, what is stored as schemata in his long-term memory. He must, for example, know the language well enough in its written form and know enough about the subject matter of the text to insure that the text will be (or could be) comprehensible to him. His knowledge of form will provide him with certain expectations about the

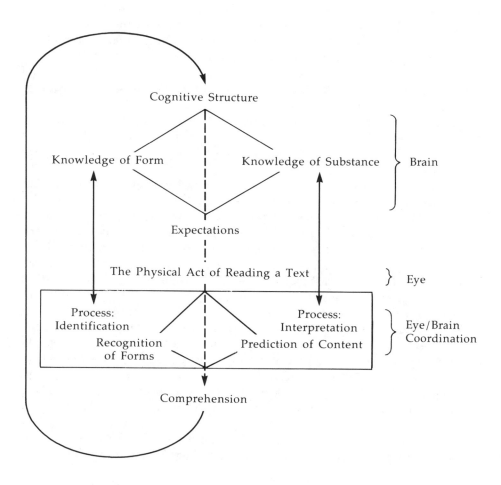

Figure 1: Reading as Cognitive Behavior: an Interactive Model

language of the text. Given these expectations, he can, during the physical act of reading, make accurate identifications of forms from a minimum number of visual cues, and if his reading skills are well developed, he can do this quickly and automatically. Simultaneously, his knowledge of substance will provide him with certain expectations about the larger conceptual structure of the text. Given these expectations, he can, while reading, make accurate predictions in interpreting the meaning of the text as a whole, that is, in achieving comprehension, a personal reconstruction of the meaning of the text, the depth and richness of which will largely be determined by this reader's knowledge and reasoning powers. In this approach to reading, the word "interactive" refers to both the interaction of the reader's several kinds of knowledge (with no directional bias, bottom-up *or* top-down) and the interaction of the reader and the text. But as the arrow from Comprehension back to Cognitive Structure suggests, these two kinds of interaction blend into one as, in the normal process of reading, the reader makes the text a part of what he knows.

Consider, for example, what is involved in reading the following remark by Oscar Wilde:

If you tell the truth long enough you are bound to be found out.

The reader to begin with must know both the written forms and the meanings of the structures and words of which this sentence is composed (and this of course *pre*supposes some knowledge of the alphabetic system we use), as well as the conventions (left-to-right word order, capital letters, punctuation, etc.) of English-language manuscripts. More specifically, he must, for example, know that the grammatical form of the sentence signals a cause-and-effect relationship between the introductory dependent ("if") clause, and the following independent clause — that is, that the main clause must be understood as the result of the introductory clause. He must recognize and accurately decode the passive form of the verb phrase in the main clause — that is, he must understand that the sentence is about someone finding you out and not you finding out something. He must know that the *you* employed here refers to anyone (and not just to the reader) and that the phrase *to be found out* implies (in addition to its basic meaning of "discovered") that its subject is involved in wrongdoing of some kind.

Beyond this linguistic knowledge, however, he must also know something about real-world attitudes toward behavior — that, for example, telling the truth is normally regarded as a praiseworthy action, one for which a person might expect to be admired. And he must know that a certain kind of humor (call it ironic) is based on the sudden turning upside down of widely held conventional beliefs and attitudes. In the absence of such knowledge, the main force of the sentence — the contrast between the expectation set up in the introductory clause and the surprising reversal of that expectation (and hence the humorous effect) in the main clause — will be lost to the reader, even the reader with a good dictionary. Comprehension of just this one sentence thus depends on a complex interaction between a rapid-fire identification of forms, based on one kind of knowledge (knowledge of form), and the setting up and sudden reversal of a semantic expectation/prediction, based on another kind of knowledge (knowledge of substance). And a breakdown, during the physical act of reading, in *any* part of the system can result in mis- or noncomprehension of the sentence.

1.6 THE SECOND LANGUAGE
READER (2)

The implications of this model for second language readers, and for the teachers of such readers, constitute the subject matter of the rest of this book. Although what these readers do when they read is not different in kind from what native speakers do, they tend as a group to have particular problems that the second language teacher needs to be aware of and sensitive to in designing and in teaching second language reading courses.

The comprehension gap

For most second language readers, the major problem in reading will simply be the gap between what they know and what a comparably educated native speaker knows in relation to the language and the content of texts written, as nearly all authentic texts are, for the native-speaking reader. This "comprehension gap," as I have chosen to call it, naturally varies from reader to reader and from text to text, but every second language reader who has not yet achieved full bilingual and also bicultural status (clearly, the vast majority) will suffer from particular deficiencies of knowledge in one or more of the major categories of knowledge — linguistic, pragmatic, and cultural — required for the full, or at least native-like, comprehension of written texts in that language. Figure 2 displays in schematic form what these categories of knowledge are (and concurrently provides a more detailed breakdown of the two kinds of knowledge introduced in Figure 1). Notice that in moving from left to right in this figure, we are also moving from the kinds of lower-level cognitive skills required for the identification of forms to the higher-level skills required for the interpretation of meaning, or from bottom to top in the language of the models. And it is true that as the second language learner acquires greater knowledge and greater proficiency in reading, he can devote less of his cognitive attention to the simple identification of forms (like individual words) and more to the higher-level processes required for interpreting texts (like predicting, relating, evaluating, and so forth). But the little research that has been done on the problems of adult, academic second language readers (e.g. Clarke 1978) suggests that such readers — even those with considerable knowledge of the language — still suffer from deficiencies at the level of identification which interfere, despite all of their higher-level skills, with their attempts to comprehend the texts they must read.

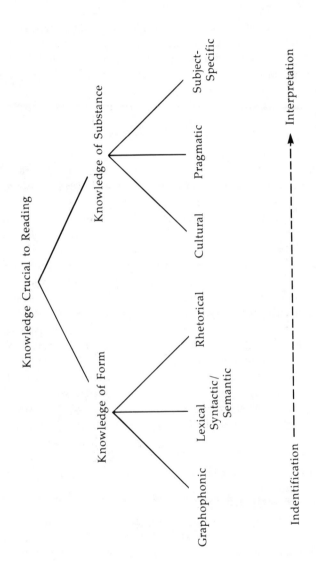

Figure 2: Categories of Knowledge Crucial to Reading

In a study of Israeli university students reading textbooks in English, one team of researchers (Cohen *et al.* 1980) identified three specific problem areas, one at the purely lexical level, one at the lexical-syntactical boundary, and one involving lexical-rhetorical markers. The first was the one-word, one-meaning problem. Since the second language learner does not always acquire the full range of meanings that a given word may have, he may always assign a single meaning to that word and he may therefore misinterpret that word when it appears in a context where a different meaning is called for (for example, a context where the word *tolerance* clearly refers to the strength of some material, not to the absence of prejudice). The second was the problem of so-called "heavy" noun phrases (like "that such treatments as holding cells in buffer after irradiation before placing them in nutrient agar plates") in which a sequence of words functions as a single complex nominal, which obscures the logical-syntactical relationships between them (for example, the facts that (1) someone holds the cells in buffer after (2) someone has irradiated them but before (3) someone places them on nutrient agar plates). The third was the problem of assigning proper meanings to lexical cohesion markers (like *however* and *thus*) which signal certain logical relationships between parts of the text as a coherent piece of discourse. One subject, for example, had no idea that the sentence connector *thus* signals anything different from the conjunction *and*. For readers like this, the general problem of what a colleague of mine calls "holding in the bottom" is a very real one. To ignore these kinds of problems and to concentrate instead, and exclusively, on teaching higher-level interpretation strategies is, it seems to me, to risk converting reading into a real guessing game.

The confidence problem

On the other hand, many second language readers do suffer from a lack of confidence in their skills when they sit down to read authentic texts in the language. Such a reader is typically an insecure reader who all too frequently believes that to comprehend a text, he must first comprehend every word in the text. He may therefore deliberately read very slowly, proceeding word by word, with frequent trips to the dictionary to look up every new word, a strategy which, as I have tried to make plain, practically precludes successful reading comprehension and practically insures a high degree of frustration. In practice, such a reader must be induced to abandon this word-by-word strategy and to take the normal risks that fluent reading requires. In reading any given text, he must be encouraged to make the best use he can of the knowledge that he has in reconstructing the probable meaning of that text (without, however, being told that mere guessing is reading). A very large part of the reading teacher's job is therefore a kind of confidence building, which is partly a matter of preparing students well but mainly a matter of directing them to a quantity of appropriate materials to read, a point to which I will return below.

Reading as a gradually developing skill

The process that I have been describing in this chapter is obviously one that learners must develop a knack for gradually. Being able to read is not like being pregnant — an either-you-are-or-you-aren't kind of thing — but a skill that every learner must develop over time and with a great deal of practice. To make sense of a text, beginners must, of course, depend more extensively than fluent readers do on the visual information provided by the print, but as they become more familiar with both the language and conventions of the printed page, and the subjects they have chosen to read about, they put that knowledge to use in reconstructing the meanings of these texts (in relation to their own understanding of the world). Thus the reading that a truly proficient reader does is a very different thing from the reading — which is more like simple decoding — that he once did as a beginner. And since the second language reader is, almost by definition, in the process of acquiring reading skills in that language, the second language reading teacher must develop a sensitivity to what his students know and what his students can do, and adapt his approach to the level of the students he is trying to help. For the second language reader, as a developing reader, the proper mix of bottom-up and top-down strategies will vary in accordance with his knowledge and skills, and also with his purpose in reading the text (compare reading a novel purely for pleasure and reading to prepare for a test on that novel) and with the density and complexity of the information embedded in that text (compare a textbook, a journal, and a simple adventure story).

Thus there is no one approach to reading appropriate to every kind of student in every kind of situation, but there is, as I have noted above, one pedagogical constant, and that is quantity of reading. Once reading material appropriate to the level and interests of a particular student has been identified, the more of that material that student reads, the better — and the more quickly his reading skills will develop. The latter point cannot be emphasized too strongly. There is no way that a reader can develop better comprehension skills, and greater confidence in his skills, without doing a lot of reading, just as there is no way that a swimmer can develop his skills and confidence without getting in the water and doing a fair amount of swimming. Knowing what to do is one thing, doing it is another, and the teacher's dual task is to find the right materials for his students to read and to find ways of inducing those students to read them.

1.7 READING AS MEANS AND END

Thus the major implication of this first chapter for the teacher of second language reading is, I would say, that the point of the reading class must be reading — not the reinforcement of oral skills, not grammatical or discourse analysis, and not the acquisition of new vocabulary. Improvement in any of these areas can make reading easier, but none of them is reading and none contributes directly to the one legitimate goal of such a class — the development of a genuine reading habit in the language. If the students stop reading when the reading class ends, the course has not achieved what such a course should achieve, no matter how well the students may have scored on a test of the grammar or vocabulary or even of the content of the reading in that class. Although readers themselves are mainly interested in content, it is a skill, not a content, that a reading class should teach. The more knowledge that the reader can acquire, the better — knowledge of the language, and of the culture and the world — but no amount of knowledge guarantees fluent reading. Reading is a skill which must be developed, and can only be developed, by means of extensive and continual practice. People learn to read, and to read better, by reading.

FOR STUDY AND DISCUSSION

1. List three ways in which reading in a second language is different from reading in a first language, and discuss the implications of these differences for teaching second language reading.

2. How can cultural attitudes toward the nature and purpose of reading affect the reading habits of students from various cultures? Discuss, using examples.

3. Distinguish between the skills of identification and interpretation in reading. Give specific examples of skills of each type.

4. What is schema theory and how does it relate to the reading process?

5. Distinguish among sensory store, short-term, and long-term memory. Discuss these concepts in relation to the reading process.

6. How do interactive models of the reading process differ from bottom-up and/or top-down models? What are the implications of these differences for the teaching of the second-language reading?

7. Can you think of activities besides reading to which the bottom-up/top-down controversy is relevant? Discuss, using examples.

8. What arguments can be made for engaging in such oral language activities as lectures, films, and discussion in a reading course? Consider both pre- and post-reading contexts.

9. Prepare a questionnaire for your students (or any group of second language readers) to elicit such information as: how much the students read in their native languages; how much they read in English; their reasons for reading in their own languages; their reasons for reading in English. After administering the questionnaire, discuss the results in relation to the problem of designing a reading course in English for these readers.

10. Prepare a similar questionnaire to elicit such information as: what problems they believe they have in reading English; what they believe would be the best means of solving these problems. After administering the questionnaire, discuss the results in relation to the problem of establishing realistic attitudes toward reading in a class of such readers.

11. One obvious approach to the teaching of academic reading would be to determine what the students will actually have to read and then to build the course around making that material more comprehensible to them. Discuss the merits and limitations of such an approach.

12. Discuss some ways in which second language readers can be induced to do enough outside reading on their own to make the teaching of reading to such students meaningful and effective.

FOR FURTHER READING

Mitchell 1982 is a detailed but very readable discussion of our current understanding of the reading process. Pearson 1984b is an excellent survey of current reading research, a collection of state-of-the-art articles in such areas as research methodology, basic processes, and instructional practices in reading.

For an overview of the top-down approach and for a general introduction to the most popular current model of reading, Goodman 1967 and 1970 and Smith 1982 are basic. Though not the last word on the subject (no one has that), anything by these two authors is recommended. Gough 1972 is a clear presentation of a bottom-up model, though such models have few supporters today. The interactive approach was first introduced in Rumelhart 1977. In McClelland and Rumelhart 1981 this model is developed in greater detail, but this is heavy going for the non-specialist. For a comparison of models and some development of Rumelhart's approach,

Stanovich 1980 is excellent, though again somewhat demanding for the non-specialist.

An excellent discussion of the role of memory in second language learning can be found in Stevick 1976. Further discussion of memory, in specific relationship to reading, can be found in Smith 1982 (also cited above).

For discussion of the problems of the second language reader, Carrell and Eisterhold 1983 and Carrell 1984c provide a clear introduction to a schema theoretical approach. Though dating rapidly, Mackay, Barkman and Jordan 1979, a collection of papers on second language reading, provides a good general introduction to the subject. Thonis 1970 deals with younger learners but is even more dated. Good recent commentaries include Hosenfeld *et al.* 1981, Krashen and Terrell 1983, and especially Nuttall 1982.

Chapter 2

The Transition from Theory to Practice in Teaching Reading

William Grabe
Northern Arizona University

2.1 INTRODUCTION

Over the last ten years the topic of reading has emerged as a major issue for both first and second language educators/researchers, reflected in the voluminous literature covering both theoretical research and practical instruction. Much less emphasis, however, has been placed on bridging the gap between theory and practice. The causes for this lacuna are many. One primary reason is the interdisciplinary nature of reading theory, involving an array of underlying assumptions, experimental paradigms, and data interpretations from various disciplines such as psycholinguistics, sociolinguistics, information science, cognitive psychology, education, and the humanities. The input from such a range of disciplines has created considerable disagreement about reading, both in theory and in practice. On the practical side, reading instruction has its own complex range of literature that well-nigh defies synthesis. Results of various group treatments with different means of instruction, and involving such variable factors as age, level, motivation/affect, social/cultural background, and language/dialect all allow a broad range of interpretations, as well as much ground for debate. Any attempt to formulate a coherent view of reading and reading instruction represents a daunting challenge.

Reading instruction requires the synthesis of theoretical assumptions and approaches, practical curriculum design, and procedures for implementing the design in day-to-day teaching. At the same time, any attempt to join theory and practice must be held up to close scrutiny; it is clear that there can be no definitive solution to such a task. However, given the need to teach reading, we must pursue the issue with the means at our disposal. One productive way to explore the synthesis of theory and practice is provided by Richards and Rodgers' (1982) framework of *approach, design* and *procedure,* a framework particularly appropriate to the issues of second language reading instruction. By *approach* we adopt a theory of reading that takes into account the processes readers use. By *design* we prepare an analysis of needs, propose a taxonomy of micro-skills, and establish overall aims for teaching these skills. By *procedure* we suggest activities and techniques needed to implement effectively the syllabus objectives deriving from curricular aims.

This chapter draws on the assumptions made by interactive models of reading (Stanovich 1980; McClelland and Rumelhart 1981; Mitchell 1982; Taylor and Taylor 1983; Perfetti 1985; see Eskey, this volume, for discussion), and explores briefly a number of questions central to forming a consistent underlying approach. Starting from such a theoretical assumption and working through the approach, design, procedure framework, the chapter delineates the movement from theory to practice. That is, theoretical assumptions are translated into a comprehensive plan of instruction, taking the second language learner from a high elementary reading level to a level where a student will have a reasonable chance of success in a university environment.

The *approach* component will address the following questions:

1. How will reading be defined such that it may guide instruction?
2. Is reading the same or different in different languages and in different cultures?
3. How does L1 reading development differ from L2 reading development?
4. Do reading and writing involve the same cognitive skills and processes?

These questions represent issues that must be resolved if a principled curriculum design is to be constructed and implemented.

The *design* section of this chapter addresses such questions as:

1. How important is reading instruction in an academic setting?
2. What should be taught to help make a better ESL reader?
3. How would one want to design a reading curriculum?
4. What is the role of commercially prepared materials in such a curriculum?
5. What is the role of the administrator?

6. What is the role of the teacher?

The *procedure* section addresses such questions as:

1. How are the reading objectives and curriculum design to be interpreted into an explicit set of instructional procedures?
2. What are the sorts of instructional procedures available?
3. What is the best balance of procedures for an effective overall program?

We would not claim that the information given here represents a final statement as much as a working statement, one which offers a coherent rationale for second language reading instruction. In a field such as reading there will inevitably remain debatable issues as theory evolves, but ongoing practical decisions must be made at the same time (in light of professional experience and the research literature) if viable reading programs are to be developed. What is clear is that any attempt to bridge theory and practice must respond to the questions raised here.

2.2 AN APPROACH TO READING INSTRUCTION

A number of the issues relating to a theoretical approach have been discussed in Chapter 1. The purpose here is to view these theoretical perspectives from a practical orientation so that they may be related to instructional issues. Accordingly, this section commences with a somewhat more practical discussion of what reading is.

On the nature of reading

There are various definitions of reading, or of the reading process, to choose from. Perhaps it would be most honest to suggest that there is not yet a completely valid explanation of reading, but such a position does not offer a useful direction for instruction. Therefore, however imperfect definition construction may be, making a working definition constitutes a necessary first step if a set of assumptions is to be formulated and built upon.

A good place to begin is with the basic definition and description offered by Mitchell.

> Reading can be defined loosely as the ability to make sense of written or printed symbols to guide the recovery of information from his or her memory and subsequently use this information to construct a plausible interpretation of the written message . . . .

> A skilled reader may be familiar with 30,000 or more words and yet he or she is normally able to identify any one of these words within a fraction of a second. He can do this despite the fact that the constituent letters are frequently represented by different shapes from one text to another and even, in the case of handwriting, from one instance of the letter to the next. He can even identify words that have been misprinted or misspelt . . . . (1982: 1)

Extending this initial definition somewhat, the views of a number of researchers, in combination, suggest a somewhat more complex definition of reading and provide the wherewithal for both general curricular aims and specific objectives.

1. Reading is an anticipatory, selective, purposeful and comprehending process (Smith 1982).

2. Reading is a process of interpreting/understanding the text in terms of the questions that the reader formulates about the text. That is, readers find answers to the questions they pose (Smith 1982).

3. Reading is a process of matching information in a text to internally activated information. Thus, reading is not information processing but rather information interpreting—what we understand from a text depends in part on what we knew previously, as well as on how we allow the text to extend and refine our knowledge of the topic. Reading is the interaction of the text and the reader (Widdowson 1979; Carrell and Eisterhold 1983).

4. Reading involves the use of different levels of internal information as well as various types of information, all interacting simultaneously to allow optimal interpretation. The reader relies on perceptual processing, phonemic processing, and internal recall of many types (syntactic knowledge, lexical knowledge, story grammars, descriptive scripts, schematic arrangement and connecting of related sets of information, intentions of the text and of the reader, affective mechanisms, etc.). In addition, issues of accuracy and speed of processing are major components of recent overall models of reading (van Dijk and Kintsch 1983; Taylor and Taylor 1983).

It is clear that reading can be defined and described in a variety of ways; in the present context all of these definitions offer useful insights into reading instruction, and thus support decisions made in developing curricula and classroom procedures.

Finally, it is also important to maintain a realistic perspective on the importance and utility of reading models when considering reading theory (see also Eskey, this volume, for discussions of reading models). Much dis-

cussion on constructing models of reading is basically the attempt to specify the assumed processes involved in reading as well as their operational
interaction. As such, they play a vital role in the exploration of reading;
they both force more careful consideration of the assumptions and more
explicit explanations of the contribution made by the various processes that
are postulated. However, it is important to keep in mind the view of Samuels and Eisenberg (1981:32) on the practice of model construction for reading theory.

> There is a danger . . . in trying to describe the reading process as
> a whole. In the past, comprehensive descriptions of the reading
> process have attempted to explain so much that they suffered
> from the serious flaw of being untestable. The partial models, on
> the other hand, sacrificed comprehensiveness, but they were
> testable. Thus, the partial models were altered as new informa-
> tion became available so that the models more accurately re-
> flected nature.

Thus, as Samuels and Eisenberg suggest, it is important to develop theory
which is open to validation, and which makes use of prior research. One
wants a model of reading that is not only intuitively plausible, but also
compatible with ongoing research. At the same time, perhaps the greatest
danger in going from theory to practice is the human propensity to remain
too committed to any theoretical orientation in the face of what does seem
to work in the classroom, and how students react to these process-
es/procedures. The essential point is that reading practitioners cannot expect fully adequate explanations of the reading process, nor can they expect
any exact blueprint for action from theory. Rather, it is for the practitioner,
informed by theory, to find the most productive and reasonable avenues to
effective curriculum design and classroom procedures.

Reading in different languages/cultures

The issue of a unitary, universal reading process must be viewed in at
least two different ways. First, there is the more linguistically constrained
issue of whether different languages, and their different orthographic systems, require different reading strategies, different learning strategies, or,
at least, suggest the likelihood that various universal processes interact differently for optimal processing in different languages. The second issue is
whether different cultures impose particular constraints on the development of the reading process(es) that, in turn, affect foreign student reading
proficiency in the EFL class.

On the former issue there is a growing body of literature on the real
and apparent differences invoked by readers of different languages, and
different orthographic systems. Among the issues most often researched

are the differential effects of alphabetic, syllabic, and logographic writing systems on reading; the effects on reading that occur when students come from languages with multiple orthographic systems (Japan, Korea, Yugoslavia); the effects on reading when a second language uses a different orthographic system; and the effects on reading from scripts written in left-to-right, right-to-left, and top-to-bottom directions. Moreover, there are issues of whether different languages require different learning strategies for reading (Tzeng and Hung 1981; Taylor and Taylor 1983), and whether linguistic reading skills in a first language are readily transferable to a second language. The standard assumption in the '70s was that they are (Al-Rufai 1976; Goodman 1981). More recently the assertion has come under some question (Clarke 1978; Elley and Mangubhai 1983; Alderson 1984).

The second issue is how different cultures use their orthographic systems differently (i.e., read for different purposes). This issue is quite different from issues of language structure and orthographic systems, though there must necessarily be a level of interaction between the two issues. The primary concern on the sociocultural level is whether or not students come from a society with similar technological and academic assumptions (Kaplan 1982, 1983; Grabe and Kaplan 1986). Such assumptions have a strong impact on how American educators view reading (Cf. Singer 1981a, for a historical view of reading instruction and its purposes in the U.S.). Since the U.S. is a post-industrial society, the emphasis in the U.S. is on (1) access and processing of large amounts of information; (2) being critical of printed information; (3) comparing the variety of different views available in the research literature; (4) understanding that research and information exist within an ever accumulating mass of printed material wherein today's facts may be tomorrow's speculations and questions; and (5) recognizing that effective research involves a synthesis of the information resources as well as a creative analysis of this information. Thus, one important aspect of cultural constraints on reading development is the amount and type of world-background knowledge that students are expected to bring to their academic reading.

While there may be other hidden assumptions in effect in post-industrial academic institutions, these suffice to illustrate the obstacles faced by students from countries where these assumptions do not operate fully. In other countries of the world many of the above assumptions are not in force in the training of students. Guthrie (1981b) notes both that third world students' reading abilities are less proficient and that they do less reading. Students from a number of societies do not read extensively for knowledge, but rather, they receive the absolute truth from the teacher's class lectures. It is not the student's place to question these sources of authority and they are not expected to look elsewhere for "alternative" explanations. In some societies, typically diglossic ones, writing occurs in a less than complete range of uses in the communicative needs of the community (Ferguson 1959). Some writing systems still maintain strong religious overtones/constraints, and other writing systems — those of languages of wider communication — are used only in specific socioeconomic, political, or academic environments. In some cultures reading is not used to gather information but rather as the basis of belief. Further, reading implies equality of access, which may not be desirable in societies which espouse information control as a doctrine.

In yet other societies the argument can be made that literacy itself is as yet a barely understood technology. For example, two refugees from Vietnam in the same class—one Hmong, one ethnic Chinese—will have very different assumptions and understanding on the nature and uses of writing systems, and by extension, reading.

Even in societies that are "developing," where literacy is pursued to varying extents, practical matters make students' orientations to reading less like the American experience than might be expected. Accessing, using and critiquing massive amounts of information requires a major economic investment, societal openness to alternative interpretations of the world, and the organizational infrastructure for adequate dissemination (Kaplan 1983; Grabe and Kaplan 1986). Few countries in the world can offer all those necessary, if not sufficient, criteria for the use of information as is the case in the U.S., Europe and Japan (Galinski 1982).

If the foreign student coming to the U.S. to study is bewildered by the hidden assumptions of the American higher education system, we should not be surprised. At the same time, we must recognize both what these hidden assumptions are and what foreign students will have to cope with if they are to succeed in this system (Obah 1983).

Both major issues, the linguistic differences and the sociocultural differences, must be given careful consideration for any attempt to develop a realistic and feasible reading curriculum. What is obvious from this set of issues is that reading instruction requires much more effort and focused attention than it presently has received if there is to be an honest commitment to teach foreign students to read and interpret material in a way that does not handicap them (that lets them approach native-like reader abilities). Given the range of obstacles to be overcome, and the possible differences from student to student in any ESL classroom, one can readily perceive the difficulty involved in constructing a second language reading curriculum.

Differences between first and second language reading

The difficulties of the foreign student learning to read in the American academic environment lead naturally to another major issue, specifically, how second language (L2) reading differs from first language (L1) reading. Again, the literature on this issue is relatively small, but growing. The reported findings and views of researchers are also not homogeneous. The most discussed topic is whether reading abilities of L1 transfer to L2. As was seen earlier, linguistic and sociocultural factors will have a major impact on transfer to L2 reading. Certainly students who assume they read well in L1, or are literate, may not transfer abilities to L2 that have not been fully developed in L1, or may encounter unanticipated processing difficulties in the second language. Research evidence does not prove conclusively that transfer of all abilities occurs. Research, however, is at best suggestive and should never be taken for absolute truth. Rather than say that transfer does not occur, we hold here that no certain proof can be advanced for or against transfer (cf. Alderson 1984). A healthy scepticism is essential for interpreting research claims in the literature.

The uncertainty of assumptions about the reading process, however, does not leave us without a research agenda. There are a number of points to note on the differences between learning to read in a first language and in a second language. (1) Reading research in both L1 and L2 suggests that cognitive capacity and organization may be culturally shaped. Building from assumptions of schema theory (Brown and Yule 1983; Carrell and Eisterhold 1983; Widdowson 1983), research is growing on the cognitive differences of different L2 readers, and what that might mean for L2 reading instruction. (2) L2 reading can be subject to interference from L1 assumptions, knowledge, expectations, etc. (3) L2 reading apparently requires a reasonable grammatical and lexical base upon which to build (Alderson 1984; Cooper 1984; Berman 1984). The general claim is not controversial. Certainly there is a major difference from L1 reading, where syntactic patterns and a large lexicon are already in use. (Singer 1981b, for example, states that L1 children already have a vocabulary of 5000 words, a sophisticated control of syntax, and an adequate phonological system for communication, and that such a base should be assumed for realistic reading instruction.) (4) Reading recognition and lexical access which is needed for an adequate linguistic base must be addressed by direct instruction and extensive reading (Beck 1981; Calfee and Pointkowski 1981; McKeown, Beck, Omanson and Perfetti 1984; Nagy, Herman, and Anderson 1985). (5) The logical consequence of the need for an adequate lexicogrammatical base is the determination of when and what to read in an L2 context. The question of when students are adequately prepared to begin reading is one of the more confusing issues in second language reading. The views range from beliefs in immediate reading practice with graded materials, to the early use of unsimplified materials, to delayed reading instruction with whatever type of material, to delayed instruction with authentic-difficult-reading material for various purposes. (6) L2 reading can be taught to the extent that a reading curriculum can lead the L2 readers to read in a manner that approximates that of a native reader of the target language. Thus, L2 reading research should carefully consider the current L1 reading research, and attempt to define and substantiate those issues which appear most promising for the L2 context.

The relationship between reading and writing

A final major issue of concern is whether or not learning to read can be taught by having students learn to write and by studying discourse grammar. This issue is important since many assumptions about reading instruction follow from an underlying assumption that reading and writing are mirror-image processes, and instruction in text features is adequate for both skills (Ibrahim 1979; cf. deBeaugrande 1984). Reading and writing abilities are highly correlated; however, correlations do not mean casual relations; particularly in the direction from writing to reading. What will be suggested here is: (1) that the relation between reading and writing is not close enough to assume full development of abilities in one from the other—and (2), by extension, that ESL students cannot learn to read by learning to write, by learning discourse grammar only, or by any purely "intensive" approach to reading—since all such approaches assume the reading-writing relationship consists only of converse manifestations of the same process.

While closely related and highly correlational for achievement results (Stotsky 1983), reading and writing are probably not cases of the same process going in different directions. The evidence, though not overwhelming (cf. Taylor and Taylor 1983), does suggest this view.

1. There is little casual evidence for the assumption of a reading-writing mirror-image interface.

2. There are numerous statable differences between reading and writing (Blau 1983; Goodman and Goodman 1983).

3. Recent literature and research support differences in reading and writing processes. As interactive models develop and make more precise claims about reading, the distinctions from writing become clearer (deBeaugrande 1984).

The point of this discussion is that simple assumptions on correlations noted between reading and writing can be dangerous. While there is good evidence that aspects of reading can be developed through writing practice and discourse study, such evidence cannot be taken to assert a mirror-image interface between reading and writing. Essentially, reading must be viewed as an independent concern requiring its own instructional design.

Summary

From the discussion to this point, and in Eskey, we can state the following claims from current reading research:

1. Interactive processes are real.
2. Perception and visual cues are important.
3. We bring much background information to any reading task.
4. Information is probably organized by schemata, scripts, plans, and goals.
5. A knowledge of discourse grammar is important for reading.
6. A knowledge of syntactic structure and vocabulary is important.
7. Reading requires practice—time on task.
8. Reading requires purpose—motivation (interest, need).

The goal for curriculum design is how to translate these views into actual practice.

To summarize this section, four areas of immediate impact on curricular design and classroom practice have been discussed. These are:

1. How reading may be defined in a way that suggests curricular and classroom preferences, and provide support for a focused reading instruction rationale.
2. How students from different backgrounds, both linguistic and sociocultural, will have different assumptions about reading, and what this might mean for design and procedures.
3. How L2 reading acquisition might differ from L1 reading acquisition, and what this suggests for second language curriculum design and classroom procedures.
4. How the relation between reading and writing — two critical academic (over and above functional L2) skills — might affect curriculum design and classroom procedures; and how a careful consideration of this relationship should lead us to rethink past assumptions and practices in second language reading instruction.

All four points represent major factors affecting how an ESL reading program will be designed, rationalized, implemented, tested, and evaluated. The views concerning these four areas provide the impetus for the curricular design to follow.

2.3 CURRICULAR DESIGN IN READING

According to Richards and Rodgers (1982), the design aspect is the attempt to identify the component micro-skills which constitute our competence as readers, and which allow objectives to be defined for teaching. The discussion of theory in this chapter, and in Eskey, suggests that we need a focused approach to second language reading instruction. The issues addressed here, therefore, center on a rationale and needs analysis for curriculum design, how one could develop such a design and what such an explicit reading curriculum would mean for the teacher, the administrator, and the curriculum and materials developer.

A curriculum rationale, and generalized needs analysis for reading instruction

There are a number of arguments for stating that reading is a (or perhaps *the*) critical skill needed by second language students for academic success. The first major argument for teaching reading comprises three parts, or strands. It asserts that extensive reading provides the means for developing what I am terming a "Critical Mass of Knowledge" of the English language and of world-background knowledge. This hypothesis of content needs and student needs, in turn, provides the key for both an independent reading ability and greater proficiency in the other language skills.

The first strand of this argument develops from observations discussed in Asimov (1971) and Bateson (1979) on the nature of knowledge and discovery. (See also Anderson 1973; Waldrop 1984.) Basically, discovery and creative thinking are emergent processes where the mind, almost of itself, makes nonobvious connections and relations between previously independent domains of knowledge in the mind of the person. It is always striking to note the inability of foreign students to discuss new or complex notions in English, even when their language abilities begin to allow for this. What is being noted is the rather formulaic thinking and expressions of opinions that often occur in advanced ESL classes. In short, second language students usually opt for "safe" responses. While there are many causes for this phenomenon, a chief one is the lack of background knowledge assumptions which form a basis from which to begin more speculative thinking, and which form the basis for many English language assumptions. The point is that prior reading experiences are crucial for having the information base to make nonobvious connections.

A second strand emerges from cognitive psychology and psycholinguistics. The development of schema theory, script theory, and frame theory all assert that knowledge is organized in large interrelated groupings. (See deBeaugrande 1980; Brown and Yule 1983 for discussion.) These clusters of topics are the internal information that is called upon to interpret and comprehend texts. The more refined the array of schemata and scripts at all levels of organization, the more likely it is for a student to understand a text better (Rumelhart 1980, 1984; Wittrock 1981; Widdowson, 1983). A simple demonstration of this principle is the study by Hudson (1982): students practicing a prereading task performed better than other students, essentially because their internal organizational schemata had been activated. These students were able to incorporate information from the text to adjust what might otherwise have been rather crude knowledge based schemata of the subject matter. In this way they were better able to anticipate and interpret when they were asked to read the material. (Research in L1 reading supports this view as well; e.g., Graves, Cook and LaBerge 1983.)

A third strand to this critical mass hypothesis comes from practical experimental research which shows positive, perhaps causal, relations between reading and writing abilities, and reading and general language proficiency (Stotsky 1983; Krashen 1984). The primary reason why Smith (1984) says we learn to read by reading, and we learn to write by reading, is that both crucially involve calling on the full range of world-background knowledge, language conventions, and vocabulary development which can only be internalized by exposure through reading.

The three strands combine to form a "critical mass" hypothesis for reading instruction. The more reading done, of the greatest informational variety and range of purposes, the quicker the reader will achieve, at some point (the critical mass point), the capacity for creating, refining, and connecting diverse arrays of cognitive schemata. Second language students will then be able to read in ways similar to successful students reading in their own language. Another view of this "critical mass" concept is to see it as the point where a student stops learning to read and only reads to learn (Singer 1981b; Eskey 1983; deBeaugrande 1984b).

This hypothesis is essentially an instructional one, and one that, over time, can be either validated or refuted. This hypothesis also subsumes and explains the basic claims that "reading is learning" and that extensive reading develops good writing skills. Given the support for the hypothesis in the reading research literature, it is reasonable to consider its impact on curriculum design and instruction.

The second argument for reading instruction follows from recent survey research at U.S. universities. Ostler (1980), Johns (1981), and Robertson (1983) all stress the importance of reading as a skill needed by students. Ostler indicated this in a survey of university ESL students. Johns obtained similar findings when surveying university faculty. Robertson, surveying all groups (students, teachers, administrators), came to the conclusion that ESL students used reading skills most, and that all concerned considered it the most important skill for future academic success. The remarkable point of these surveys is that reading is stressed at all, despite the tendency of teachers to ignore the less obvious "receptive" language skills, as well as the tendency by some to assume all students can read well enough if they just use their dictionaries.

A third reason why teaching reading is important is a more practical one. Emphasis on reading instruction is often ignored in the curricular design of many ESL programs. It is often somehow assumed that students will just acquire reading, and do not require extensive explicit instruction (cf. Downing 1979; Berman 1984; Pearson 1984a). What can be said about haphazard reading instruction is that students may acquire a range of bad habits which prevent them from learning to read the way we do as native readers, and also probably prevent them from learning to read the way they do in their own language. While Goodman and others suggest that the fluent reading process may be the same across languages, such a claim does not guarantee tranference of native language reading skills to L2 reading tasks.

A fourth reason for teaching reading derives from reflection on fluent native reading abilities. Reading requires rapid processing of text if the information is to be stored, incorporated, combined and retrieved in a manner similar to fluent L1 reading. It is quite true that students in many situations will have to read slowly and carefully. This applies to both native and nonnative students. The fluent native reader does not read James Michener and Noam Chomsky in the same way, at the same rate (Gibson and Levin 1975). However, in both cases the native reader can rely on a full range of comprehension strategies. He can skim back over material, he can scan back for some important information, and he can read at a faster pace to see where the argument or explanation is leading. In all cases, he can read the prose forms on the page rapidly enough that his time is not consumed by trying to understand the prose itself, but in trying to understand and relate the concepts being presented by the text. He may read Chomsky at a slow page rate, but this longer time is not being consumed by trying to understand the print itself. Thus we should recognize a distinction in slow reading between language processing difficulties and information processing difficulties. This argument ties in well with Smith's (1982) discussion of a minimal reading rate of around 200 WPM, and the variety of arguments for such a claim. Students who read engineering texts and science texts still need access to the full range of native reading skills.

A final reason for focusing on reading skills in an academic setting is that all students will be required, at certain points, to read exhaustively in classes. (The obvious apparent counterexamples here are the undergraduate and graduate natural science and engineering students.) Undergraduates at almost all universities require freshman writing classes, as well as a number of general education classes in social sciences and humanities. In these classes reading skills are essential. Graduate students have a much greater need for reading skills. Research work of an acceptable standard requires much reading. The notion of textbooks, or even books generally, being the major source of information recedes as the graduate student progresses and develops. There can be little doubt that a large majority of advanced graduate students need high-level reading skills to cope with the large mass of reading material on research in their respective fields.

These five points, taken together, argue strongly for an explicit, comprehensive reading curriculum in an academic setting. Unfortunately, recognizing the need to teach reading does not tell us how actually to do it.

Establishing a reading skills taxonomy

To this point we have established that reading is important for academic success, that current theory suggests important reading sub-skills, and that certain skills and capacities should be addressed explicitly. We can now begin to consider what these skills might be, and in turn, how these skills might be presented as parts of a comprehensive L2 reading curriculum design.

A Taxonomy of Micro-skills for Reading

1. Perception and Automatic Recognition Skills:
   a) recognize distinctive features, letters, parts of words, or whole words;
   b) discriminate between the similar orthographic patterns of different words;
   c) recognize synonymity, collocation, and other lexical/semantic relations between words (i.e., general-specific, part-whole, part-part, same semantic field, etc.);
   d) chunk smaller units into larger single processing units;
   e) limit regressions to normal amounts used by native readers;
   f) read rapidly enough to have adequate informational input to form or call up various schemata, scripts, plans, or goals;
   g) recognize different script and print styles;
   h) recognize orthographic cues (punctuation, capitalization, indentation);
   i) read charts, tables, graphs, maps, directories, etc.;
   j) find a specific item of information quickly.

2. Vocabulary:
   a) recognize vocabulary items similar to forms they know;
   b) guess the meanings of unknown items from context;
   c) guess the meanings of unknown items from derivational affixes;
   d) recognize variance of meanings in vocabulary items;
   e) guess meanings of vocabulary items that require cultural information to define.

3. Syntactic Skills:
   recognize the various syntactic patterns of the language.

4. Cohesion:
   recognize ellipsis, transition forms, reference, etc. (the range of cohesive devices, as in Halliday and Hasan 1976).

5. Coherence:
   a) recognize different word order patterns occurring for functional and stylistic purposes;
   b) detect topical words from less important ones;
   c) read rapidly over a text to determine the topic and its usefulness for reader's purpose;
   d) infer situations, goal, participants—local inferencing procedures from the text;
   e) use real world knowledge and experience to work out purposes, goals, settings, and procedures;
   f) predict outcomes;
   g) infer links and connections between groups of events/objects;
   h) detect coherence relations such as main idea, supporting detail, given information, new information, and basic cognitive relations such as cause and effect, time sequence, spatial sequence, condition, etc.;
   i) recognize larger logical rhetorical patterns such as definition, exemplification, classification, comparison and contrast.

6. Author's Stance:
   a) distinguish between literal and implied meaning;
   b) determine author's goals, intents, biases.

7. Application Skills:
   a) critique particular texts and compare them to other texts;
   b) synthesize and integrate material.

8. Meta-skills:

   a) read at different rates for different purposes and tasks;

   b) use various reading sub-skills simultaneously and interactively;

   c) absorb large amounts of material over a reasonable amount of time (concentration on the reading task);

   d) use the dictionary properly, and recognize its limitations.

At this point it is important to note that taxonomies, of themselves, do not make a curriculum design. In fact, as Widdowson (1983) strongly argues, a taxonomy provides very little guidance on how to arrange and implement it into instructional practice. In this regard, there is also little in the way of L1 research on program design to refer to for support.

> Because few comparative evaluations of comprehensive programs exist, practitioners lack basic information needed for intelligent program selection, and researchers lack data that could alert them to important program components. Some well-conceived empirical program evaluations would do little damage and might possibly raise the present state. (Jenkins and Pany 1980:572)

In its present state, the taxonomy of micro-skills should be seen as a tentative outline of candidates for practical reading instruction. As has been suggested above, there is a need to establish and study comprehensive reading programs before any skills taxonomy can be firmly established (cf. Hoffman and Rutherford 1984).

Designing a reading curriculum

On the questions of either curriculum design or teaching procedures, L1 reading researchers typically have little to offer the second language teacher. Goodman and Smith, for example, leave it to the law of natural selection among students, implying that formal instruction is of limited use to reading acquisition. Other researchers, however, take issue with the notion that direct instruction is pointless, and also with the notion that reading instruction cannot be provided within a multi-skills framework.

Attempts to derive instructional procedures from recent theory in L1 are few, and much more work is needed before it can do more than suggest instructional practice for second language reading. Apart from the limited L1 research, good practical advice for second language reading instruction can be found in Eskey (1973); Clarke and Silberstein (1977); Mackay (1979); Dubin and Olshtain (1980); Mahon (1980); and Carrell and Eisterhold (1983). In addition, a number of recent texts for reading instruction provide material and procedures designed to teach a range of important skills.

Despite these articles and texts, we still lack the critical overall design for reading curricula which will incorporate the procedures we want, in ways that systematically develop those skills observed and hypothesized for reading (e.g., see Brown and Hirst 1983). Whatever design is constructed will also have to account for time contraints, monetary contraints, and constraint from other student priorities; that is, a reading design will have to build in flexibility as well as comprehensive systematic development over the entire range of program courses. One drawback to reading instruction that must be recognized at the outset is that achieving success requires a long time commitment, beyond the limits of "a reading class" for one semester.

Recalling the basic insight of interactive models, that many skills are used interactively in reading, we want to set up a curriculum which develops these skills most effectively. A reading curriculum should be set up among four interacting components teaching the various skills from the taxonomy presented earlier. The first task is to teach students how to read at a normal rate, using the relevant reading skills and strategies. These include scanning, recognition practice, reading rate practice, etc.; thus, this component is related to the skills of recognition and various meta-skills.

The second task is to include the standard, recognizable task of teaching appropriate grammar and vocabulary development in whatever way is most compatible with individual biases. The point is that such a strand cannot be blithely ignored in second language reading instruction. This component relates to the major skills of vocabulary and syntax in the taxonomy.

The third task is to teach students to read and work with extended pieces of texts comfortably, applying those skills and strategies that are part of the native reader's skills — for example, reading for general information and maintaining concentration over extended periods of time. This strand forces students to read in a manner similar to the way native readers process longer texts. This may be the most crucial part of a successful reading program. Certain coherence skills, application skills, and meta-skills apply to this component.

The fourth task is to teach students to use careful, analytic reading skills such as forming inferences, noting textual relations, synthesizing information, recognizing discourse information, and forming reasoned opinions. Cohesion, coherence, author's stance, and application skills most closely match this component.

The best way to see the set of tasks globally is to form a 4 X 3 matrix. (See Figure 1.) The goal of the curriculum design is deciding how to fill each cell in the matrix, and how this can best be done given the particular constraints of any program. Setting up a program following this design is admittedly somewhat complex and difficult. One must define goals at all levels, define the interaction between both levels and tasks, recognize the relation between overall curricular aims and syllabus objectives, and recognize the relation between syllabus objectives and teaching procedures. There is support in the literature for teaching each of these components. Suffice it to say here that a good reading curriculum will try to include and combine these four components at all levels of instruction.

	elementary	intermediate	advanced
recog/reading rate	X	X	X
analytic reading	X	X	X
extensive reading	X	X	X
grammar/vocabulary	X	X	X

Figure 1: A 4 X 3 Matrix

The role of commercially prepared materials

It is evident that a reading curriculum cannot be successfully devised by creating a few reading classes and using commercial reading texts as the full program. Second language materials are seldom comprehensive from beginning through advanced levels. Materials especially designed for particular skills for a semester's use are written with no expectation of coherence and continuity across the full range of second language class levels. In addition to the continuity limitations of commercial materials, no reading texts on the market are capable of accounting for all four tasks outlined at any level. Recent commercial materials are relatively good at teaching analytic reading skills, and some are reasonably good at teaching reading rate skills, but most impede the development of extensive reading practice. Specifically, there are three paradoxes that arise out of using commercial texts for teaching reading, if they are adopted as the total reading program.

1. "I suppose you have a better way."
   All texts tend to focus more or less on teaching discourse grammar as a means to teach reading (though this may be better suited to writing instruction). This is the status quo of reading materials on the market. The primary paradox is that a partial approach is accepted as a complete program. We give students part and expect the whole in return.

2. "I wonder if they can really read."
   A look at most texts on the market proves the truth of this paradox. Any text is obviously constrained by space and money considerations, but that doesn't mean that we are free to ignore the problem. We want students to be able to read and absorb large amounts of text, as native readers are able to do, but we teach them with materials that offer relatively small amounts of text material.

3. "See no evil."

   We try to teach students all the right habits in class, and then let them go home with their dictionaries to plow through the short texts in the textbooks by translating everything. Textbooks often try to teach reading skills with passages of two to four pages. Almost always, students return to class two days later with the texts having translations scribbled all over them. Any reading teacher is used to seeing the texts in front of the students in the next class covered with translations, and politely ignores the fact that the student cannot be reading those texts the way we do. We pretend not to see this, or refuse to admit that it is such a problem. But it is clear that students are deciphering texts in a nonnative manner.

These paradoxes do not imply that teachers should abandon good reading textbooks on the market. The textbooks are useful, but their limitations should be recognized, and attempts should be made to create a more rational overall reading curriculum. One major way to round out a reading program is to introduce extensive reading material into the curriculum, especially at intermediate and advanced levels, where textbook readers are typically deemphasized and discourse grammar becomes the more prominent focus of reading instruction.

The role of the administrator

The major implication of the arguments for a strong curriculum design is that reading instruction cannot be limited to one "reading" course at any particular level. Adequate treatment requires a well planned coordination of reading texts among the levels of a program that reflect integrated goals and a single philosophy. Such a requirement goes beyond the organizational capabilities of any teacher in a program and is, rather, the province of the higher administration and the curriculum coordinator. As Hoffman and Rutherford (1984) have argued, a committed administrator is crucial in successful reading programs.

Reading is a skill which, if it is to be taught directly, demands extensive attention, persistence, continuity and ongoing support. The efforts of a good teacher will not extend far beyond that particular classroom if the student's next teacher does not intend to build on the work already done, or if the next teacher is not aware of the complexities and demands of successful reading instruction. In a similar way, students will experience confusion and frustration when they move from a class where they recognize progress in their reading to a class that seems to ignore reading instruction altogether.

Program supervisors and curriculum designers must plan actively for a curriculum that intelligently addresses the perceived needs. For reading, this is not an easy task given the different claims about second language reading instruction, and the range of other priorities calling for attention in a second language program. A good administrator must realize in this context that an effective reading program cannot be carried out by a single teacher or a single course. At some point, it is necessary to have a comprehensive program design which integrates different course levels.

The role of the teacher

Briefly, the role of the teacher is to facilitate reading, raise consciousness, build confidence, ensure continuity and systematicity, show involvement, and demand performance. Admittedly, the word 'facilitate' is a worn word in ESL. Nevertheless, since we cannot define reading exactly, it is a little too strong to say we teach the reading process directly. Rather, we try to get students to read and to develop skills aimed at improving their ability to read (see Eskey, this volume).

The teacher in a reading program is often faced with the problem of students who do not always recognize the difficulties they face in an academic program, but who experience frustration when these difficulties are encountered. (Students in programs which emphasize writing or speaking, as opposed to reading, consciously recognize those shortcomings.) For the teacher, heightening students' awareness and supporting students' efforts are essential.

Moreover, any program attempting to reach the level of automaticity in reading skill production (see Eskey, this volume) must insist on continuity and systematicity. Continuity is the process wherein reading instruction begun in week 2 will still be emphasized in week 12. Systematicity is the process wherein procedures lead naturally from one to the next, and wherein procedures are repeated regularly. Both processes are essential to a reading program. Continuity ensures that students' efforts and commitments will not be disregarded at a later point and demonstrates the integrity of the commitment on the part of the teacher. Systematicity shows students that teachers have a coherent teaching plan in which procedures are seen as purposeful and effective over the longer time. It also offers students guideposts against which to measure their progress in comparison with prior performance on similar tasks.

Finally, the teacher must show involvement and demand performance—two sides of the same behavior. A blasé or detached attitude will destroy students' enthusiasm and jeopardize instruction. Since reading instruction must begin with a fair amount of faith and good intentions on the part of the student, overt signs of involvement and interest are all the more important. Progress in reading is only recognizable over a period of time, and often in less overt ways than direct production or application. Teachers must be willing to believe in the process as well. One clear indication of faith and commitment is to demand performance. Reading is a personal experience and the teacher cannot peer over the shoulder of the student. But the teacher can require assignments to be prepared, require participation, and place expectations on the students. Most students rightly interpret such behavior as commitment and involvement on the teacher's part. What we have outlined here are general requirements placed on the teacher in a reading curriculum. While much more may be said in this regard, the above serves as an adequate overview.

To summarize, we have explored why it is important to teach reading, what skills are involved in teaching ESL reading, how these skills would translate into general curricular aims, how one should view commercial reading materials, and the role of both the administrator and the teacher. Yet to be discussed are the teaching procedures available to the teacher for planning the syllabus and organizing the reading class.

2.4 PROCEDURES FOR INSTRUCTION

Given that the goal of design is to generate a taxonomy of basic reading skills and insructional aims, the difficult practical issue becomes how to move through a curricular design to instructional practice. In this discussion I will only suggest a general outline for instructional procedures in a reading program. Detailed discussion follows in the chapters by Stoller, Mahon, Jensen, and Dubin. There are essentially two major issues involved in the discussion here:

1. How do we translate reading as discussed in this chapter and in Chapter 1 into instructional practice?

2. How are the different parts of instructional practice to be balanced and combined for the most effective results?

Reading, for instructional purposes, is the ability to recognize vocabulary and syntax automatically, the ability to read at a reasonably rapid rate, depending on the context, the ability to grasp the main idea and scan for a piece of information, and the ability to adjust rate and adapt strategies for careful analytic reading and critical evaluation.

Given the more practical view of reading above, classroom teaching procedures can be defined along three axes: proper orientation, effective materials, and realistic goals.

First there must be major confidence building work. Students must be sold on the need for reading; unless they understand the need, or the difficulties involved with teaching this skill, reading instruction will not succeed. There are four things that can be done in this regard:

1. "Sell" both teachers and students on the idea.
2. Set up progress charts. Typically, students will initially accept on faith the exercises that will lead to improvement.
3. Use charts to show progress later on as students see some improvements.
4. Have a rationale for all exercises given to students.

The second major requirement is a set of materials to focus on the crucial habits that we want students to develop. Exercises must be somewhat challenging but never too difficult. This advice may appear obvious but is all too often disregarded by producers of reading materials in the efforts to offer 'authentic' texts. An overriding consideration in instruction is for students to develop the confidence that they can indeed read. For this reason there must be a balance between challenge and frustration. The types of materials for reading instruction should include:

1. guessing from context
2. skimming and scanning
3. vocabulary development
4. reading rate materials
   a) prereading
   b) reading rate recognition drills
   c) phrased reading
   d) paced reading, pacing exercises
   e) cloze identification exercises
5. extensive outside reading material (also including ESL texts and reference materials)
6. analytic reading materials
   a) literal comprehension
   b) interpeting complex information and presuppositions
   c) drawing low-level inferences
   d) drawing global inferences
   e) synthesizing information
   f) evaluating information
7. a good place where students can read
8. materials that continually recycle habit-forming exercises

The final aspect of teaching reading is a proper set of curricular aims. Three listed here should be part of any reading program.

1. reading fluency to a relative degree (e.g., 200 WPM)
2. students' confidence in their own ability to read new material
3. a set of nonconscious processing habits that, in fact, allow them to read new material in a manner similar to L1 readers.

2.5 CONCLUSION

All of the discussion in this chapter has been an attempt to answer the first question noted at the beginning of this section, "How can we translate reading as discussed in Chapter 1 and this chapter into instructional practice?" Chapters 3-5 will explore this issue in much greater depth.

The second question, "What balance of instructional procedures is most effective?" is much more difficult to answer. There is little in the way of current research to inform us of the best instructional mixture over the length of a comprehensive program. This should perhaps not be surprising considering the few comprehensive L1 reading programs currently in use, and the total lack of an explicit, theoretically informed curriculum design for second language reading instruction. A major task of the three practically oriented chapters that follow is not simply to suggest ways to teach reading, but to suggest a possible "most effective" combination of instructional practice, which becomes, at least, a starting point for future experimental research and practical refinement.

FOR STUDY AND DISCUSSION

1. What framework is proposed by Richards and Rodgers (1982)? How does this framework offer us a way to bridge the gap between theory and practice? Why does a taxonomy of skills create deceptive problems for curriculum design?

2. How is reading defined in this chapter? How does this definition allow us to find practical implications for reading instruction? What are these practical implications?

3. How important is reading instruction in an academic setting? What arguments can be presented for emphasizing reading? How is the concept of "Critical Mass" central to the concerns of academic reading instruction?

4. Why is the question "Is reading different in different languages?" not the same as "Is reading development different in a first language and in a second language?"

5. How would one want to design a reading curriculum? What skills would be practical at each proficiency level and in each of the curricular components discussed in the chapter?

6. Why do commercially prepared materials only partially resolve problems in reading instruction? What can be done in place of, or to supplement, commercial textbook materials?

7. Select a proficiency level and construct a reading program which provides the best balance of procedures. Be prepared to argue for your program design (you may want to refer to Part II, this volume).

8. Select a curricular component and explain how you would develop instruction for that component through all proficiency levels (again, you may want to refer to Part II, this volume).

9. Why is an interested administrator crucial for a successful reading program?

FOR FURTHER READING

There are a number of sources which should prove useful for individuals wishing to pursue particular topics. A suggestion for further reading must begin with Richards and Rodgers' (1982) and Richards' (1983, 1984) instructional framework and discussion of curriculum as a means for moving from theory to practice. Theoretical perspectives on reading may be pursued in Lesgold and Perfetti (1981b); Taylor and Taylor (1983); van Dijk and Kintsch (1983); Perfetti (1985), and sources cited in Eskey (this volume). On the issue of developing "a Critical Mass" for reading, deBeaugrande (1980); Rumelhart (1980, 1984); and Brown and Yule (1983) all discuss schema theory and related cognitive organization theory essential to reading.

On a more practical level, research by Berliner (1981); Guthrie (1981a); Samuels (1981); Elley and Mangubhai (1983); and Hoffman and Rutherford (1984) all point to important instructional/curricular design variables in successful reading programs. Discussion of numerous teaching procedures may be found in Grellet (1981) and Nuttall (1982). Finally, for instructional procedures that seem to work well, readers may turn to a number of good current texts noted in other chapters in this volume.

Part II

PART II: OVERVIEW

It is not possible to provide a simple recipe for reading instruction which applies in any context. We can, however, set up guidelines for reading instruction in a number of different contexts, and draw from these instructional designs which are likely to meet a particular program's needs. In these three chapters, Stoller, Mahon, and Jensen present designs for reading instruction in three distinct contexts. Together they present an overview for planning instruction according to parameters of student proficiency levels, types of reading programs, and the focus of instruction.

Stoller presents a general model of instruction for high elementary/low intermediate students within the context of a reading lab. Emphasis is placed on identification/recognition skills as one important foundation for reading proficiency. Mahon presents reading instruction aimed primarily at intermediate students who are in a separate class for reading skills study. She stresses the skills and the practice that are essential for reading rate development. Jensen presents reading instruction for advanced students as part of an integrated skills class, in which all language skills are taught together. Her focus is partly on reading rate but also on critical reading skills. All authors make the point that the skills and techniques they discuss are adaptable for other proficiency levels and other types of programs.

The three articles together provide a set of instructional options for any reading program. Their contributions, as a whole, add substance to the movement from theory to practice which was introduced in Part I of this volume. They present the basic instructional techniques assumed in much of Part III of this volume.

Chapter 3

Reading Lab: Developing Low-Level Reading Skills

Fredricka Stoller
Northern Arizona University

3.1 INTRODUCTION

Because of its inherently flexible character, a Reading Lab[1]—an independent reading program with time built in for extensive reading—provides an ideal setting for students to practice reading as well as receive instruction in both bottom-up and top-down skills. (See the Eskey and Grabe chapters for discussion of these skills.) Recognizing reading as a skill in and of itself, a Reading Lab allows reading to be addressed directly, giving this vital skill the focused attention it deserves. A Reading Lab is of particular importance to academically oriented students who will inevitably have heavy reading loads and a pressing need to develop efficient reading skills and strategies (Eskey 1979; Ostler 1980; Johns 1981; Robertson 1983). It must be stressed that a Reading Lab need not be a mere adjunct to other ESL/EFL courses. Rather, it should be seen as an independent course that focuses specifically on the reading skill itself.

In a focused setting such as a Reading Lab, both teachers and students can make a conscious effort to develop and improve reading skills. Here teachers have an open forum to promote the importance of reading as one of the keys to academic success. Teachers can provide students with a variety of well-defined activities for practice and can discuss and later remind students of what they should do to become efficient readers. Such a focused approach to reading permits students to monitor their reading progress easily, which, in turn, builds their confidence, another key to academic success. Once students recognize the need, and understand what it takes to become better readers, visible improvement will follow through practice and the use of progress charts and graphs.

In this chapter, a prototype Reading Lab will be presented, one whose format can easily be adapted to many kinds of ESL/EFL programs. The prototype description will include an explanation of its basic components and their respective goals, the role of the instructor, and administrative concerns. A detailed review of the individual Reading Lab components will include the rationale for the activities, available materials, actual procedures, and the sequencing of activities. Attention will also be given to the physical set-up of the Lab. The prototype Reading Lab presented here can easily be adjusted to meet the particular needs of students at more advanced or more elementary levels.[2]

3.2 THE PROTOTYPE READING LAB

My primary concern here is to present a prototype Reading Lab designed for low intermediate students (400-450 TOEFL). It is, however, a design which is potentially useful in any language program and at any language proficiency level. For purposes of illustration, I will present a Reading Lab program that follows a typical semester time frame.[3] This should by no means be interpreted as a fixed restriction on Reading Lab programs.

The Reading Lab can be divided into two principal parts, in-class activities and out-of-class activities. The in-class activities can be further divided into teacher-guided and individualized activities (See Figure 1.)[4]

The set of activities listed in Figure 1 introduces many reading skills necessary for effective reading. The skills and corresponding goals for each activity are summarized in Figure 2.

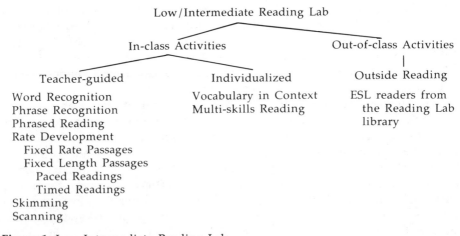

Figure 1: Low Intermediate Reading Lab

Reading Lab Activities

Skills/Goals	Rapid word recognition	Rapid phrase recognition	Phrased reading	Rate development activities	Skimming	Scanning	Multi-skills reading	Vocabulary in context	Outside reading
Simple word perception	X								
Simple phrase perception		X							
Breaking habit of reading word by word		X	X	X	X	X	X		X
Recognition of clues which signal phrases		X	X						
Reading in meaningful units		X	X	X					
Deducing vocabulary in context				X			X	X	X
Breaking dependency on the dictionary				X			X	X	X
Skimming for the main idea(s)				X	X		X		X
Scanning for specific information				X		X	X		
Comprehension improvement			X	X	X	X	X	X	X
Recollection of facts and ideas				X			X		X
Making inferences				X			X		X
Conceptualization of reading rate				X					
Rate improvement	X	X	X	X	X	X	X		X
Critical reading				X			X		X
Independent reading				X			X		X
Confidence building	X	X	X	X	X	X	X	X	X

Figure 2: Principal Goals of Reading Lab Activities

3.3 THE INSTRUCTOR'S ROLE IN THE READING LAB

From the activities listed in Figure 1, one might conclude that only a portion of the Reading Lab activities requires the presence of an instructor. However, the instructor is an indispensable part of the Reading Lab and plays an integral role in all activities. The instructor should be present at all times, whether the students are working on teacher-guided activities or individualized activities.

In the Reading Lab, the instructor promotes the importance of reading, thereby motivating the students and setting a mood conducive to reading. The instructor also helps the students develop a positive attitude towards reading. The importance of such an attitude cannot be overemphasized; it represents one of the instructor's primary responsibilities. In addition, it is important that the instructor be accessible and able to monitor student progress, providing feedback and encouragement at the appropriate time (Coady 1979; Eskey 1979). Yet, the teacher should never be on "center stage" (Stevick 1980, 1982 discusses this notion more fully). That is, the instructor cannot play a traditionally active role while students are reading. If the instructor does, that reading becomes some other task (Chastain 1976; Gaskill 1979).

In the Reading Lab students need sufficient time to sit and read. Therefore, the teacher has to strike a proper balance between active instruction, teacher-guided activities, and individualized reading activities. The balance naturally shifts during the semester. At the onset of the semester, the individualized activities are actually teacher-guided, since the instructor has to introduce the materials and procedures to the students. As the students begin to feel more at ease with the materials and procedures, the balance begins to shift, and the students increasingly take control of, and responsibility for, their own reading. A healthy balance seems to rest somewhere between 30-35% of the time devoted to teacher-guided activities and 65-70% devoted to individualized activities. Of course, the percentage of time allotted to teacher-guided activities and individualized activities should be flexible, determined by students' needs and the nature of the ESL program in question. For example, if the students are doing extensive outside reading for other ESL courses or academic courses, more teacher-guided activities in the Reading Lab might be appropriate.

Introducing the Reading Lab activities and getting students started require careful and consistent preparation by the instructor. The instructor must, of course, know the rationale for each activity, be convinced of its effectiveness, and communicate this to the students. Once the Reading Lab activities have been introduced, it is the instructor's responsibility to make sure students follow the correct procedure for each activity. Most Reading Lab activities have their own procedure and their own particular progress chart or graph, making a teacher orientation essential.

This notion of charting progress through tables and graphs is a critical aspect of the instructor's responsibilities. This visual representation of a student's progress serves as an excellent motivating tool and is, therefore, an essential part of the Lab. Becoming familiar with all procedures and all methods of noting progress is essential for both the instructor and students.

3.4 FROM THE ADMINISTRATOR'S VIEWPOINT

Program administrators and supervisors must realize that the instructor's attitude towards reading and reading instruction is crucial for an effective Reading Lab program. Many ESL/EFL instructors' views of reading instruction stem from exposure to and/or the teaching of traditional reading texts in traditional reading classes; these traditional classes typically have been organized around a short reading assignment, followed by numerous comprehension questions, a number of vocabulary exercises, and two or three grammar points. ESL instructors' limited exposure to a focused reading program most often results in a shallow perception of reading and reading instruction. Further exacerbating the problem is that most traditional ESL reading texts are devoid of focused reading skills exercises or only have a limited number. Textbooks have only recently come out which seriously and conscientiously approach ESL/EFL students' reading needs. In addition, teacher's manuals that accompany programmed materials, and textbook introductions are typically inadequate; these teachers' materials need to be supplemented with a detailed orientation to focused reading instruction and the Reading Lab.

A further potential problem for ESL/EFL teachers is that many reading improvement materials, ranging from texts to programmed reading packages, are designed for native readers.[5] Consequently, these ESL teachers must be sufficiently well-informed to evaluate existing materials, those written with both the native and nonnative reader in mind, in order to decide if the materials are appropriate or not for their particular ESL/EFL students. Being sensitive to the specific needs of ESL/EFL students, the teachers must evaluate materials in terms of (1) vocabulary level; (2) cultural assumptions; (3) general level of assumed background information; (4) general format, including illustrations, titles, etc.; and (5) syntactic complexity. Instructors must be able to identify inappropriate materials. At the same time they should identify materials that could be adapted to meet the needs of their ESL students. (See Nuttall 1982:25-32 for discussion of issues related to text selection.)

For a Reading Lab to be successful, a detailed orientation to reading must be provided for all instructors. In a properly organized orientation, teachers will (1) develop a strong sense of what the reading process is, (2) appreciate the importance and purpose of the Reading Lab, (3) understand the importance of focused reading skills development for academically oriented students, (4) learn the rationale for each Reading Lab activity, (5) learn the proper sequencing of activities, (6) become familiar with procedures for each activity, (7) learn to evaluate reading development materials, and (8) learn to adapt materials for an ESL/EFL student population, if necessary.

3.5 DISCUSSION OF THE PROTOTYPE READING LAB COMPONENTS

In-class teacher guided activities

Devoting a portion of the Reading Lab to teacher-guided activities is crucial. There are a number of skills that the entire class can practice together, with the guidance and encouragement of the instructor. At this level, it is beneficial to concentrate on rapid word and phrase recognition exercises, phrased reading, rate development activities, and skimming and scanning.

Rapid word and phrase recognition exercises

Rapid word and phrase recognition exercises are the first of the teacher-guided activities to be introduced to the students in the Reading Lab. Recent reading research has indicated the importance of accurate and rapid word recognition. Much research indicates that "comprehension deficits can at least in part be traced to deficiencies within the word recognition process" (Chabot, Zehr, Prinzo, Petros 1984:148). Many researchers actually claim that accurate and rapid, ideally automatic, recognition skills distinguish skilled from less skilled readers (Stanovich 1980, 1981b; Lesgold and Perfetti 1981a; Perfetti and Roth 1981; Schuberth, Spoehr and Lane 1981; Spoehr and Schuberth 1981; Mitchell 1982; van Dijk and Kintsch 1983; Chabot, Zehr, Prinzo, and Petros 1984).

The word and phrase recognition exercises are intended to help students develop their so-called "bottom-up" skills. That is, students learn to react rapidly and accurately to the appearance of English words and then English phrases as a whole. From these activities, students develop a sense of the visual image of key words or phrases. These exercises also serve as a means for introducing the importance of rate, a notion that will be reinforced continuously throughout the Reading Lab program. Since reading at a faster rate improves comprehension (Smith 1982), the Reading Lab furnishes exercises to improve rate on a continual basis, beginning with recognition exercises, followed later in the course with other types of rate improvement exercises. These recognition exercises are not to be mistaken as actual "readings," nor are they to be confused with vocabulary enrichment exercises. They are simply recognition exercises, sometimes referred to as perception or identification exercises, one of the first crucial steps in a reading skills development program.

The word recognition exercises, later followed by the phrase recognition exercises, should be introduced early in the semester and continued throughout much of the Reading Lab course. The introduction should include: (1) a rationale for these recognition exercises; (2) a discussion of the procedure; and (3) an explanation of the overall importance of developing efficient reading skills. The latter point must be emphasized early in the Reading Lab course; understanding the importance of efficient reading skills will prepare the students psychologically to tackle the challenge of the Reading Lab and future reading commitments. Furthermore, it will help students develop a positive attitude towards the Reading Lab and reading in general.

To reinforce the importance of rate development, all recognition exercises should be timed, and the times recorded. Ideally, three recognition exercises should be done consecutively. The first can be considered a warm-up exercise; the students strive to proceed faster and more accurately with the last two. No more than ten to fifteen minutes should be devoted to these exercises in any given Lab period. If both the students and instructor do not confuse these exercises with vocabulary expansion exercises, the three exercises can be done quickly yet be effective (and enjoyable). With practice and encouragement, in addition to consistent record keeping, students will quickly notice improvement in both their recognition rate and accuracy. As they progress through the exercises, their perceptions will become surer and their choices more accurate. The entire process builds confidence.

There are a variety of recognition exercises that can be used in the Reading Lab. Some useful texts for this purpose are Adams (1969, 1980, 1981), Harris (1966), Yorkey (1970, 1982), Miller, Steeber, and Ladd (1981), Miller, L. (1984), and Miller and Steeber (1985a, 1985b).

Ideal circumstances would probably dictate the use of individual teacher-generated exercises incorporating words or phrases to be encountered by the students in their actual reading passages. These exercises could easily be modeled after the exercises in the texts mentioned above. The word recognition exercises found in these texts vary only slightly and all strive to accomplish the same goals. Below is an abbreviated sample of a rapid word recognition exercise:

Key word

1. class	close	cloze	class	clash	crash
2. sold	told	bold	mold	sold	cold
3. book	bike	book	bake	beak	boot
4. worst	watch	waste	wasp	washed	worst
5. read	real	red	rate	read	raid

This exercise, similar to those found in the texts mentioned above, runs from left to right, getting the students used to sweeping their eyes across the page. The students are directed to look at the key word, then sweep their eyes to the right until they spot the word. The moment they see the word, they mark it and continue immediately on to the next line. Instructors should encourage the students to locate the word as quickly as possible but also to strive for accuracy. Students should time themselves and record their time.[6] The exercises are always corrected, either as a class activity, in small groups or individually, and the results recorded by the individual students.

The texts mentioned above also have a wide variety of phrase recognition exercises. Even though they vary in format, and the chunks of meaningful language are larger than single words, the goals are similar. In all the exercises the students are asked to focus on the visual image of the phrase as a whole rather than the individual words. This progression from word recognition to phrase recognition, in theory, bridges the gap between reading word by word and reading in phrase groups.

The following phrase recognition exercise is patterned after an exercise in Harris (1966):

1. pay day	pay day	Ⓢ D
2. big cat	big rat	S D
3. put on	put in	S D
4. on the way	in the way	S D
5. in the bag	in the rag	S D

The students read the phrases, from left to right, as quickly as possible, to determine if they are the same (S) or different (D). These exercises, like the ones to follow, provide students with practice in responding rapidly and accurately to phrase units.

The second set of example exercises, modeled after the Miller, Steeber, and Ladd (1981) and Miller and Steeber (1985a, 1985b) exercises, also runs from left to right. The students look at the key word and spot the identical phrase. In these exercises, a tiny dot appears above each phrase. The slower students, who tend to see phrases as separate word units rather than a whole unit, fixate on the dot and use their peripheral vision to see the entire phrase.

Key phrase

1. to have lunch	to make lunch	to have brunch	to have lunch
2. fast dancing	fast dancer	fast dancing	fast dancer
3. to get tan	to be tan	to get tan	to be tanned
4. central heat	control heat	central heat	controlled heat
5. a can opener	an open can	an opened can	a can opener

The last set of examples, drawn from a format in Adams' (1969), are in vertical columns. In the single column exercise (A), students look at the key phrase and run their eyes down the list, which can be as long as thirty-eight words, as quickly as possible, in order to identify the key phrase, which may appear more than once. In exercises B and C, involving multiple columns, the students read from left to right, from one column to the next, and mark the key phrase every time it appears.

A. Key phrase: lazy day

   crazy day

   hazy day

   cloudy day

   ~~lazy day~~

   windy day

   nasty day

   ~~lazy day~~

B. Key phrase: on the floor

on the book	in the flood
on the bay	in the blood
on the door	on the floor
in the door	on the door
on the floor	on the flower
in the lore	in the flour
in the flood	on the floor

C. Key phrase: drive a car

drive a truck	rent a car	drive cars
drive a bus	drive a car	car driver
dry a car	wash a car	drive a tractor
park a car	drive a truck	drive two cars
buy a car	buy a truck	drive a car
drive a car	buy a bar	drive a bus

Phrased reading

Once the students understand the importance and purpose of the recognition exercises and work through a number of them, building their recognition rate and accuracy, phrased reading exercises are introduced. Recognition and phrased reading exercises are not introduced simultaneously, as the latter are more effective if preceded by recognition work. The phrased reading exercises add a comprehension variable, focusing on the importance of reading in meaningful phrase units as opposed to reading word-by-word. Reading in meaningful units, in turn, positively affects their reading rate and comprehension. (For a more detailed discussion of phrased reading, see Mahon, this volume.)

Rate development activities

The recognition exercises and the phrased readings prepare students for a directed and systematic rate development program. Complete reading passages, whether simplified or authentic, and series of rate development activities encourage students to read faster. Yet, because reading speed should not be developed at the expense of comprehension, it is important that the students practice both simultaneously in these Reading Lab activities. A properly constructed rate development component, in addition, reinforces other valuable reading skills. Because the readings are timed, (1) students are obliged to determine the meaning of unfamiliar vocabulary items from the context of the passage rather than depend on the dictionary, (2) students are forced to read in meaningful phrase units, and (3) students can recall facts and make inferences with follow-up comprehension questions.

Rate development materials can take on many forms. One common format is to have a *fixed rate* imposed on a series of reading passages that get consecutively and progressively longer, though not necessarily more difficult. The fixed rate should be challenging but not frustrating for the students. As they progress through a series of fixed rate passages, their rate improves due to the added length of the text. In order to coordinate rate and comprehension improvement, these reading passages should also be followed by a set of comprehension questions; these should be general in nature, not questions calling for small details which are really tests of memory. The questions should be answered within the imposed rate limit.

Any number of materials can be used for the fixed rate component of the Reading Lab—for example, textbooks that have reading passages which get progressively longer or the SRA *Multi-Read II* "Rate Builders" which are designed specifically for this purpose.

Another common format is to have a series of *fixed length* passages read with progressively faster reading rates. Like the fixed rate materials, fixed length passages should include a set of comprehension questions. These fixed length passages can be used in two different manners, either as paced readings or timed readings, the difference being that the reading pace is controlled by the teacher in the former, whereas students work completely on their own in the latter.

When initiating the fixed length reading rate development activities in the Reading Lab, students should begin with paced readings and then move on to timed readings. The 10-book series entitled *Timed Readings: Fifty 400-Word Passages with Questions for Building Reading Speed*, Spargo and Williston, has proven useful for this particular purpose. Of course, any set of passages of equal length can be used in a similar fashion to facilitate pacing. The passages in this particular series, all 400 words in length, are marked with dots at every 100 words. The pace is controlled by the teacher who signals an agreed-upon pace at given intervals by lightly tapping the table. Upon hearing the signal, students should have read the 100 words between the dots. The students who are reading slower jump ahead and attempt to read the next 100 words in the designated time period; the students who find themselves reading faster slow down and try to read the next section more carefully. For example, when reading a 400-word passage at 100 words per minute, the teacher will signal the students every 60 seconds. Within four minutes, the students will finish reading the passage. Using these passages in this manner, students learn to conceptualize a reading pace by reading at a specific rate between the dots. (See also, Jensen, this volume.) With continual practice, the teacher is able to set a faster pace and students gradually build up their reading rate which, in turn, improves their comprehension. Once students complete the passage, they continue on their own to answer the comprehension questions. These questions help students recall facts and understand ideas presented in the passage, as well as make inferences.

Two consecutive paced readings should be given at the beginning of the paced reading component. As the students progress, the instructor can use the same materials to pair one paced reading with a timed reading. After reading the paced exercise at an imposed rate, the students read a new passage, of the same length, without the imposed rate. The paced reading exercises actually help students set realistic goals for themselves. Generally, the students' goal should be to read the new passage at the same rate as their paced reading, if not faster, maintaining the same degree of comprehension or better. This second reading will be timed on an individual basis and the results recorded. These recorded times are an indication of a student's actual reading rate.[7] With encouragement and diligence, students show a marked improvement over the course of a semester. Even though the passages are short in comparison to the students' future reading assignments, in either ESL courses or other academic courses, rate development with such exercises gives them the confidence for reading longer passages.

The rate development activities used in the Reading Lab, whether they be fixed length or fixed rate, prove to be most effective if the actual reading exercises are preceded by pre-reading activities, led by the instructor. Soliciting an oral or written response, the instructor can (1) ask students to focus on the title and any illustrations that may accompany the text; (2) ask students to skim the entire passage quickly for the main idea—this is particularly important if the title is not straightforward and/or if there are no illustrations; (3) ask students to scan the passage for specific details considered crucial for overall comprehension; and/or (4) introduce "loaded" cultural presuppositions which would otherwise mislead or confuse students, or perhaps go unnoticed. The incorporation of these pre-reading activities supports the notion of "conceptual readiness," that reading activities must either relate to the students' knowledge of the world or the teacher must fill in the gaps before the reading task begins (Clark and Silberstein 1979:49; see also Goodman 1970). If there are gaps to be filled, and most likely there are, these previewing activities help ESL students prepare for their actual reading tasks by helping students access appropriate content and cultural schemata (Hudson 1982; Carrell and Eisterhold 1983). Since comprehension depends partially on the reader's prior background knowledge (Adams and Collins 1979; Coady 1979; Rumelhart 1980; Carrell and Eisterhold 1983), pre-reading activities can be used to establish a frame of reference facilitating comprehension when the students actually begin reading the passage.

Skimming and scanning

Skimming and scanning are skills that should be addressed in the Reading Lab, for all efficient readers utilize these skills. There are many ways to incorporate skimming and scanning practice into the Lab. One effective manner in which to provide practice in these skills is to coordinate it with actual reading passages. The pre-reading activities suggested above for the rate development component oblige students to skim and/or scan. By skimming and scanning for the main idea, key words and/or concepts in these passages, the students activate those content schemata they do control and form reasonable hypotheses about the content of the passage. Consequently, they will be better prepared to read. Furthermore, the comprehension questions which follow the fixed rate passages get students to scan the text, reinforcing the skill in a very natural way. Other materials, both prose and non-prose, can be used in the Lab for skimming and scanning practice. As will be explained in the next section of this chapter, students will also practice skimming and scanning with the multi-skill individualized reading materials and the outside readings.

In-class individualized activities

Devoting part of the Reading Lab to individualized activities is important. In a class made up of students whose reading abilities inevitably vary, it is imperative to have materials and activities that allow students to begin at their own level and proceed at their own rate (Coady 1979). With individualized materials, students are not forced into a rhythm artificially imposed on an entire class, rather, they set their own pace. In addition, allowing students to choose their own reading materials and/or texts is psychologically satisfying. Most importantly, students need to have time to sit quietly and read materials without interruption. In the long run, students learn to read by reading (Eskey 1983).

Multi-skills readings

A number of commercial multi-skill reading packages designed for individualized reading are available. Some of these programmed reading materials are listed in Appendix A at the end of this chapter. Ideally, an individualized reading program (1) includes a placement test for accurate level assignment; (2) accomodates a wide range of student reading levels; (3) permits students to progress at their own pace; (4) has clear, self-explanatory directions; (5) allows for a systematic progression from one level to another; (6) has a large variety of reading selections at each levels, including nonfiction and fiction readings; (7) has a selection of high interest topics that are appropriate for ESL students, that is, topics that are not too culturally specific or biased; (8) includes exercises that require students to practice a variety of reading skills and strategies; (9) includes a self-correction system; and (10) includes charts and graphs for easy record keeping.

A good example of a multi-skill reading package that has proven effective is the SRA *Multi-Read II* "Power Builders." This package provides a progressive and systematic training program which is initiated the first week of the Reading Lab and is continued until the end of the course. There are eight levels in the "Power Builders"; the degree of difficulty increases with each level. Twelve cards at each level allow students to select a different reading card even if several students are reading at the same level. Each card comprises a different text, the length varying according to the level. The text is followed by questions, the number of which varies with the level. These questions are divided into two basic groups: (1) "How Well Did You Read," which deals with the central idea of the text, simple identification and inference; and (2) "Learn about English," which deals with the lexical and grammatical content of the text.

In the initial phases of the "Power Builder" component, the instructor assigns each student a beginning level, determined by the results of the SRA *Multi-Read II* "Power Builder" placement test. After the materials and procedures are introduced, the instructor monitors the students' work to ensure that the procedure is understood and followed. Even though students proceed at their own pace, the instructor must continually encourage the students to work as quickly and accurately as possible, with maximum concentration. Like most Reading Lab activities, the "Power Builder" passages are timed and the times recorded. The standardized worksheet conveniently provides the students with a space to note both their beginning and finishing time, making rate calculations very simple. The students can also correct their own work by referring to the "Power Builder" answer cards. They then record the results, producing a series of graphs to show their performance. Gradually, a picture of their progress emerges. For this to be meaningful, the instructor must check, throughout the course, that the students are proceeding through the materials in the correct order, and charting their results properly. This is important because students, working on their own, can unintentionally skip a level, forget to calculate their reading rate and comprehension, or forget to chart their results. Even though the instructor is not "actively" involved while the students are reading, the instructor is present for supervision and demonstrates concern for and involvement in the students' progress.

Vocabulary in context

Efficient reading sometimes requires the reader to deduce the meaning of unfamiliar lexical items through contextual clues. ESL/EFL students tend to rely on the dictionary (or instructor) rather than deal with new vocabulary independently, making the most of contextual clues and textual redundancy. A few progressive and systematic developmental reading programs (commercial packages) designed to teach students to use context clues and textual redundancy to deal with unfamiliar vocabulary items are available for individualized work. (See Appendix B at the end of this chapter.) It is important to remember that there is a limit to what a student can deduce if an exercise or passage is too complex, either lexically or syntactically. With the needs and proficiency levels of students in mind, evaluate potential materials carefully in order to avoid "exercises in frustration." Criteria similar to those listed for multi-skill packages should be considered when selecting materials for this Reading Lab component. (See *Multi-skills readings* in this section)

The SRA *Reading for Understanding Junior (RFU)*, appropriate for low-intermediate students, will serve as an example of such materials. With the *RFU*, students use contextual clues and textual redundancy to select the correct word for completing a series of sentences and/or short paragraphs. The *RFU* package is made up of 400 lesson cards, arranged in 100 levels, with four lesson cards at each level. Each card contains ten incomplete sentences and/or short paragraphs. The level of difficulty increases with each level. A placement test, administered during the first week of the Reading Lab, determines each student's initial level.

As with the SRA "Power Builders," after the placement test has been corrected, the instructor assigns each student a level, introduces the *RFU* materials and procedure, then monitors students individually to ensure that the procedure is understood and followed. The students correct their own work once they are done, using the *RFU* answer keys, then record the results on their *RFU* progress charts. When the students score more than

80% on two cards within one level, they move on to the next level. These progress charts serve multiple purposes. Principally, they allow students to monitor their own progress and build the students' confidence.

Out-of-class activities

Individualized outside reading

The individualized outside reading program encourages independent reading and promotes reading for enjoyment. (See Krashen 1982:164-167, for a discussion of the merits of pleasure reading.) Furthermore, because class time is limited and the amount of reading needed to achieve fluency and efficiency is great (Nuttall 1982:23), outside reading is crucial. To facilitate such a program, it is important to have a Reading Lab library, comprising a variety of ESL readers, grouped according to level of difficulty. Readers published by Collier Macmillan, Collins, Heinemann Educational Books, Longman, Newbury House, Oxford University Press, Regents, and Scott Foresman, to name a few, are extremely useful for this purpose. Selecting their own reading materials is something that students enjoy. With a large selection of fiction and nonfiction readers on the library shelves, students find themselves skimming the back covers in order to find a book that interests them.

From the onset of the Reading Lab course, students are required to check out a minimum of one reader per week. Such a requirement obliges students to read at least thirteen readers during the semester and keeps them reading continuously. The checkout procedure is similar to a public library checkout procedure, each book having a checkout card. Over the course of the semester, this individualized outside reading builds confidence and personal satisfaction.

As with other Reading Lab components, students should keep a record of their weekly outside readings. One option is for the students to keep a record in the form of an informal, brief, written book report. (See Figure 3 for an example of a simple book report form.) It is important to remember, however, that the actual written work should not be given too much weight; if the students' written performance is emphasized too much, the fear of the book report will undermine the reading focus of the activity.

Name_____

OUTSIDE READING

Title of book:
Author of book:
Fiction_____ Nonfiction_____

Date book was begun:
Date book was completed:

A. Write a paragraph that tells what the book is about.

B. Did you enjoy the book? Explain in 1-2 sentences.

C. Would you recommend this book to others? Why?

Figure 3: A Simple Book Report Form

3.6 SEQUENCING OF READING LAB COMPONENTS

The sequencing of all the Reading Lab components discussed in this chapter should be considered of primary importance, for without it, the Reading Lab would lose its effectiveness. In general, the sequencing permits students to develop and improve their reading skills gradually, easing the students into an effective reading program, continually building their confidence and positive outlook towards reading. The sequencing of the Reading Lab components discussed is summarized in Figure 4.

The most delicate sequencing occurs with the in-class teacher-guided activities. Rarely is more than one activity introduced at a time, as each activity introduces a new skill and/or aspect of reading. It is important that the students understand the need for each skill and become comfortable practicing it before being introduced to a new activity. These teacher-guided activities lead the students from simple word perception to reading a complete passage at a reasonable rate with good comprehension. One cannot expect the students to be competent at both of these extremes simultaneously at the beginning of the Reading Lab program. For that very reason, the Reading Lab activities are sequenced to build upon and reinforce one another. It should also be noted that exercises are not ended abruptly in order to introduce the next set of exercises. Rather, there is a period of overlap which allows an easy transition from one activity to the next.

The sequencing of the in-class individualized activities and out-of-class activities is much more straightforward. There is a very specific reason for introducing these activities at the beginning of the course and letting them continue throughout the entire course. It is important that students continually have the opportunity to read on their own both in the Reading Lab and at home. Both activities allow students to work at their own pace, rather than at a pace artificially imposed on the entire class.

As suggested in Figure 4, the first week of class is dedicated to administering placement tests for the individualized in-class activities. In this manner, students can begin reading at a level appropriate to their entrance proficiency level immediately. During the last week the same placement tests are readministered; the results of the first tests can be compared to the results of the last to give some indication of the students' reading progress.

Week:	1	2	3	4	5	6	7	8	9	10	11	12	13	14	15
In-Class Teacher-Guided Activities															
Word Recognition	X	X	X	X	X	(X)	(X)								
Phrase Recognition				X	X	X	X	X	X	X	X	(X)			
Phrased Reading						X	X	X							
Rate Development Activities															
Fixed Rate							X	X	X						
Rate Development Activities															
Fixed Length: Paced Readings									X	X	X	X	X	X	
Fixed Length: Timed Readings												X	X	X	
Skimming									X	X	X	X	X	X	
Scanning									X	X	X	X	X	X	
In-Class Individualized Activities															
Multi-Skill Readings	X°	X	X	X	X	X	X	X	X	X	X	X	X	X	X*
Vocabulary in Context	X°	X	X	X	X	X	X	X	X	X	X	X	X	X	X*
Out-of-Class Activities															
Outside Reading	(X)	X	X	X	X	X	X	X	X	X	X	X	X	X	(X)

°Week 1:   Placement test to determine each student's level.
*Week 15: Readministration of the placement text to determine student's progress.

Figure 4: Sequencing of the Reading Lab

3.7 PHYSICAL SET UP OF THE READING LAB

For the Reading Lab to function smoothly, the physical set up of the lab should be taken into consideration. Ideally, the Reading Lab should be situated in a room of its own. A traditional classroom, with immobile desks/chairs is not at all conducive to reading. The Reading Lab should have large tables, with plenty of room in which to spread out the Reading Lab materials, and moveable chairs. The room should have adequate light for reading. Multiple book shelves are necessary to house the Reading Lab library and there should be additional space for the other Reading Lab materials, including the programmed materials and class sets of books. (See Nuttall 1982:174-182 for an elaborate description of library organization.) A file cabinet is convenient for storing additional materials such as worksheets, graphs, charts, and outside reading report forms. Individual student folders, used to keep an organized set of progress charts, graphs, and exercise worksheets, can be kept in the file cabinet as well.

3.8 SUGGESTIONS FOR MORE ELEMENTARY AND ADVANCED READING LABS

A Reading Lab for more or less advanced students can be developed in any language program functioning either in isolation, that is, not preceded or followed by another Reading Lab, or in sequence with other Reading Labs. Ideally, a progression of Reading Labs could be organized to address all the reading skills a student might need. Naturally, the focus of Reading Labs shifts as students move from one proficiency level to another. For example, in more advanced Reading Labs, activities will not only require more linguistic sophistication, they will also be directed towards specific academic reading needs, including analytic, critical and interpretive skills, inappropriate for the elementary student. No matter what the level, the prototype model outlined in this chapter, comprising an in-class teacher-guided component, an individualized component and an out-of-class component, is feasible, and desirable, at all proficiency levels. Both elementary and advanced students need time to read on their own, at their own pace; they can all benefit from teacher instruction and guidance.

Many of the exercise types introduced in this chapter are suitable to both a more elementary and more advanced Reading Lab. In some cases, the only major difference might be the degree of difficulty and/or length of the exercises.

In-class teacher-guided activities at other levels

Rapid recognition exercises are valuable in Reading Labs at all levels. Even though the format/content of the exercises may differ substantially at each level, the goals remain the same. For elementary students, word recognition might be preceded by more basic recognition exercises including:

1) Number Recognition

1	2	3	7	~~1~~
3	4	3	9	2
5	6	4	5	8

2) Number Cluster Recognition

27	28	72	73	~~27~~
39	93	38	39	89
40	20	40	10	90

3) Letter Recognition

A	S	F	~~A~~	D
V	W	B	O	V
G	O	G	Q	P

4) Letter Cluster Recognition

stu	ste	sto	~~stu~~	sta
ght	hgt	gth	gbh	ght
bro	pro	bra	bro	bru

A series of exercises like these prepare students for word recognition exercises and later simple phrase recognition. Both number and letter recognition exercises can be found in Yorkey (1970, 1982); Miller, Steeber, and Ladd (1981); and Miller and Steeber (1985a, 1985b).

Advanced students benefit from rapid word and phrase recognition exercises that add the comprehension variable. For example, exercises of this type require students to recognize a synonym or antonym of the key word:

1) Synonym Recognition

agree	~~consent~~	discard	delay	relax
inactive	trivial	weak	dormant	dense
group	maze	clique	explode	stage

2) Antonym Recognition

similar	disparate	~~different~~	direction	alike
unnecessary	required	replicate	abundant	brevity
shorten	widen	lessen	soften	lengthen

Exercises of this sort can be found in Adams (1980) and Miller, L. (1984), in addition to the texts listed above.

At all levels, phrased reading exercises provide instructors with a means by which to draw attention to and emphasize the importance of this skill. At lower levels, the procedure would be similar in nature to the intermediate level, although simplified; at higher levels, this activity might be used as a warm-up activity before moving onto more sophisticated readings.

A rate development program, including paced and timed readings, should be included in all Reading Labs. The timed and paced reading series by Spargo and Williston (1980), mentioned previously, has many passages in books 4 through 10 that are appropriate for more advanced students. They can be used in a similar fashion to that described in this chapter. The incorporation of pre-reading tasks is useful at all levels, although some research indicates that its effect is much more significant with lower level students (Hudson 1982).

In-class individualized activities at other levels

For a more advanced Reading Lab, the SRA *Research Lab* is an excellent multi-skills reading program designed for individualized work. Not only does the *Research Lab* reinforce crucial reading skills, it also gives students an opportunity to develop and then use research techniques and library skills necessary for academic work. The Grolier Educational Corporation's programmed materials, especially *Reading Attainment Systems* 2 and 3, provide a progressive and systematic reading skills development program appropriate for individualized work at the more advanced level.

Out-of-class activities: individualized outside reading at other levels

Besides simplified ESL readers, the Reading Lab library might include introductory texts for university classes, ESL texts, and reference materials, including English-English dictionaries. For more efficient management, all the readers should be marked to indicate the reading level; that is, the readers for elementary students should be distinguished from the intermediate level readers and the advanced readers should be similarly distinguished from the others. For easy identification, this can be achieved by color coding the books, using colored tags on the book bindings. Each color can identify a level of difficulty. If desired, a more elaborate color-coding system could separate fiction and nonfiction reading material within a particular level. A second way to approach the organization of books might be by implementing a simplified letter/number system, replicating the university library system.

As in the low intermediate Reading Lab discussed in this chapter, at other levels some sort of informal book report should be required of the students. This helps them synthesize the content of their outside reading and facilitates outside reading record keeping. The format of the report may be altered, but care must be taken to avoid making the writing aspect more important than reading.

3.9 CONCLUSION

The importance of reading in today's academic world and the close relationship between academic success and efficient reading support the need for a focused reading skills development program for ESL/EFL students. The Reading Lab represents a feasible and effective approach to a focused reading skills development program. It allows reading to be addressed directly, permitting students to practice reading as well as receive instruction in skills which aid the reading process. Moreover, it is flexible enough to accommodate and address the specific needs of students at all levels. The combination of teacher-guided activities and individualized activities, both in the Lab and at home, helps students develop a positive attitude towards reading in addition to better reading skills.

NOTES

1. I use the term "Reading Lab" to refer to a reading *course*, to be described in detail in this chapter. This should not be confused with the more traditional characterization of a "reading lab" which refers solely to multi-level reading *materials*, designed to "enable each individual student to start where he is in reading achievement, and to have the opportunity to move ahead as fast and as far as his reading rate and capacity will let him." (Parker 1959. See also Anderson 1972.)

2. Other considerations such as the incorporation of computers in the Reading Lab and formal reading assessment are beyond the scope of this chapter. See the Dever and Allerson/Grabe chapters in this volume for these and related issues.

3. The prototype Lab program discussed here follows the semester and program constraints at the American Language Institute (ALI) at the University of Southern California, Los Angeles. The low intermediate students at the ALI (ALI level 200) have twenty-eight hours of ESL instruction per week, during a fifteen-week semester. Four of these hours are devoted to the Reading Lab, which meets twice a week, in two-hour blocks. Another six hours are devoted to a Reading/Writing class. These two classes, the Reading Lab and the Reading/Writing class, are designed to complement and reinforce one another.

4. Gaskill (1979) distinguishes between two different types of in-class reading components. He proposes two separate and distinct, but closely coordinated reading classes, one focusing on "reading skills" and the other on "reading comprehension." These labels make me a little uncomfortable, as Gaskill's description of the "reading skills" component includes comprehension factors. Yet, no matter what labels we assign to these reading activities, it is more realistic and efficient to combine the two rather than separate them totally. I should add that a number of Gaskill's other observations coincide with mine, though we have worked independently.

5. Most first language reading teachers now faced with second language readers for the first time are already familiar with these materials and corresponding procedures.

6. For greatest efficiency, the teacher can direct students to begin their recognition exercises at exactly the same time, ideally referring to a large classroom clock. If the teacher starts everyone off when the second-hand is on the '12,' students can look up at the clock as they finish and easily calculate their time. If the class is small, students can indicate they are done by looking up at the teacher at which point the teacher can read off individual times quietly.

7. The results of timed readings should not be construed as a student's actual reading rate for other materials of an extended length. It does, however, represent a real change in a student's ability to read shorter texts and, therefore, represents a true improvement.

APPENDIX A

Reading packages for individualized instruction: multi-skills

1. Boning, Richard. Specific Skill Series, Programs for Individualized Instruction. Picture Level Through Level H. Baldwin, N.Y.: Barnell Loft, Ltd.

2. College Reading Program II. Chicago: Science Research Associates.

3. Dimensions: An American Album. Chicago: Science Research Associates.

4. Dimensions: Countries and Cultures. Chicago: Science Research Associates.

5. Harris, Matteoni. Reading Dexterity Kit. Oklahoma City, Ok.: Bowmar/Noble Publishers.

6. Jolly, David. 1982. Reading Choices. Cambridge: Cambridge University Press.

7. Multiple Skills Series. Levels Pre-1 Through 9. Baldwin, N.Y.: Barnell Loft, Ltd.

8. Multi-Read II: A Multi Level Reading Kit. Chicago: Science Research Associates.

9. Olympics Reading Kit. Oklahoma City, Ok.: Bowmar/Noble Publishers.

10. Reading Attainment System #2. Danbury, Conn.: Grolier Educational Corporation.

11. Reading Attainment System #3. Danbury, Conn.: Grolier Educational Corporation.

12. Reading Attainment System Comprehension Skill Building Lessons. Danbury, Conn.: Grolier Educational Corporation.

13. Reading Attainment System Starter Program. Danbury, Conn.: Grolier Educational Corporation.

14. Reading Comprehension Series: Aviation; Cars and Cycles; Crime Fighters; Dogs; Escape; Fads; Marguerite Henry's Horses; Special People. Oklahoma City, Ok.: Bowmar/Noble Publishers.

15. Research Lab. Chicago: Science Research Associates.

16. Sports Reading Series: Big League Baseball Reading Kit. Oklahoma City, Ok.: Bowmar/Noble Publishers.

17. Sports Reading Series: NFL Reading Kit. Oklahoma City, Ok.: Bowmar/Noble Publishers.

18. Sports Reading Series: Pro Basketball Reading Kit. Oklahoma City, Ok.: Bowmar/Noble Publishers.

APPENDIX B

Reading packages for individualized instruction: vocabulary in context

1. Cloze Connections. Baldwin, N. Y.: Barnell Loft, Ltd.

2. Reading for Understanding. Chicago: Science Research Associates.

3. Use of Context Clues: Developing Reading Comprehension Skills. Dobbs Ferry, N. Y.: Oceana Publications.

4. Using the Context: Specific Skills Series. Baldwin, N. Y.: Barnell Loft, Ltd.

FOR STUDY AND DISCUSSION

1. The Reading Lab described in this chapter allots approximately 30% of class time to teacher-guided activities and about 70% of class time to individualized activities. What circumstances would dictate a change in this time allotment?

2. How would you define the teacher's role in the Reading Lab? What are the teacher's major responsibilities? How and to what extent should the teacher get involved in the Lab?

3. What is the relationship between the effectiveness of the Reading Lab and the instructor's understanding of the reading process?

4. Many educators claim that reading is the most important skill for academic success. *How* would you convey this importance to your Reading Lab students?

5. In order to maintain the reading focus of the Lab, it is best to play down the importance of written work. Do you think book reports should be assigned for outside reading? Why or why not? If reports are assigned, do you think the instructor should provide the students with feedback on the written report? If so, what sort of feedback?

6. What does the author mean when she refers to "exercises in frustration?" How can an instructor determine if materials are too difficult and therefore "exercises in frustration?" What can be done to alleviate this problem if such exercises are actually being used?

7. Some researchers claim that accurate and rapid recognition skills distinguish skilled from less skilled readers. How do Reading Lab recognition exercises address this issue? What distinguishes the recognition exercises from all other activities suggested for the Reading Lab?

8. Although dictionary use is not discussed in this chapter, what kind of dictionary use policy, if any, do you think should be enforced in a Reading Lab? Should students be allowed to use a bilingual dictionary or should they be limited to a monolingual dictionary? Under what circumstances should students be able to use a dictionary in the Lab? Should dictionary use be restricted to certain Reading Lab activities? Explain.

9. The focused approach to reading in the Lab allows students to monitor their own reading progress easily; this is facilitated by the use of progress charts and graphs. Why is this monitoring process an important aspect of the Lab?

10. If you were in the position to stock a Reading Lab library, what kinds of reading materials would you order? What criteria would you use in your selection process?

11. How does this Reading Lab program reflect what you know of reading theory? How does this program address the bottom-up and top-down skills involved in the reading process?

FOR FURTHER READING

Very little has actually been written about Reading Lab programs; therefore, readers cannot be directed to articles about different Reading Lab approaches. Yet, a number of sources are relevant to issues concerning Reading Labs. On a general level, Nuttall (1982) provides good advice on reading instruction and feedback which applies to Reading Lab programs. More specifically, there is extensive research on rate and recognition, providing support for this type of instruction. Much of the research is summarized in Mitchell (1982); an important recent study is that of Chabot, Zehr, Prinzo, and Petros (1984). The relevance of these exercise types was noted early on by Harris (1966) and Yorkey (1970). The importance of previewing and the utilization of background knowledge is discussed extensively in Coady (1979) and Hudson (1982). Coady also stresses the importance of feedback, motivation, and encouragement. On a practical level, materials published by Jamestown Publishing Company and Little, Brown, and Company provide important textbook resources for Reading Lab materials.

Chapter 4

Intermediate Skills: Focusing on Reading Rate Development[1]

Denise Mahon
University of California at Berkeley

4.1 INTRODUCTION

In recent years, with the realization that English language instruction alone seldom produces fluent readers of English, ESL theorists have revised their opinion of the place of reading in an ESL curriculum. Their consensus is that reading should be taught as a skill in its own right and should not be used solely as a device to teach other language skills (Widdowson 1978; Eskey 1979). With this realization have come suggestions on how to teach reading and what to include in an ESL reading class. Many authors—among them Rivers and Temperley (1978); Eskey (1979) and Grellet (1981)—have advised including rate development in the curriculum, a suggestion which can be difficult to follow. For while many articles discuss the value of teaching students to read faster, they seldom explain how to do so.

A successful reading rate component involves more than opening a textbook, telling students to read faster and timing them. Such an approach seldom results in much rate improvement and often causes both teachers and students to feel frustrated, reinforcing the attitude that nonnative English speakers cannot improve their reading speed significantly. But ESL students can make impressive improvements. Most rate components, however, ask students to do too much at once, demanding that they change their concept of reading as well as their reading strategies, without teaching students how to change or convincing them that change is desirable. To be successful, reading instruction must also teach students the skills they need for a new style of reading and introduce the skills gradually to circumvent the students' natural resistance to change. This chapter will both review the rationale for including a reading rate development component in an ESL reading program and discuss the form that program should take.

Reading rate development is a phrase that must be carefully defined. It does not mean speed reading, which we associate at its worst with tricksterism and at its best with a luxury, something that would be nice for our students to know how to do, but inessential for good reading. Though speed reading at 1,000 words a minute may be a luxury, however (and one we don't really know is possible—see Brown, *et al.* 1981, for discussion of the controversy), the ability to read at an efficient rate is a necessity. An adequate reading rate — perhaps not less than 200 WPM — is essential (Smith 1981)

1. for good comprehension. Readers who read quickly place fewer demands on their short-term memories (see Eskey, this volume, for discussion). Because of language redundancy or repetition, the reader is able to condense the information available, to process out the repetitions, retaining the essential underlying meanings. The reader who reads quickly for meaning rather than concentrating on individual letters or words can extract information from a greater amount of the text and condense it into denser, more meaningful chunks than can the word-by-word reader. S/he therefore transfers more meaning to long-term memory in a given period and understands more of what s/he reads.

2. for concentration. The mind is capable of processing great amounts of information in short periods of time. Readers who feed their brains only isolated words at a slow rate of speed will find that they are not keeping up with their thought processes, that their minds wander, and that they will become sleepy or bored (Smith 1982:22; 1978:37).

3. to affect a strategy change. Smith describes a good reader as a risk taker who is willing to take chances, to make decisions about meaning without absolute certainty from the page. But some readers are afraid to take risks, demanding almost total certainty before they will hazard a decision.

This description of the overly-cautious reader applies to many ESL students who read slowly, processing each word before they go on to the next, often rereading again and again to make absolutely certain they got the message. (See Seliger 1972 and Vorhaus 1984 for description of students' reading process and insights into underlying issues.) Reading rate work forces students out of this overly analytical word-by-word approach. Under a time pressure, students do not have time to translate and memorize and thoroughly digest each word. Instead they must adopt some of the risk-taking strategies used by more confident, fluent readers. (See Cohen and Hosenfeld 1981:296 for a comparison of strategies used by good and poor ESL readers.)

4.2 OBSTACLES

Teachers have good reasons then for including rate development in an ESL reading program. However, they may encounter difficulties when they try to do so, for ESL students often resist reading English any faster than the 80 WPM rate they are likely to enter the classroom with. Students with a developing though imperfect knowledge of English, who, in addition, define reading as a word-by-word analysis, instead of a sampling or searching of the whole text for meaning, will feel anxious and resistant when they are encouraged to read quickly. No matter how they say they would like to read faster, when the time comes to alter reading strategies, they resist change. They become skeptical, even more unwilling to take risks, and reluctant to exchange their approach to reading for one that makes them, initially, uncomfortable. A teacher must short-circuit this resistance to produce results.

4.3 APPROACH

The following program takes student resistance into account. The curriculum is based upon the assumptions about the reading process and the reading strategies of fluent readers outlined in Chapter 1, and is structured to help students acquire and use these strategies.

The curriculum includes:

1. Testing
2. Orientation
3. Making students aware of resources
   a) graphic, syntactic, semantic information
   b) knowledge of the world
4. Presentation of alternate reading strategies
   a) prediction
   b) vocabulary in context
   c) phrased reading
   d) eye sweep
   e) previewing

Through each activity students learn to use reading skills or strategies which make faster reading possible. Some activities remind students of skills they use when they read in their first language and teach them to apply these skills to the reading of English. Others teach new reading strategies. Figure 1 outlines these strategies/activities and their interrelationships.

An essential element in the curriculum is confidence building. Students are introduced to a new reading style gradually. They practice each component skill in exercises and timed readings until they feel comfortable with it, before attempting the next.

Activities

Reading Skills/Strategies	cloze	sentence completion	vocabulary in context	reading in phrases	previewing	timed reading	rapid phrase recognition	skimming	scanning
using resources	X	X	X						
recognition of phrase signals	X			X			X		
reading larger units of print				X			X		
risk taking	X	X	X			X		X	X
tolerance for inexactness			X			X	X	X	
prediction	X	X		X	X		X	X	X
making inferences	X	X	X		X				
knowledge of organization					X			X	
reading for meaning	X	X	X	X	X	X		X	
comprehension	X	X	X	X	X	X	X	X	X
fluency	X	X	X	X	X	X	X	X	X
rate development	X	X	X	X	X	X	X	X	X
sustained reading						X			

Figure 1: Strategies/Activities Interaction

4.4 CURRICULUM

Testing

A reading rate assessment serves two purposes: it gives students information and it provides motivation. A rough assessment is sufficient for the purposes of this class. Passages for the nonfiction assessment can be chosen from course texts, preferably from those which will be used at the midpoint of the course, since they will be representative of the level of difficulty students will eventually encounter. By the time students arrive at the place in the syllabus where these materials appear, their reading rates will usually have exceeded the one assessed on the first day, so they will have a concrete measure of their progress. In an intermediate class, a passage from one of the Hirasawa and Markstein readers (1983a, 1983b, 1983c, 1983d) is appropriate. Students read the passage and mark the time at which they finish it. They then calculate their nonfiction reading rates by dividing the number of words in the passage by reading time (in minutes). They record these rates on individual charts. (For further discussion, see Jensen, this volume.)

Orientation

To increase their speed, students must be willing to change their reading habits. They will be more open to change if they have confidence in the teacher, the class activities, and their own abilities. A short three-part orientation is the first step in confidence building:

1. Needs/Interest Inventory: Students must understand that the course will address their particular problems. The teacher can assess student difficulties through a questionnaire such as the one in Figure 2, or by asking students directly: "What problems do you have when you read English?" "Is reading English the same for you as reading your first language? If not, how is it different?" At the lower levels, where language is limited, a simple checklist works best. Though student groups change, the problems they identify are predictable:

   a) slow reading rate

   b) need to reread

   c) poor comprehension

   d) poor concentration

   e) insufficient vocabulary

   f) fatigue and boredom

   g) need to translate

   h) inability to pronounce each word correctly

During the discussion which follows, the teacher should let students know that their problems are common to most ESL readers of English and will be addressed during the course. She will capture students' attention, motivate them, and help them remain open-minded toward the next step.

---

1. How well do you read in your first language?
   ___very well ___well ___average ___poorly ___very poorly

2. How well do you read English?
   ___very well ___well ___average ___poorly ___very poorly

3. How fast do you read English?
   ___very fast ___fast ___average ___slowly ___very slowly

4. How well do you understand what you read in English?
   ___very well ___well ___average ___poorly ___very poorly

5. How well do you concentrate when you read English?
   ___very well ___well ___average ___poorly ___very poorly

6. Do you have to reread material in order to understand it?
   ___Often ___Sometimes ___Rarely

7. Do you get tired easily when you read English?
   ___Often ___Sometimes ___Rarely

8. Do you read English other than class assignments?
   ___Often ___Sometimes ___Rarely

A less complicated alternative is the following:
Mark your main difficulties in reading English.
   a. vocabulary
   b. comprehension
   c. concentration
   d. speed
   e. fatigue
   f. boredom

Figure 2: A Performance Questionnaire

2. Introduction to Reading Style: This can take the form of a mini-lecture or a discussion based on a handout, such as the ones in Figures 3 and 4, written in simple English, which is best for lower level students. Though the sample handout resembles a multiple-choice quiz it has no right or wrong answers. It is a discussion stimulus, an instrument

through which teacher and students can compare their reading approaches. Again, the students' responses to the "quiz" are usually predictable. Most feel that a reader must use his dictionary frequently, look closely at each word, translate, know all the words on the page in order to read English, be able to pronounce them all correctly.

As teacher and students compare their "answers" to the quiz, the teacher can explain, simply, the relationship between reading rate, comprehension, and concentration. (See Seliger 1972 for a discussion of this relationship.)

She can also describe the reading style which she will teach during the class:

a) reading without dictionaries;

b) reading for information rather than grammar knowledge;

c) reading for general idea rather than details;

d) reading under time pressure.

This short discussion on the first day of class short-circuits the surprise, confusion, and resistance which occur if students are left to gradually discover that their definitions of reading do not match the teacher's and that this reading class will be quite different from those they have had before. (See Widdowson 1983 for an interesting discussion of schema theory as it applies to intercultural communication.)

Please answer the following questions:

1. The best way to read is to
   a. translate all the words from English into your own language.
   b. use the dictionary frequently.
   c. guess the word meanings.

2. In order to understand what you read you must
   a. look closely at each word and translate it.
   b. read one or more sentences at a time.

3. In order to read well you must
   a. know all the words on the page.
   b. read easy books.
   c. be able to guess what words mean by reading several sentences.

4. In order to concentrate well you must
   a. read slowly and carefully.
   b. read a little more quickly than you want to.
   c. write the meanings of all the words on the page.

5. Reading class is similar to vocabulary class.	T	F
6. There is only one way to read.	T	F
7. You should always read every word on the page.	T	F
8. You should read newspapers the same way you read texts.	T	F

Figure 3: Reading Handout #1

How Do You Read English Now?
Do you look up all the words you don't know in the dictionary?
Do you translate from English into your first language?
Do you read quickly or slowly?
Is reading English fun or no fun at all?

Purpose of the Class
* To learn how to read English more easily and quickly
* To learn how to read without translating every word
* To learn how to understand more when reading
* To learn how to find necessary information quickly

Why It Is Important to Learn These Things?
A college student must read _____ words during his freshman year. A student must read quickly and easily in order to finish his assignments.

How to Learn to Read Quickly and Easily
1. *Lots of reading practice in class* (The more a person reads, the better he will be able to read.)
2. *Timed readings* (To help the student read more quickly)
3. *No dictionaries* (The dictionary is a very useful book. But, using it takes a lot of time.
   Students will learn how to decide what words mean without using dictionaries.
   Students will also learn how to read without knowing all the words on a page.
   Students will learn how to read without dictionaries.)

A Final Word About Reading
Students who want to learn how to read more quickly and easily should be PATIENT. We have all been reading for over 10 years and so we all have our own reading habits. Habits are difficult to change. Eight weeks is a very short time to learn *new* reading habits. But students can *begin* to learn how to read more quickly and easily during this term.

Figure 4: Reading Handout #2

Moreover, if students understand why the teacher is asking them to do an exercise or to read in a certain way, they will be more willing to give it a try. Widdowson's observation holds here: "The acquisition of abilities requires the learner to assume a more active and responsible role involving . . . an awareness of his own learning processes and of the relevance of particular exercises to their development" (1978:109). This is especially true of teaching faster reading to adult learners, who have used their own particular reading strategies for a number of years and are reluctant to alter them without sufficient cause.

Setting the tone of the class

Students will have a hard time improving their reading rates if they are afraid of making mistakes. Students should understand that their purpose in the class is not to achieve a high reading rate or to answer all questions correctly, but to try out a different approach to reading. They should therefore experiment with new strategies. But most importantly, they should relax and enjoy themselves. They should be told to relax, to enjoy the readings, and not to worry. The anxiety they usually bring to the reading "chore" will diminish and they will be more willing to take the risks that are necessary for faster reading.

The teacher should also tell students that reading in a new way may make them at first feel awkward or insecure. To make the transition easier, they will read materials which will be easy to comprehend, with familiar vocabulary and simple sentence structure. Students sometimes feel that such materials will not help them with the kind of technical reading required in their fields. However, they should understand that the easy-to-read passages will be used only until they become comfortable with a new reading style, and that during the semester, they will read gradually more complex prose. The skills they acquire will be transferable.

After presenting the program and enlisting the cooperation of the students, the teacher can begin the first series of exercises.

4.5 TYPES OF ACTIVITIES

Blackout exercises

The first series consists of several easy-to-read paragraphs in which every fifth word is deleted—simple cloze exercises. Their purpose is to prove to students that they do not have to analyze each word on a page:

> Bob learned to swim _____ year. He went to _____ beach with
> John. John _____ swimming. It was good _____ and it was fun.
> _____ watched John. He tried _____ learn. He kicked his _____;

he moved his arms. _____ swallowed some water. John _____ swallow any water. Bob _____ sad. He asked John _____ the sport. "How does _____ swimmer move his arms? _____ does he kick his _____? When does he turn _____ head?" John explained it _____ Bob. They practiced together _____ day. Bob swims well _____, and he doesn't swallow _____. He is going _____ become a good swimmer.

a. What is Bill doing?

b. Who is helping him?

The students read a paragraph quickly and answer the simple questions which follow. The teacher should point out that they were able to comprehend the main idea of the passage even though every fifth word was missing; not every word in the passage is essential to the meaning of the whole.

After this initial reading, the teacher should read the paragraph through with the class, asking the students to call out words to fill in the blanks. With every suggestion, she should ask students to explain why the word they suggested fits.

For example, a class discussion might bring out the following information:

a) Sentence 1: Grammar clue. The past tense verb *learned* indicates *last*, *one*, or *this* as an appropriate choice.

b) Sentence 2: Grammar clue. prep + article + (adj) + noun. While the name of the beach could be placed in the blank, *beach* would then have to be capitalized.

c) Sentence 3: Grammar and semantic clues. The syntax requires a verb which can be followed by an -ing word. Within those restrictions *liked* or *enjoyed* makes sense in the story.

d) Sentence 4: Semantic clue. Which word makes sense? *Exercise* is a possibility.

e) Sentence 5: Grammar clue. Tried + to.

f) Sentence 6: Personal knowledge and semantic clues. When you swim you use your arms and legs/feet. In English *kick* and *feet* have an affinity.

Through this discussion, students become aware of the grammatical and semantic cues they use to make sense of a passage. They also learn about redundancy in language and the role their own knowledge of the world plays in comprehension. Using these resources rather than dictionaries and translation strategies is a skill necessary for faster reading. Students should read several of these short passages, beginning with very easy ones.

After reading three or four, students will approach them more confidently, reading them more quickly. They will then be ready for more sophisticated passages which can be adapted from intermediate readers (or, later in the course, taken from Fry's *Reading Drills*). (For additional suggestions on using cloze exercises, see Weaver 1980 and Y. Goodman 1980; see also Grellet 1981 for other sensitizing exercises to break student dependancy on each word.)

After this and every other skill exercise, students should do a timed reading, using materials described in "Easy to Read Materials" below.

Sentence completion exercises

After the blackout exercises students do sentence completion exercises such as the following:

You can trust Henry to take good care of your money for he is very ____.

    a) angry   b) honest   c) evil   d) distant

                                                  (Harris 1966)

This is another exercise to get the students used to the idea that they can predict meanings in context and to persuade them to relax their word-by-word analysis. Students can do these exercises individually or in small groups. Group work is particularly helpful in persuading resistant students to adopt new reading strategies. When exceedingly skeptical students work with students who adapt more easily to predicting, using language resources, and reading quickly for information, they are less likely to remain closed-minded. Their initial reaction—"this is impossible"—is tempered when they talk to students for whom the task is indeed possible. The students are given about 25 items which they answer as quickly as possible. The exercises should be timed to prevent students from overanalyzing.

The class discussion which follows will again bring out redundancy features and the syntactic and semantic cues which the mind uses to fill in unknowns (for a thorough summary of language redundancy in reading, see Haber and Haber 1981). The discussion should proceed in much the same way as that for the cloze exercises with students giving answers as well as their reasons for them. Throughout all these exercises, it is important to maintain a sense of momentum and not become immersed in overlong discussion. A teacher's sense of pace is important. (See Berliner 1981 and Samuels 1981 for further discussion of factors underlying a successful reading program.)

Three or four of these exercises over a few class periods are usually enough to build students' confidence in their ability to assign meaning to the blanks. Later in the course, they are good warm-up exercises, focusing students' attention and getting them in the right frame of mind for timed readings.

Vocabulary in context

Clarke and Silberstein consider guessing word meanings from context, "the most important of the vocabulary attack skills" (1979:145). This involves using contextual clues to guess at the general meanings of words instead of resorting to dictionaries. Though dictionaries can be helpful tools in vocabulary building, not all words are in the dictionary and not all definitions apply to all contexts. Overreliance on dictionaries makes reading a tedious translation exercise and fluent reading impossible.

Guessing meanings from context teaches students that they can often obtain a general understanding of an unfamiliar word if they continue reading (Clarke and Silberstein 1979:145).

Students should understand the advantages of inferring word meanings and be aware that while context will not always provide them with exact meanings, they will often get sufficient meaning to understand a passage.

It is important when choosing vocabulary in context exercises to select items that are directly solvable from context (see Jensen, this volume, for sample exercises). The goal of the exercise is to help students realize how much they can accurately infer and to build their confidence in their ability to comprehend without looking up every word they have doubts about. So answers, at first, should be obvious.

Pacing is also important. Discussion should not center on detailed or involved grammatical explanation. Students often know the information the teacher points out and need only be made aware of its application in this new situation.

The sequencing of blackouts, sentence completion and vocabulary guessing is deliberate. ESL students are often in awe of unknown words. If confronted at the outset of a reading course with vocabulary guessing exercises they can freeze or close their minds to the idea of guessing meaning, for their answers, however accurate, seem dangerously vague. They may go mechanically through the exercises during class but remain unconvinced, continuing to use their dictionaries at home. The blackout and sentence completion exercises help get around this word barrier. Students see only blanks which are somehow less intimidating than unknown words. They readily fill them in and discuss their strategies with classmates, considering alternatives. When the teacher later asks students to assign meaning to words in the vocabulary from context exercises, they willingly take part, treating the new words like blanks and feeling confident that they can do the task.

Reading in phrases

Reading specialists agree that word-by-word reading hinders comprehension (Eskey 1973; Weaver 1980; Smith 1982). Phrased reading—the processing of meaningful groups of words at a glance (Saville-Troike 1979:31)—encourages students to look at units of the text larger than the individual word. It teaches as well as reinforces skills which students need to read fluently with good comprehension. Since in English grammatical phrases often coincide with semantic units, work in phrased reading teaches students how to process larger units of meaning. It also teaches them to recognize grammatical clues which signal phrases and to predict what will follow within the phrase (Elias 1975:312). (Noun phrases, for example, are often introduced by numerals, possessive pronouns, articles; infinitive phrases are introduced by *to*, and so on.)

If phrased reading helps comprehension, it also improves reading speed. Reading in phrases sharpens readers' prediction skills, helping them process text more quickly. It also increases the amount of text they take in per fixation, reducing the number of fixations per line. Phrase-readers can therefore read at faster rates than readers who stop at every word.

Work in phrased reading involves both recognition and practice. Students should first understand what a phrase is—a meaningful group of words which often forms a grammatical unit. In English common phrases are noun phrases, verb phrases and prepositional phrases. (Several phrase recognition exercises are described in Stoller, this volume.) For low-level classes, recognition exercises can include those like the following in which students answer questions by marking the appropriate phrase:

Where do you go to buy bread?
___ to the store   ___ to school   ___ to church
(Harris and Sipay 1980)

Teachers can read passages pausing between phrases, the students marking the phrase boundaries as they listen. (See also McPartland 1983 for phrase recognition exercises appropriate for low-level students.)

Phrased reading practice may include exercises like the following:

1. (Be sure) (that your eyes) (move across the page)
   (with a smooth,) (even rhythm.) (You should be able)
   (to develop speed) (if you continue) (to practice.)

2. About 1660   Robert Hooke   put a thin slice
   of cork under his microscope.   He was amazed
   to see tiny divisions rather like a honeycomb.
   With this in mind, he gave these divisions   the name of cells.

3. Many foreign students find that their studies in English take so
   much time they have little time for the other pleasures of college
   life. This is unfortunate because many of the most useful and per-
   manent lessons you will learn at college do not come from books at
   all. They come from your association with teachers and students
   outside of class.

(Yorkey 1970)

The complete exercise includes two of each of the above examples. Students read through the entire page of exercises at a fairly good speed. By
the time they reach example 3, they can usually focus automatically on
phrases without stopping to think about how to do it.

The teacher should present phrased reading as a unit, having students
do exercises in each class for a few minutes over several days. She should
caution students to concentrate not on grammatical analysis but on meaning. She should choose exercise materials which are not too difficult. When
students become used to the idea of reading in phrases, she can use the
exercises as warm-ups before timed readings (Saville-Troike 1973; Elias
1975; Hatch 1979).

Eye sweep

Research has shown that the eye proceeds through the text in a series
of uneven movements (the series of saccade/fixations described in Chapter
1). While the eye movements of native speakers of English and ESL readers
have yet to be fully explored, many ESL readers seem to share with inefficient native speaker-readers certain characteristics. When ESL students—especially those for whom reading English is a burden—describe
their reading strategies, they often say that they proceed slowly and cau-
tiously, reading two words, rereading one, reading a phrase, rereading a
word, using an erratic pattern of stops, rereadings and starts. Inefficient
native readers use similar strategies. Though some regression is normal in
reading (Rayner 1981) inefficient readers regress excessively and inappro-
priately (Y. Goodman 1975). While a full explanation for these reading patterns is necessary, a focus on risk taking is a start. Poor readers searching
for security regress more than efficient readers who take risks (Seliger
1972:51). The eye sweep is directed at inefficient readers who regress more
than is necessary for comprehension.

To introduce the technique, the teacher should give students one-page
passages, the easier the better. (Those from graded readers are suitable: see
Figure 5 below). She asks students to take a chance as they read by moving
their eyes steadily across the lines without rereading any word, phrase, or
sentence, no matter how much they would like to. She also asks them to
read just a bit faster than they usually do or than they feel comfortable

doing. Since students have gone through the orientation exercises, they generally feel confident enough to try the technique.

However, this is a hazardous step for overly-cautious readers which takes them uncomfortably into the realm of the risk takers. Having the habit of reading at a plodding pace, with unlimited regressions, they often feel awkward with the new strategy and uncertain about their comprehension. Many students will have a hard time following instructions because their insecurity and subsequent desire to regress is so strong. The teacher, therefore, must encourage them, pointing out their ability to process information quickly. She should also caution them about their reading speed. Students should not read so quickly they lose contact with the material. They should aim for a steady pace which they achieve by eliminating unnecessary rereadings. If they practice the technique on several easy-to-read passages—some followed by simple true/false questions—their confidence will gradually build. Practice should be intensive at first, two or more readings in the introductory lesson, followed by longer readings in successive classes. When students feel fairly comfortable, they can transfer this strategy to the reading of graded readers, novels, and other materials described below. Most students find that they quickly increase their speeds without losing comprehension and that after a little practice they become more comfortable.

Notes from the Sea

In 1956 a young sailor at sea was feeling very far from his family and friends. He wrote a note and put it into a bottle. Then he closed the bottle and threw it into the ocean. The note in the bottle asked any pretty girl who found it to write to him.

Two years later a man was fishing on a shore in Sicily. The fisherman saw the sailor's bottle and picked it up. As a joke, he gave it to his pretty daughter. Still as a joke, the girl wrote the lonely sailor a letter. More letters went back and forth. Soon the sailor visited Sicily. He and the girl were married in 1958.

This is just one of the many stories about drifting bottles that have changed people's lives.

Strange as it may seem, a sealed bottle is a good traveler at sea. It can travel safely through storms that destroy ships. And glass will last almost forever.

The speed of a drifting bottle changes with the wind and the ocean current. A bottle drifting in a quiet place may not move a mile in a month. Another bottle may move 100 miles in a day.

But no one can be sure just where a bottle will go. For example, two bottles of the same size, shape and weight were dropped at the same time into the ocean near Brazil. The first bottle drifted east for 130 days. It was found on a shore in Africa. The second bottle went northwest for 196 days, and was found in Nicaragua. Two other bottles, which were thrown into the middle of the Atlantic Ocean, landed 350 days later in France, only a few yards from each other.

Probably the longest trip ever made by a bottle began in 1929. In that year, a bottle was thrown into the South Indian Ocean. A note inside the bottle could be read through the glass. The finder was requested to report when and where he picked it up, and then to throw the bottle back into the sea without opening it.

This bottle first went east, to the southern tip of South America. Someone found it, reported it and threw it back into the sea. Then others found it, reported it and threw it back. This happened several times. From Cape Horn the bottle moved into the Atlantic Ocean. Then it went to the Indian Ocean again, passing the place where it had first been dropped.

Finally this bottle reached western Australia, in 1935. It had traveled 16,800 nautical miles in 2447 days. That was about 6.8 miles each day.

410 words
(Reader's Digest, *Reading*, Book 4)

1. This story tells about a pretty girl who married a sailor.   T   F
2. Storms often destroy bottles.   T   F
3. All drifting bottles travel at the same speed.   T   F
4. Two bottles of the same size, shape and weight may drift in different directions.   T   F
5. Probably no bottle has ever traveled for more than two years.   T   F

Figure 5: An Easy-to-Read Narrative

Easy-to-read materials

In every class, after the strategy/skill exercises, students should practice their skills during timed readings. Each passage should be about two pages long, and should include easy true/false questions which focus on ideas rather than small details. The purpose is to build confidence, not test students on content. After every reading, students should record their rate on charts, which are excellent motivators because they keep students aware of their progress.

The early readings should be narratives since "passages with a story line . . . will be easier to understand and will, in consequence, build up the reader's confidence in his ability to handle 'the rules of the game' " (Yorio 1971:114). Though through most of the course students read natural unedited prose, passages for the first two weeks may be taken from simplified readers such as Lewis' *Reading for Adults* (1973). Passages should be chosen for their simplicity, too easy being better than too hard to promote rapid silent reading (Seliger 1972:52; Eskey 1973:73). When students practice on easy-to-read materials first, they learn the mechanics of the new approach without battling syntax. When they have read successfully, they are motivated to transfer their strategies to more complex material.

Passages should also be unglossed. Unglossed material is more natural, more closely approximates "real" prose, and encourages the students to guess and search for contextual clues rather than depend on dictionary definitions supplied by authors. (See Widdowson 1978:85-88 for a discussion of various types of glosses and how they hinder independent reading.) Unglossed materials are appropriate for a rate building class because nothing in their format distracts the eye from its steady, forward progress. Glossed materials encourage the reader to break off his left-to-right eye movements, to skip to the bottom or side of the page to find synonyms or definitions. The interruption of thought flow and concentration is what the reading teacher is trying to help her students avoid.

Once students are used to vocabulary guessing, minimum regressions, and a slightly faster pace, they are ready for more extended practice. Daily 10-minute timed readings provide this and persuade students that they can transfer their new style to the reading of "real" books.

Students should choose any easy-to-read novels which interest them (lower-level students can use graded readers) and follow the steps outlined in Figure 6.

I. Preparation
   A. Determine the number of words per novel page
      1. Count the number of words in 3 full lines.
      2. Divide the total by 3. (This is the number of words per line.)
      3. Count the number of lines on a full page.
      4. Multiply the words per line by the lines per page. The answer is the words per page.

II. 10-minute reading
   A. Read for 10 minutes, being sure to mark beginning and ending lines.

III. Record Keeping
   A. Calculate reading speed
      1. Multiply words per page by number of pages read to determine number of words read.
      2. Divide number of words read by time (10 minutes) to determine reading rate (words per minute).
   B. Record rate on a separate fiction rate chart.

Figure 6: Timed Novel Reading

The teacher should encourage students to read at a steady, quick pace, keeping their eyes moving forward. Though she should encourage them to increase their rates, she should warn them not to be overly enthusiastic; a 10 to 15 word-per-minute increase every few days is a realistic and achievable goal, though many students will experience greater increases. After each reading, students determine their reading speeds and record them on their charts. They should also do a daily timed 10-minute reading at home.

The teacher should emphasize that these in-class readings are not tests but a chance for students to relax and enjoy themselves, which for the analyzer-student will be a new experience. Students have read and enjoyed Hemingway's *A Farewell To Arms*, Orwell's *Animal Farm* and Steinbeck's *The Red Pony*, and then gone on to novels with more challenging syntax. If the story lines are interesting — such as in spy, mystery or adventure stories — students will read them quickly and enjoy them, without worrying about complex syntax. (See Carrell and Eisterhold 1983:567 for further discussion of the value of self-directed silent reading.)

Though to this point materials in the component have been fiction, future science or business students should not feel that the reading they have been doing is not appropriate to their needs. After several weeks of practice with narratives and fiction, they can transfer their skills to more difficult nonfiction and academic material, which is the focus of the next part of the rate building program.

Previewing

Students better understand nonfiction if they know the organizational plan and point of view of the author, and the sequence of ideas in the passage (Dubin and Olshtain 1980:358-359), and if they can apply their own background knowledge and experience to the text (Weaver 1980). This combination of organizational information and personal knowledge helps them to form expectancies about the passage and read with better speed and comprehension. (For an explanation in terms of Schema Theory, see Carrell and Eisterhold 1983 and Carrell 1984a.) Previewing acquaints readers with content and organization before they read a passage thoroughly (Seliger 1972:53).

To preview, students should:

1. read the introductory paragraph completely;
2. read the first sentence of each of the body paragraphs;
3. read the entire concluding paragraph.

Previewing should be a quick reading for general familiarity, and should take only a few minutes. After they preview, students should immediately return to the beginning of the passage and quickly reread every sentence in it.

To teach previewing, nonfiction materials with a minimum of four paragraphs are best, so that students can practice reading the first sentence of body paragraphs. However, three-paragraph passages work for beginning and low intermediate and slower students. Books such as Fry's *Reading Drills* with passages arranged in levels of difficulty and *Developing Reading Skills* and *Expanding Reading Skills* by Hirasawa and Markstein have been used successfully.

If readings include comprehension questions, it is best to begin with true/false questions to build student confidence. If textbook passages include multiple choice questions, the instructor should check them carefully before asking students to answer them. Often they require memorization of insignificant details — the kind of reading which contradicts the purpose of this course.

Once students become used to previewing they should preview every piece of nonfiction they read. Those who do, find that the few extra minutes it takes increases their comprehension, frees them from the anxiety of having to take it all in in one reading, and increases their reading speed.

4.6 SEQUENCING AND INTEGRATION OF ACTIVITIES

At this point it may seem that developing reading rate in this manner will demand too much time. However, initial concepts can be presented in only a few class sessions, and the reward in student rate gains will be well worth the time and effort spent in presentation.

Daily activities

Every class is structured to include the following activities:

1. warm-up exercises;
2. strategy/skill practice;
3. timed reading;
4. charting of reading rate;
5. teacher-student consultations.

The warm-up activities mentioned are used to put students in the appropriate frame of mind for rate development activities and strategy practice. They can be taken from strategy exercises similar to those done in weeks 1-6 (recognition, sentence completion, vocabulary in context, cloze exercises) or from rapid phrase recognition exercises (like the one in Figure 7; see Stoller, this volume, for further examples), or skimming or scanning exercises. They should be timed. Working at short, timed exercises also prepares students for a longer, timed fiction or nonfiction reading in class. After students have begun reading their novels, 10-minute novel readings can be alternated with other activities as warm-ups.

Figures 8 and 9 describe

1. the sequencing of skills for the reading rate development component;
2. segment models for activities from weeks 6-15.

> the coal miners
> her purple dress
> strange question
> source of income
> graduate students
> They don't know
> What time is it?

Students cover the column of phrases with a 3 x 5 card in their left hands. They move the card down and up again with a quick flick of their wrists, so that the first phrase in the column is exposed for an instant. They write down what they think they say. If they are not certain, they should make a guess.

(Judson 1972)

Figure 7: Rapid Phrase Recognition Exercise

Activity	Week														
	1	2	3	4	5	6	7	8	9	10	11	12	13	14	15
Introduction	X														
Cloze Exercises	X	X	X												
Sentence Completion		X	X	X											
Vocabulary in Context			X	X	X										
Reading in Phrases				X	X	X									
Previewing						X	X	X	X	X	X	X	X	X	X
Skimming		X	X	X	X	X	X	X	X	X	X	X	X	X	X
Scanning		X	X	X	X	X	X	X	X	X	X	X	X	X	X
Timed Fiction Reading	X	X	X	X	X	X	X	X	X	X	X	X	X	X	X
Timed Nonfiction Reading	X	X	X	X	X	X	X	X	X	X	X	X	X	X	X

Figure 8: Skill Sequencing

Warm up exercise (word recognition) 10-minute reading of novels Chart rates (20 minutes)	Warm up exercise (sentence completion) Preread and read Fry 2C Answer comprehension questions Chart rates (20 minutes)	Skim Fry 3C to preview Read Fry 3C Answer comprehension questions Define selected vocabulary in context Chart rates (30 minutes)
Warm up (word recognition) Preread and read Fry 4C Answer questions and compare answers Scan to correct discrepancies Chart rates (25 minutes)	Skim questions of Fry 5C to preview Read Fry 5C Answer questions Define selected vocabulary Chart rates (30 minutes)	Warm up (phrase recognition) Preread and read Fry 6C Answer questions Chart rates (20 minutes)
Warm up (Scan Fry 7C to answer comprehension questions) Preread and read Fry 8C Answer questions Chart rates (30 minutes)	Scan Fry 9C for specific facts Read Fry 9C Answer questions Define specific vocabulary in context Chart rates (25 minutes)	Warm up (sentence completion) Preread Fry 10C Devise questions to be answered on 2nd reading Read Fry 10C Answer questions Chart rates (25 minutes)

Figure 9: Segment Models

After week four it is possible to start following timed readings with multiple choice questions, provided students have not been introduced to a new skill on the same day. By weeks 11 or 12, students may be ready for inferential questions or those associated with critical reading, for by this time they will be able to read a passage quickly and give opinions about it or apply the information. Students will therefore be able to use their faster reading skills to accomplish tasks assigned in other parts of the reading program. For example, they will be able to read quickly for the main idea, preview to predict organization and structure, gather information from several articles quickly in order to summarize, analyze or synthesize it. By this time, then, the component will no longer seem a separate entity but an integral part of the overall reading program.

The reading rate component serves as one part of a comprehensive reading program which includes work in other comprehension and language skills conducive to good reading. A structured rate component can be the core of a reading program. In this case, the teacher should emphasize reading rate and include other work, such as paragraph analysis, discourse signals, etc., as an aid to speed improvement. Such a program would be especially appropriate to prepare students in short term college orientation courses for heavy college reading loads. Or she can present reading rate as one of several elements equally important for successful reading. In any case, an essential part of the component is daily timed readings to provide students the opportunity to practice new strategies so they will be convinced of their effectiveness and will use them outside of class. (See Hudson 1982 for a discussion of the need to experience skills as usable in order to abstract principles for successful reading.)

Though the program described here was designed for intermediate students of English, similar components can be a part of lower-level reading programs as well. Students at these levels too can improve their reading ability if they change their attitudes toward reading. If materials for the program are appropriate — if they progress gradually from very easy material to material which is just at the students' reading level — a rate development component can successfully help students develop crucial new reading skills.

4.7 TEACHER'S ROLE

Methodology aside, the teacher is the most important element in a reading class, for her attitude influences students and their performance.

The teacher of this component should provide her students:

1. an anxiety-free atmosphere so they will feel free to experiment with a new reading style;
2. practice so they will master new strategies;
3. pressure in the form of persuasion and timings.

Anxiety-free atmosphere

To provide such an atmosphere, the teacher should understand what she is trying to do and how she is going to do it. She should also be convinced of its worth. The teacher is asking students to change long-established reading patterns, a process which will cause them discomfort and insecurity. If she is insecure and unfocused, students will feel unconvinced, uncertain, and insecure.

Secondly, the teacher should relieve the students of the burden of detailed tests. She cannot teach them to read quickly for general understanding if they feel they must memorize details. She should also relieve them of competition with other students or for grades. She should make clear to her students that their purpose in the class is to develop their *own* reading skills. Students should therefore try out new reading options. Success should not be based on who has the fastest rate or who can answer the most questions correctly.

Thirdly, the teacher should build success into the program and keep her students aware of what they have achieved. Students should practice new skills on easy-to-read materials and only gradually apply them to more difficult prose. Following this progression students will gain confidence and will be willing to take risks when they are reading anything. Needless to say, what is easy for one student may be difficult for another, so the teacher should be aware of her students' individual differences and provide materials with which students feel comfortable.

She should also keep students aware of their progress, comparing their achievements with their abilities on the first day of class, providing charts and reviewing them with students.

Fourth, she should provide support, through encouragement and clarification. She should keep up a dialog with students. What is difficult about this activity? What is helpful about that? More importantly, did a student miss a question because he misunderstood the reading or merely interpreted it differently than the test author? Was the question unclear, too detailed? These considerations are important for students to be aware of—one missed question does not mean they did not understand a reading; maybe they understood better than everyone else.

A few minutes of consultation time should be put aside in every class session to talk to students individually about their materials, their progress, and their ability to comprehend.

And fifth, she should make the class enjoyable by providing engaging readings and an engaging attitude. It will be difficult to help the students read for enjoyment if they feel the reading is tedious or irrelevant.

Practice

Students learn to read by reading. In order for students to learn to use new reading strategies, they have to practice them. However, reading practice at home, especially in the first weeks of class, is rarely effective, because students will too often employ their analytical word-by-word reading style instead of the new strategies. At home it is too easy to pick up a dictionary. So students practice these strategies best while reading in class with a teacher's guidance. During the second part of the course, when students are ready to read novels, they will be sufficiently comfortable with their new style, and sufficiently involved in the stories they are reading, to time themselves and practice their reading strategies in 10-minute readings at home.

In-class reading is also important to help students develop the ability to read English for sustained periods. Often students' experience in reading English has been limited to reading a few pages and then doing exercises, analyzing grammar or defining vocabulary, tasks which require short periods of concentration. Some therefore have not developed the ability to sit and read English for longer periods of time, searching out ideas and information. This ability is necessary for academic success and one that will be fostered through in-class readings.

Pressure

The pressure described here is different from the anxiety produced by overly-detailed tests and the burden to answer correctly. This pressure comes instead from timed readings and from the constant persuasive coaxing that the teacher should employ. The purpose is to create a situation in which students are constantly asked to read quickly, so that the habit takes hold and they will do so independently. Therefore, the teacher should time many class activities the students do—warm-ups, skimming, scanning exercises, reading of directions. This should be a gentle pressure. If students need an extra minute to do an assignment, they should have it. The timings should produce positive results, make students feel that they have accomplished what even the day before may have seemed an unrealistic task—reading and comprehending quickly, without analyzing.

4.8 CONCLUSION

It is important to state that such a component is not intended to teach speed for speed's sake. Nor will an increase in reading rate solve all comprehension problems; it does not substitute for teaching language, or prediction, or other reading skills. But it is an important part of an overall reading program. Though students' ability to read fluently depends upon their knowledge of grammar and semantic cues, it also depends upon their reading habits, their approach to the printed page, their reading strategies. Students may learn all they can about English, but if their approach to reading remains the same, if they continue word-by-word processing and translating, they will remain plodding, inefficient readers, reading too slowly for good comprehension. When we teach students to read for rate we are helping them to change their reading strategies, so that they will predict more quickly and regress more purposefully, trusting their growing language competence instead of their dictionaries.

NOTES

1. I am indebted to Trudy Laney of San Francisco State University who showed me where to start.

FOR STUDY AND DISCUSSION

1. How would you answer a student who complains that he can't understand what he's reading if he doesn't use his dictionary?
2. What suggestions can you make to students who say they must pronounce every word they are reading in order to understand the passage?
3. Discuss the advantages and disadvantages of glossing. What is its place in a reading rate development program?
4. Discuss some of the implications of giving students time to do sustained in-class reading.
5. Why is a rate development component a necessary part of a reading curriculum?
6. Rate development is only for students who have full mastery of English. Discuss.
7. Discuss the statement, "Slow and careful reading will result in maximum comprehension."

8. Review reading materials you are familiar with. Which of them could be used in a rate development class such as the one described. Why? What are your criteria for selection?

9. Find vocabulary in context exercises. Do them yourself. Describe the clues in context which led you to your answers. Is more than one answer appropriate for any of the blanks? What problems are created by vocabulary in context exercises?

FOR FURTHER READING

For information on redundancy features, eye movements, schema theory, and the working of memory as they relate to reading, see Pirozzolo and Wittrock 1981.

For articles on the social psychology of reading, including the teacher's effect on student performance and her need for self-awareness, see Edwards 1981. This anthology also contains a sensible summary of the rapid reading controversy by Brown 1981.

Widdowson's discussions of the role of schemata in cross-cultural communication (1983) offers insight into cultural barriers which can affect rate development classes. And Seliger 1972 is an excellent discussion of the effect of student anxiety on reading strategies and comprehension.

For well-thought-out exercises appropriate to many parts of this reading course see Grellet 1981.

Chapter 5

Advanced Reading Skills in a Comprehensive Course

Linda Jensen
University of Southern California

5.1 INTRODUCTION

The focus on reading in the language classroom has swung with the pendulum of methodology from being the principal means of language study in the days of grammar-translation to suffering from benign neglect during audio-lingualism, and now to being recognized as an important and necessary skill, especially in an academic program (Ostler 1980; Johns 1981; Robertson 1983). The number and variety of recent EFL/ESL reading textbooks testifies not only to an interest in reading but also to a rekindled awareness of the importance of reading (Hamp-Lyons 1982). Given the renewed concern for reading, this chapter addresses the question of how reading should be taught in an academic program, especially in comprehensive courses at the advanced levels.

In a comprehensive language course, the four language skills — listening, speaking, reading, and writing — are taught together in some combination with varying degrees of emphasis on each skill, depending on the specific needs of the students and the type of language program. Ideally, each skill should be coordinated with and related to the other language skills. A typical link has been the study of grammar, but more recently, connecting threads are communicative functions (such as requesting, apologizing) or themes (extensive work on a single topic). In these more recent cases, the four skills should be presented so as to reinforce each other whether integrated within one class or course, or taught within separate classes.

The amount of class time spent on any one skill can vary depending on the type of language program, needs of the students, or teaching philosophies of the administration and instructors. Since reading is of such importance for university bound students (see Grabe, this volume), more time should be spent on reading skills than has been traditionally allocated to them; good reading skills should be considered as important and necessary as good writing skills in the academic world.

Traditionally, reading in the comprehensive language classroom has consisted of students reading a passage either in class or at home, and then answering comprehension questions in a true/false or multiple-choice format. There might be some grammar exercises and vocabulary work, followed by a class discussion and writing assignment. The frequent practice of using reading as a springboard for writing is not uncommon since there are many pedagogically sound reasons for the practice, especially in a comprehensive skills course. But what is often missing in this "first read, then write" sequence is the overt teaching of reading skills and strategies, as well as the setting of the proper psychological atmosphere for students to understand the need to read well and to enjoy reading.

Although now changing, teachers and material writers have tended to place reading skills on a continuum ranging from reading for language practice to reading for meaning. At the beginning to intermediate levels, students need to read for language practice, that is, reading as an activity to increase knowledge of vocabulary and structure. Then at the intermediate to advanced levels, students need to read for meaning, that is, reading as an activity to gather information. By the intermediate level, teachers, programs, and even text materials assume the student is able to read. However, there is often a gap between "reading" which is really just language practice and real reading for meaning; to fill this gap, students need to be made aware of a variety of reading skills and strategies and to practice good reading habits. As Johnson (1981) concludes in a recent reading comprehension study, "the problems in reading comprehension of the ESL students at the intermediate/advanced levels . . . demonstrate the need to facilitate the development of reading skills in the foreign language classroom."

5.2 PROTOTYPE

Based on a perceived need for focused reading instruction at the high intermediate-advanced level, this chapter presents a description of an approach to teaching reading in a comprehensive skills classroom. The description consists of a prototype, a basic format designed to simulate a university course, a list of the necessary academic skills, a detailed description of procedures, a discussion of the role of the instructor, and implications for lower levels.[1]

University simulation

The prototype described here has been designed to address the needs of university ESL students. Students in a university program need both the language and academic skills that are required for academic success. These skills can be taught within a comprehensive language course which simulates a university class. Instead of focusing on a topic for a brief period of time by means of commercial language textbooks with limited topic development, thematic units can be created which allow students to explore a topic in-depth, similar to a university course. By using ESL texts and authentic materials such as academic textbooks, magazines, journals, and newspapers, thematic units can be developed which allow students to practice both academic and language skills in a university environment.

Thematic units such as "Culture Shock," "Media," and "Social Change" can be stimulating topics. For example, if the unifying theme were "Culture Shock," listening skills could be practiced by students listening to a lecture on culture shock; note-taking skills could be addressed by students taking notes on the lecture; speaking skills could be focused on by students discussing examples of culture shock or ethnic stereotypes; and finally, writing skills could be practiced by students writing a composition based on the lecture/discussion/reading. This chapter, however, will focus on the reading component in these thematic units.

Prototype components

What reading skills do academic students need? Experienced ESL teachers have their own mental lists of reading skills necessary or useful for students to learn. Students are taught the skills that are appropriate for their needs and abilities. The advanced-level academic student in particular needs to be able to read rapidly with good comprehension; this requires skills ranging from the basic perceptual skills, to skimming and scanning, speed, and such in-depth comprehension skills as critical reading. To develop this reading facility, the course includes a Rate Development Component to improve rate and comprehension, a Core Reading Component to develop analytical and critical skills, and an Extensive Reading Component to give the students the opportunity to pursue core reading topics and to practice reading skills on their own (see Figure 1).

Rate Development Component		Core Reading Component	Extensive Reading Component
Paced Readings	Timed Readings	Authentic Materials Textbooks	Authentic Materials Textbooks

Skills	*Skills*	*Skills*
previewing	previewing	previewing
skimming	skimming	skimming
scanning	scanning	scanning
rate and comprehension	vocabulary in context	rate and comprehension
	recognizing rhetorical patterns	vocabulary in context
		recognizing rhetorical patterns
		critical reading

Figure 1: Prototype Components

Skills rationale

Rate development component

The Rate Development Component focuses on rate and comprehension skills as well as previewing, skimming, and scanning skills by using paced and timed readings with a variety of exercises to improve rate and comprehension levels (see Mahon, this volume, for a discussion of rate development at lower levels). The difference between a paced and a timed reading is that students read a paced reading at an imposed rate, whereas they read a timed reading at their own rate.

Rate and comprehension skills are very important for academic students. Given the amount of required reading for most university students, it is imperative for the nonnative student to approximate native speaker reading rates and comprehension levels in order to keep up with classmates (approximately 300 WPM for university students). At the end of the course, even advanced ESL students may read only 100 words per minute or less; but with consistent practice, students can double their reading rates over the course of a semester. While they may never read quite like native speakers, any efforts to close the gap between them are worthwhile.

Previewing, skimming, and scanning are practiced in the Rate Development Component since these skills also facilitate rate development; as necessary reading skills, they merit further practice in the Core Reading Component as well.

Previewing, also referred to in the reading literature as prereading or surveying, is practiced with all reading materials in the Rate Development and Core Reading Components. Previewing helps to determine appropriate reading strategies, as well as to provide a general idea of the text content. Before reading, students must learn to preread a text in order to determine whether skimming or critical reading is the more appropriate strategy.

Skimming and scanning are similarly practiced in both the Rate Development and Core Reading Components. Skimming exercises teach students to read quickly for meaning, allowing a general understanding of a text. Scanning exercises teach students to read quickly to locate a specific piece of information such as a fact or a figure within a text.

Core reading component

The Core Reading Component uses authentic materials and ESL textbooks built around thematic units to develop analytical and critical reading abilities such as understanding new vocabulary in context, recognizing rhetorical organization, and examining a text critically.

Vocabulary in context exercises teach students to look for clues within the text to determine the meaning of new vocabulary items. Most foreign students are overly dependent on their bilingual dictionaries because they are afraid to guess and take risks. Vocabulary in context skills help break dictionary dependency and build self-confidence; essentially these are consciousness-raising exercises.

Rhetorical pattern recognition exercises teach students how to identify main ideas and supporting details as well as rhetorical forms such as description, exposition, etc. English patterns of organization, traditionally taught for writing, need to be taught for reading skills development as well. As students analyze the internal structure of a passage and understand how the parts relate to the whole, their abilities to predict and anticipate will enhance their reading rate and comprehension skills.

Critical reading activities encourage students to make inferences, draw conclusions, and separate fact from opinion. This in-depth examination of a text is probably the most difficult skill to teach because many students are from countries where the written word is not criticized or analyzed.

Extensive reading component

The Extensive Reading Component provides additional reading passages to complement the core readings. If students wish to pursue a subject further or feel a need for additional exercises, they can utilize these versatile materials. Since students learn to read by reading, this component provides extensive reading materials for out-of-class use; students also exercise responsibility for choosing various materials on their own, leading to increased motivation.

5.3 TEACHING THE COMPONENTS

Orientation

Before starting any reading activities, the students need to spend time discussing the importance of reading as well as the strategies of the fluent reader (for further discussion, see Eskey, this volume). Students must recognize that comprehension alone is not adequate; they must also be able to interpret and use text information in class discussions, seminars, research papers, and examinations. Since the students are academically oriented and possibly taking university courses, it is important to stress the amount of reading that may be required of them — up to a book a week or more — so that they understand the importance of reading quickly and efficiently.

The necessity of using different reading strategies depending on one's purpose and the type of material must be discussed. For example, students should read an assigned textbook differently from library research materials or a weekly news magazine.

Most important, self-confidence must be built. Having students do a cloze exercise at an early point in the semester can introduce them to the idea that they do not have to understand every word of a passage in order to comprehend it. Students can read a passage where every *nth* word is blank. Then they can answer some oral or written comprehension questions and discuss their answers. Students are typically surprised by how much they have understood even though many words are missing (see Mahon, this volume).

Students should be made aware that this type of exercise approximates reading a text with difficult vocabulary items or unfamilar grammatical structures; students should also be aware that even native speakers sometimes have difficulty reading certain texts for such reasons as an unfamilar topic or unfamilar vocabulary items. Students should also be made aware that they have many reading skills in their first language which may be transferable to English.

Students need to know that the good reader when reading quickly for meaning (1) does not need to go back over the text; (2) does not need to stop at unfamilar words or reach for a dictionary; and (3) does not need to subvocalize or move lips.

Teaching the rate development component

Following orientation, the Rate Development Component may be introduced, which begins with previewing, skimming, and scanning skills. In addition to being useful skills in and of themselves, they facilitate rate development.

Previewing

As the first step to reading, students preview the text material for a general idea of its topic and content. When previewing, students quickly skim the title, subtitles, first and last paragraphs, the first sentence of every paragraph, and look at any pictures or illustrations which may accompany the text.

Previewing facilitates reading by helping students anticipate or predict what they are going to be reading about; this kind of prior knowledge also makes the students feel more secure. Previewing helps students focus on the passage, increases motivation, and sparks an interest in the topic. It also provides the teacher with the opportunity to present or fill in whatever background knowledge may be necessary to understand the reading. Previewing should be practiced consistently with all materials — paced, timed, core, and supplementary readings. With constant practice, previewing should become a habit.

Skimming and scanning

Skimming is reading quickly for the main idea; for example, it is how one generally reads a newspaper. Scanning, in contrast, is looking for a specific piece of information; for example, it is how one locates an item in the *Readers' Guide* (Baudoin *et al.* 1976) or telephone book. Skimming and scanning exercises are often used as previewing activities; skimming can give the students an idea of the type of reading selection and the general content, while scanning can help them locate important or difficult items quickly.

After the students have skimmed a passage for overall meaning, they answer a few general comprehension questions. Next, they scan for a few specific items. The point of these exercises is to use these skills once or twice as part of a larger lesson. It is better to repeat work on skimming and scanning with each reading selection, rather than to present long skimming and scanning exercises independently.

Rate development

Paced Readings

Paced readings can be practiced with many types of reading passages; 400-word passages work especially well. Each 400-word passage is marked with a dot in the margin at every one-hundred words. Using these dots, the teacher paces the students by having them read each 100-word section within a set time period. For example, the teacher may impose a pace of 200 words per minute for the students to read the passage. All students begin reading the passage at the same time; after thirty seconds have passed, the teacher knocks loudly on the table and the students move their eyes down to the sentence of the first dot if they are not already there.

Thirty seconds later, the teacher knocks on the table and students are to be at or move to the sentence of the second dot. The teacher knocks two more times at thirty-second intervals while students move their eyes down to the next dots. After "reading" the passage, students turn the page and answer multiple-choice comprehension questions, ideally without looking back at the passage. If comprehension scores are below 60%, the pace is probably too fast, and the teacher may want to slow it down. On the other hand, if the students are answering the comprehension questions with 90-100% accuracy, the teacher will want to speed up the pace. (See Spargo and Williston 1980 for a comprehensive set of paced readings.)

The purpose of paced readings is to push the students to read at a faster pace than they would read on their own. Imposing a reading rate on a group of students with a variety of first languages may create problems for individual students with much faster or slower rates. One solution is to alter the goals for these students by requiring greater accuracy from the faster readers and less accuracy from the slower readers. For example, at an imposed rate of 200 WPM, a Spanish speaker who can read comfortably at 200 WPM should score 80% or higher at this imposed pace. An Arabic speaker, on the other hand, who normally reads at 100 WPM should be expected to score only 50% or so on the comprehension check at a 200 WPM imposed pace. Students' own expectations of their rate and comprehension scores can be raised as the semester progresses. It is also important to convince the students that they are competing against themselves and not each other.

In order to give students an idea of how fast native speakers read, it is useful to have the class read the first paced reading at 300 WPM and then answer the comprehension questions. There will be many groans as the pace is marked and most students will answer only about 30% of the comprehension questions correctly. The students can then reread the passage at half the pace — 150 WPM — and comprehension scores will go up dramatically to 80-90% This exercise effectively demonstrates the rate at which they should be reading as college students, and the reading difficulties they may face in the university.

Since paced readings give the students a feel for a specific reading rate, these exercises effectively push the students to read at a rate faster than they normally would. Paced readings are most effective if done regularly at least twice a week. One way to get students involved is to let the class set its own rate goals with an end of the semester goal of 300 WPM. Students also plot their own pace and comprehension scores on bar graphs after correcting the comprehension questions (see Figure 2). The bar graphs are very important psychologically because the students need to see evidence of their improvement to sustain motivation and enthusiasm. While students are filling in their bar graphs, the instructor should walk around the room checking scores and offering constructive feedback.

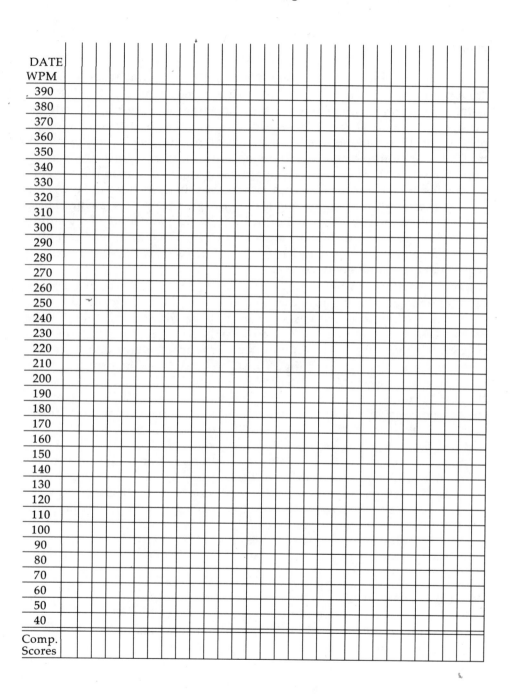

Figure 2: Bar Graph

Timed Readings

A timed reading follows a paced reading in a typical reading lesson. Students are warmed-up, having just read a paced reading at 150 WPM or faster, which should increase their timed reading rate. For timed readings, passages between 500 and 1000 words work well, but occasionally a longer reading of 1500 can be used. Timed readings are usually followed by true/false or multiple-choice comprehension questions. Since these readings are used to increase rate and comprehension, no discussion of the content of the timed reading passages is necessary in class beyond supplying some background information about the passage during previewing. These passages do not necessarily have to fit into the thematic units of a comprehensive program, but if they do, students can use them as resources similar to the extensive reading material (see 3.4 *Extensive Reading Component*) as they would in a university course.

When beginning a timed reading, students record their starting time in minutes and seconds. Ideally, there is a clock with a second hand; otherwise, the teacher acts as timekeeper by writing the starting time on the board. As students approach the end of the passage, the teacher writes the time on the board at fifteen-second intervals. When students finish the passage, they look up and record their finishing time above their starting time, then go on to answer the comprehension questions without looking back at the text. When everyone is finished, the teacher can read the answers to the comprehension questions aloud, students can correct them individually with answer cards, or they can determine the correct answers with a tally and discussion.

Students determine their reading rate by subtracting their starting time from their finishing time to find their reading time in minutes and seconds. They then divide the number of words in the passage by their elapsed reading time in order to find their reading rate in words per minute (WPM) as illustrated below:

FINISHING TIME: 2:20
STARTING TIME: -2:15
                    5 minutes = READING TIME
WORDS IN PASSAGE = 1000
1000 : 5 = 200 words per minute

Since times are recorded at fifteen-second intervals of 15, 30, and 45 seconds, these times have to be converted to the decimal system:

15 seconds = .25
30 seconds = .50
45 seconds = .75

If a student reads a passage in 4 minutes and 45 seconds, then the reading time is 4.75; this is then divided into the number of words in the passage to find the reading rate in words per minute. After a few tries, students quickly become adept at figuring out their rate, especially with pocket calculators. Rate and comprehension scores for timed readings are then plotted on bar graphs in the same manner as for the paced readings.

While students are filling in their bar graphs, the teacher should walk around the room to check the graphs. Those students who score 60% or less on the comprehension questions should decrease their reading speed in order to increase comprehension; comprehension should not be sacrificed for speed. At the same time, they must not read too slowly because that too will decrease comprehension (Smith 1982). On the other hand, if students' scores are 90-100% correct, they should speed up to improve their rate. Students should set their own reading rate goals in relation to where they are and what they hope to achieve. They are competing with themselves and not their classmates. They need to be reassured by the instructor that even if their rates are not improving dramatically, they are making progress.

A paced reading followed by a timed reading takes about half an hour; if this is done twice a week, approximately one hour per week is spent on rate development. Given the importance of quick and efficient reading skills for university students, an hour a week is a reasonable time allotment for rate development, especially if students' self-confidence is improving at the same time. With the right approach, students at the advanced levels enjoy paced and timed readings; they recognize the necessity of building up their reading rates to approximate those of native speakers. Even though students should not be encouraged to compete with each other, they take these types of exercises very seriously and tend to compete.

Paced and timed readings can be created from many types of reading passages. Rate development materials for native speakers work just as well for second language students if the content is not heavily culture-bound. Vocabulary and topic choice should not be so difficult as to interfere with the reader's comprehension. (This potential problem can sometimes be reduced by previewing.) Paced readings can be designed by marking off 400 words of a passage and placing a dot in the margin at every one hundred words. Figure 3 shows how many seconds must elapse between dots in order to set a specific pace. For example, to set a pace of 200 WPM, 30 seconds must elapse between each dot in a 400-word passage. Timed readings can be created from any relevant reading passage. A simple way to find the approximate number of words in a passage is to:

1. find the average number of words per line in 20 lines
2. count the number of full lines
3. multiply the average number of words per line by the number of full lines

For example: 12 words per line × 100 full lines = 1200 words.

Passages of different word lengths will have an effect on student's reading rate. Shorter reading passages result in faster reading rates; conversely, longer passages tend to result in slower reading rates. Short passages may be read with intense concentration but they are not typical of real reading situations. Passages of about 1,000 words seem to work best, both in terms of students' rates and classroom time spent on rate development. In addition to length, levels of language and content must also be considered when choosing reading passages for paced and timed readings.

```
To set a pace of
    100 WPM, say "Mark" every 60 seconds
    125 ...............................48
    150 ...............................40
    175 ...............................34
    200 ...............................30
    225 ...............................26
    250 ...............................24
    275 ...............................22
    300 ...............................20
    325 ...............................18
    350 ...............................17
    375 ...............................16
    400 ...............................15
    425 ...............................14
    450 ...............................13
    500 ...............................12
    550 ...............................11
    600 ...............................10
    650 ............................... 9
    750 ............................... 8
    850 ............................... 7
   1000 ............................... 6
```

Figure 3: Pacing Chart (from Spargo and Williston 1980)

Core reading component

The core reading forms the basis for the thematic units described earlier, serving as material for listening and note-taking practice, for oral discussion practice, and for background material for writing practice. Most importantly, it provides practice for a variety of reading skills and strategies. The material for a core reading can be authentic material taken from a variety of sources such as high school and college textbooks, articles, and books for general reading.

Selecting suitable core (and supplementary) readings is time consuming since authentic materials are often difficult and frustrating for the nonnative reader. One must consider grammatical structure, vocabulary, presupposed background knowledge (both world and cultural), and rhetorical style. Introductory level college textbooks often work well for core readings since they familiarize students with academic writing styles and presuppose relatively little background information. The information contained in them is basic and usually presented in a clear and well-organized manner.

Such material should be challenging but not frustrating. Any difficulties that foreign students typically have with these texts can be alleviated, to some extent, by previewing exercises and/or a discussion at the beginning of a new unit (see Johnson 1982; Carrell and Eisterhold 1983). Furthermore, vocabulary in context exercises can ease certain excessive vocabulary difficulties. Nonetheless, core reading materials have to be chosen carefully for appropriateness.

In an integrated skills course, the most common practice is to use one textbook covering all of the language skills; this practice is the least expensive for the students, but often multi-skill textbooks have limitations because they are primarily designed for the lower and intermediate levels only. A second possibility is to select a variety of textbooks for the different language skills: one for structure, reading, etc. This option is more expensive and can be difficult and time consuming for the instructor to coordinate. A third option is not to use textbooks at all, but instead to employ teacher-developed materials which are designed for the particular needs of a specific group of students; this is especially appropriate for English for Special Purposes (ESP) courses. The problem with this option is that not all teachers have the time and/or the inclination to develop materials; this choice can be time consuming, impractical, and difficult. A fourth possibility is to use a combination of these options by combining textbooks, authentic materials, and teacher-developed materials. Whether a teacher decides to use a comprehensive skills textbook, a reading textbook, or teacher developed materials, the approach described in this chapter is equally applicable.

The skills developed in this component — previewing, skimming, scanning, vocabulary in context, recognizing rhetorical devices, and critical reading — can be broken down into pre-reading, during-reading, and post-reading activities (see Figure 4).

Pre-Reading	During-Reading	Post-Reading
Previewing (Skimming/Scanning) Vocabulary in Context	Text Highlighting	Skimming Scanning Recognizing Rhetorical Patterns Critical Reading

Figure 4: Skills Focus for Core Reading Component

Pre-Reading Activities

1. Skills Focus: Previewing

The content of the core reading can first be presented in a lecture as part of the university simulation. This activity works to preview the core reading as well as to provide an opportunity to practice listening and note-taking skills. In addition to the lecture, other activities which can work as a type of previewing are opinion polls, discussions, and vocabulary in context exercises. Students may also preview the core reading in class, as described in the Rate Development Component, before working on vocabulary in context exercises in class or reading the passage carefully at home.

2. Skills Focus: Vocabulary in Context

In addition to previewing, vocabulary in context exercises are given to the students before they read the core selection. Vocabulary in context exercises should be done in class and not as homework. The students will not be tempted to use their dictionaries which tends to defeat the purpose of the exercise. There are several good reason for doing vocabulary in context exercises. First, vocabulary in context exercises act as a type of previewing by familarizing students with the topic and content of the passage. Second, students should learn that they cannot rely on their dictionaries every time they encounter an unfamilar word. In order to become risk-takers, they need to learn a variety of strategies useful for figuring out the meanings of new words within their context. Students need to recognize redundancies within the language through exercises employing a variety of contextual clues and which draw on the vocabulary from the core reading.

Some of the major types of contextual clues which are found in commercially prepared materials include:[2]

    CAUSE AND EFFECT
    SYNONYMS
    ANTONYMS
    FUNCTIONAL DEFINITIONS
    DESCRIPTION
    EXAMPLES
    USE OF BE
    CLAUSE MARKERS
    APPOSITIVES
    PARENTHESES

The following examples illustrate a few of these types of contextual clues:

Use of *functional definition:*

Joan used an *atomizer* to spray her plants with a fine mist.

Atomizer means:

Use of *be*:

An *anthology* is a collection of writings.

Anthology means:

Use of *appositives*:

Oso, my dog, is long-haired German Shepherd.

Oso means:

After students have completed a brief vocabulary in context exercise (never more than ten items, preferably fewer), the clues or key words which enabled them to understand the meaning of the target words are discussed as well as the possible definitions of the target words. The focus of a vocabulary in context exercise should be on *how* students recognize the clues as opposed to what the correct definitions are. As such, the procedure is one of conciousness raising rather than actively teaching a large amount of vocabulary.

Vocabulary in context exercises have a number of uses:

1. Students become familar with some of the new words that they will encounter in the core reading.

2. They develop a sense of the content of the core reading.

3. They learn to identify clues which should aid them in understanding new vocabulary items.

4. They become more confident in their abilities to guess at the meanings of new words.

Vocabulary in context exercises are not intended to take students away from occasionally consulting their dictionaries or asking their teacher for explanations. In fact, "guessing from context" should not become a major skill focus which takes on a life of its own. (See Haynes 1984 for a discussion of the problems with guessing vocabulary in context.)

During-Reading Activities

1. Skills Focus: Text Highlighting

When the core reading passage is assigned as homework, the teacher should instruct the students to read the passage all the way through once without stopping or using their dictionaries for unfamilar words, reminding them of the vocabulary in context strategies they have already practiced. Students will have to read the passage several times in order to understand it thoroughly; even native speakers must do this.

Students should also underline the main idea of each paragraph during the second reading, having already practiced identifying topic sentences and main ideas at an early point in the semester. As with most students in academic settings, second language readers should learn to mark or highlight the text in order to facilitate study of the important facts and ideas. As they read, students need to underline or circle important information. In addition, they should learn to write comments in the text margins for reactions, definitions, or summaries. Another study technique while reading is to take notes on a separate piece of paper or to write a summary after reading. Teachers need to stress the active role a reader must take during-reading.

Post-Reading Activities

There are a variety of activities which are possible as post-reading exercises including: skimming and scanning, recognizing rhetorical patterns, and reading critically. The most common post-reading activity is a comprehension check of the core reading — such as a true/false, multiple-choice, or short answer quiz. In addition to checking comprehension, the quizzes pressure the students to read the material beforehand and to come to class prepared. Quizzes also work well as the basis for small group discussions.

1. Skills Focus: Skimming and Scanning

Skimming and scanning exercises as a post-reading activity are useful for several reasons. They focus students' attention on vocabulary, grammar, rhetorical structure, author's style, etc., depending on the purpose of the exercise. For example, students can skim a reading passage for the main ideas and sub-points, or for the thesis statement and supporting arguments if the teacher is working on organization or rhetorical patterns. Students can scan a passage to find answers to comprehension questions; in addition to answering comprehension questions, they can also write down the number of the paragraph in which the correct answer can be found. Sequencing exercises in which students must order a sequence of events or arguments are also useful for developing scanning skills.

2. Skills Focus: Recognizing Rhetorical Patterns

Exercises which involve identifying the functions and rhetorical structures of a passage are useful not only for writing skills but for reading comprehension as well. For nonnative speakers, analyzing a well-written passage will not only improve students' writing, but it will provide a deeper understanding of the author's purpose and message.

Students can identify such typical academic functions/rhetorical devices as: defining, observing, illustrating, predicting, classifying, describing, and generalizing at both the sentence and paragraph level. In addition to identifying such devices, students can also insert appropriate rhetorical phrases or markers in a passage. Other possible activities are choosing the correct missing paragraph from a passage, choosing the correct introduction and conclusion for a passage, or choosing correct topic sentences. Exercises in which students fill in text diagrams or flow-charts are also useful when analyzing rhetorical structures.

Another example of an exercise dealing with rhetorical patterns is to have the students identify the function of each paragraph as it relates to the entire passage; students can identify the paragraph(s) which presents background information, introduction, thesis statement, examples, counterarguments, sub-points, conclusion, etc. This type of exercise can be done individually, but since it may be difficult for some students, it may work better as a small group activity followed by a class discussion. Other exercises which focus the students' attention on rhetorical structures and organization are scrambled paragraphs which must be reordered and outlines which need to be filled in. Analyzing rhetorical patterns helps students gain a deeper understanding of the reading selection and familarizes them with organizational patterns necessary to improve academic writing skills.

3. Skills Focus: Critical Reading

Critical or interpretive reading skills are essential for academic students who must read a variety of writing styles for informational purposes. The successful student needs to be able to:

1. recognize the author's purpose
2. recognize the author's point of view
3. make inferences
4. draw conclusions
5. separate fact from opinion
6. separate own opinion from text.

Exercises which focus on critical reading skills oblige students to read thoughtfully and analytically; they should be challenging and thought provoking. For students who come from cultures where the written word is the Truth, these exercises can prepare them for the critical processes needed in higher education. Students must learn to question, evaluate, and criticize as part of the reading process (Lewin 1984).

Certain reading exercises can aid students in developing critical abilities. For example, in recognizing the author's purpose, the reader should consider who the author is, and what his/her background, credentials, or place in history is. When assessing the author's point of view, the reader needs to understand that it can be implicit or explicit. If the point of view is implicit, then the reader must infer and draw conclusions. Exercises in which students identify possible inferences and conclusions in a multiple-choice or true/false format help to develop critical reading skills. In addition to multiple-choice or true/false questions, students can also identify statements based on a reading passage as assumed, implied, or not assumed or implied as in the following exercise from Nuttall (1982):

Example of A Critical Reading Exercise

Last week, Rahman's wife had an accident. Rahman's youngest child, Yusof, was at home when it happened. He was playing with his new toy car. Rahman had given it to him the week before, for his third birthday.

Suddenly Yusof heard his mother calling "Help! Help!" He ran to the kitchen. His mother had burnt herself with some hot cooking oil. She was crying with pain and the pan was on fire.

Rahman had gone to his office. Both the other children had gone to school. Yusof was too small to help his mother, and she was too frightened to speak sensibly to him. But he ran to the neighbor's house and asked her to come and help his mother. She soon put out the fire and took Yusof's mother to the clinic.

When Rahman came home, his wife told him what had happened. He was very proud of his son. "When you are a man, you will be just like your father," he said.

Read the text and then read the facts stated below. Say which facts can be inferred from the text.

1. Rahman had three children.
2. Yusof was three years old.
3. Yusof was playing in the kitchen.
4. Rahman's wife was frying something.
5. Rahman was a clerk.
6. Yusof had a brother and a sister.
7. Rahman's house was not isolated.
8. The neighbor was a nurse.
9. Yusof's mother needed medical treatment.

Later, students can also list their own inferences and conclusions from a text for small group or class discussions. Inferring and concluding exercises are also useful for recognizing the author's point of view or purpose. In addition, students can explore such questions as:

1. What is the author's aim or intention?
2. Who is the intended audience?
3. What kind of background knowledge is assumed by the author?
4. Is the author successful or not in achieving his/her purpose?

Students should ask themselves these questions before reading a passage as part of previewing and again while reading.

An exercise for separating fact from opinion involves the students underlining what they believe are facts but circling what they believe are opinions. They can also identify types of opinions such as a generally held opinion or a personal opinion. Another exercise is one in which the class is divided into groups. Each group identifies a type of opinion or point of view which can be found within the text, for example, a pro, con, or undecided view. An exercise for separating one's own opinion from the text (or the author's) is to give the students a list of statements which they must mark as true or false according to the text, not according to their own opinions. Students can also list the arguments found within a text as well as underline statements which show approval or disapproval. Critical reading is a difficult skill even for native speakers, but advanced ESL students do need to detect bias, emotional appeals, and to identify incomplete and faulty reasoning (see Wood 1984 for additional exercises examining styles of argumentation).

Newspaper and magazine articles work well for critical reading exercises since the writing is usually clear and succinct; most foreign students are aware of and interested in current events so they find these topics interesting. Using a variety of newspapers and weekly news magazines, students can compare the coverage of the same event by examining different sources with respect to point of view, bias, and selective omission of facts, etc. (Lewin 1984). The OP/ED page of newspapers also contains a wealth of material for developing critical reading skills.

After completing critical reading exercises for a core reading selection, students should learn to synthesize the information as they would in an academic course. Such syntheses of information are crucial for writing assignments as well as for participation in class discussions, panel discussions, and debates.

Extensive reading component

The Extensive Reading Component, an extension of the Core Reading Component's materials, provides students with additional readings and exercises. The most important function of the Extensive Reading Component is to encourage more reading; the more students read, the better readers they become (and the better they read, the more they enjoy reading). Students may wish to pursue the theme of a core reading by reading additional material on the topic — for example, additional articles or even books — so the Extensive Component provides additional information on the various thematic units. For example, in the thematic unit "Culture Shock," extensive readings could direct students to related topics such as comparative social customs, body language, etc. Passages which may not be suitable for classroom use due to level of difficulty or length could also be included in the Extensive Reading Component.

The Extensive Reading Component material may be accompanied by a variety of reading exercises which students choose from if they or the instructor wish to work on a particular reading skill. For example, additional timed readings can be included in this component for those students who wish to develop rate and comprehension skills on their own. Also additional critical reading exercises are very useful in this component since the critical reading skill is the most difficult to develop.

It is suggested that the Extensive Reading Component be considered as part of the required course work; students should keep a personal log of their Extensive Reading Component activities in order to be aware of the importance of reading outside the language classroom. At the same time, the instructor needs to take note of and comment on exercises that the students are choosing.

5.4 ROLE OF THE INSTRUCTOR

The function of the instructor, other than that of assigner and overseer, includes:

1. making students aware of the importance of reading in higher education;
2. building students' self-confidence in their reading abilities;
3. sustaining student motivation;
4. supplying background information for texts;
5. reinforcing good reading habits;
6. teaching text-appropriate strategies;
7. reminding students of the strategies of fluent readers;
8. pushing students' reading rates/acting as timekeeper;
9. providing individualization and one-to-one contact;
10. choosing appropriate texts.

The importance of the role of the instructor should not be underemphasized. Of course students learn to read by reading, but putting them in a classroom alone with an array of reading materials is not enough. Students must be introduced to strategies and skills by a competent and enthusiastic instructor who is knowledgeable and aware of the importance of reading.

5.5 IMPLICATIONS FOR LOWER LEVELS

The reading course prototype discussed in this chapter is useful for developing a reading component in an academic/university program. This basic format works well at the intermediate and advanced levels, since a higher level of language proficiency creates greater possibilities for using more interesting material and teaching more sophisticated reading skills. A certain level of language proficiency is necessary in order to develop such skills as rhetorical awareness and critical reading, but many of the activities and exercises described in this chapter are adaptable for lower level classes.

Students at the lower levels can benefit from comprehension exercises, slower paced readings, and shorter timed readings (see Stoller, this volume). Previewing can be done at lower levels; in fact, the sooner learned, the better. Skimming and scanning exercises are useful for all levels and are usually part of low-level reading programs. Vocabulary in context exercises are possible at lower levels with appropriate word choices. Rhetorical pattern recognition skills may be possible to teach through the introduction of outlining and paragraph organization. Even some critical reading skills are useful for the lower levels such as drawing conclusions and making inferences. At every level, extensive reading materials provide students with the opportunity to choose their own selections and to discover that reading can be pleasurable. Especially important at the lower levels is the instructor's role in building students' self-confidence.

The goal of an academic reading program is to prepare students for academic tasks by supplying them with the skills that good readers need. Through a program that develops rate and comprehension, analytical, and critical skills for second language learners, a foundation for academic success is established.

NOTES

1. This prototype is modeled after a comprehensive skills class at the American Language Institute of the University of Southern California. This class, ALI 201, is for students who have TOEFL scores in the intermediate range (450-500). Students are in class three times a week for a total of twelve hours and are usually enrolled in one class in the major field of study. A special thanks to Mary Alvin and Cheryl Kraft of ALI/USC who have supervised this course.

2. See Clarke and Silberstein (1977) for a discussion of these types of contextual clues; see Zukowski/Faust et al. (1982, 1983) for some excellent examples of contextual clue exercises.

FOR STUDY AND DISCUSSION

1. Discuss the changes in reading instruction methodology which have occured in recent years. What are some of the reading textbooks which reflect these changes?

2. What is the difference between reading for language practice and reading for meaning? Cite examples, texts.

3. What are some of the advantages and disadvantages to teaching reading skills within a university course simulation?

4. List three reasons why nonnative speakers (readers) need to improve reading rate.

5. Read a paced reading passage at 600 WPM and answer the comprehension questions. Now read the same passage at 300 WPM. How is this experience similar to a student's?

6. Read a nonfiction passage of 1500 words to determine your reading rate.

7. Why is previewing an important study habit? How do you preview various reading material? What do you do differently?

8. List the reading material read in a typical day and identify the various rhetorical forms. How do your reading strategies vary?

FOR FURTHER READING

Nuttall (1982) is a classroom oriented overview of ESL reading; the chapter on critical reading skills is of particular use to intermediate/advanced-level instructors. Grellet (1981) contains material for developing a variety of reading exercises.

Practical textbooks for developing reading rate include Spargo and Williston (1980) in ten volumes; each volume contains fifty 400-word passages with comprehension questions. The Markstein and Hirasawa texts — intermediate and advanced (1981, 1982, 1983a,b) — are excellent for timed readings and are also adaptable for paced readings. The Zukowski/Faust et al. texts (1982, 1983) are very complete intermediate and advanced-level texts which contain interesting passages and a wide variety of reading exercises.

Part III

PART III: OVERVIEW

In Part III, the focus becomes broader with chapters about the separate topics of dealing with texts in reading courses (Dubin), evaluation of learners' reading skill (Allerson and Grabe), and computers and reading (Dever). Although these three areas do not fall into a convenient pigeonhole because of their similarity of content, they all discuss aspects of second language reading that are relatively unexplored and infrequently written about in the literature. Thus, they are linked together because each ventures into fresh territory.

A feature which both the chapter by Dubin and the one by Allerson and Grabe do share is an emphasis on the teacher's role in the process of second language reading instruction. Reading success in a second language does not necessarily happen naturally; indeed, the teacher's role is crucial — in choosing and modifying selections, as well as in writing exercise material for natural texts, as Dubin points out; in carrying out ongoing, informal evaluation of the learner's growing skill in reading, as Allerson and Grabe suggest.

The reader of this book who is looking for practical suggestions, techniques to try out in the classroom tomorrow morning, will find fewer in Part III than in Part II. Although Dubin leads us into the process of analyzing a reading passage and writing exercise material to use with learners, she does not provide a recipe. In fact, the procedures described in her chapter are meant to be a general suggestion for dealing with texts. Similarly, Allerson and Grabe point out a number of measures for the teacher to employ in ascertaining learners' reading skill, but as in the field of testing in general, the questions outnumber the tried and proven procedures. And in the chapter on reading and computers, Dever can only guide us to some appreciation of the intriguing potentials of the computer age in relation to pedagogical uses. At the same time, she does not hesitate to explain why and how the *possibilities* for utilizing computers in improving students' skill in reading, at present, far outweigh what the software has to offer. Nevertheless, we understand what may develop in the future far better after reading about it.

Chapter 6

Dealing with Texts

Fraida Dubin
University of Southern California

6.1 INTRODUCTION

In building courses for developing reading skills—whether for first or second language learners—teachers draw on three basic areas of investigation: (1) the nature of the reading process, (2) the characteristics of specific learner-readers, and (3) the texts or reading materials selected for instructional purposes. Chapter 1 (Eskey) discussed the first area by reviewing theoretical models which suggest how it is that people are able to get meaning from print, while Chapter 2 (Grabe) looked at the implications of theory for L2 classroom practice. The second area, planning instruction for particular groups of L2 learners, was highlighted in Chapters 3, 4, and 5 (Stoller, Mahon, Jensen). This chapter focuses on the third basic element, the actual texts or reading materials which are used for instructional purposes.

Models about the cognitive underpinnings of the reading skill apply to both native and second language readers since both, of course, possess the same mental and neuro-physiological capacity necessary for reading. However, in considering appropriate texts for L2 reading instruction, the factor of the learners' language and cultural backgrounds becomes more crucial. Reading in a second or foreign language overlaps with first language reading, yet there are significant differences of which teachers must be aware.

Some L1 reading specialists have expressed warnings for teachers not to interfere with students' reading (Bettelheim and Zalen 1981). They claim it is a process which will take care of itself if the right ingredients are present, chiefly sufficient motivation and texts which appeal to and interest each individual learner. In an L2 instructional context, however, the goal of having the teacher step aside should come about only at quite an advanced level. Before this stage, the teacher has the responsibility, among others, to select appropriate texts for instructional purposes. In order to carry out this role, the teacher must appraise classroom materials in terms of their language complexity, their informational content, and their text-type characteristics. Each one of these topics is discussed in detail in the following major sections.

This chapter takes a wide perspective on second language reading inasmuch as it looks at both narrative and expository texts for instructional purposes, rather than to be concerned with specialized reading matter associated with academic courses alone.

6.2 LANGUAGE CONCERNS AND TEXTS

For instructional purposes, L2 teachers make use of two broad categories of texts: specially written and unchanged or natural texts. The first type provides comprehensibility for the learner in terms of structural complexity and vocabulary. The second type, on the other hand, exposes L2 readers to rhetorical and stylistic features which are usually absent from specially created texts. In deciding which type may prove appropriate with a particular group, the teacher must realize there will always be trade-offs. It is not an easy job to produce specially created texts and maintain learners' interest level and motivation for reading. While outside of intermediate-advanced levels, most natural texts require a deeper control of grammatical elements and a richer word stock than many of the learners will possess.[1]

Specially created texts

All materials in printed form which have been created for the purpose of language instruction offer possibilities for paying closer attention to reading. The most typical example is the comprehensive language textbook which is arranged by grammatical topics, or in more recent times by semantic ("notional") or functional categories. In addition, the teacher can add to the store of specially created texts by using natural sources but then adapting them in ways which aid comprehension by L2 learners.

The comprehensive language textbook

Although its effectiveness as reading material may be questioned, the universally-known, specially created material is the comprehensive language textbook. Even though the course may emphasize aural/oral or communicative activities, many learners and teachers look to it as a primary source of language examples, rules of structure, as well as practice activities. In using it, the learner probably works on decoding skills, while relying heavily on overall meaning in the native language. This is particularly the case when the material for reading highlights examples of particular grammatical elements rather than subject matter which involves the learner in some meaningful way.

Describing How Something Is Done

Estelle Jones is a sales manager for the Wren Computer Company. The computers that she sells *are made* in the United States and *are* often *sent* to other countries. Before they *are shipped,* the computers *are* carefully *packed*. They *are weighed,* and labels *are put* on them. Then they *are delivered* to the airport terminal.

At the terminal, they *are taken* to an airplane and loaded into the baggage compartment. When the computers arrive in another country, they *are unloaded* very carefully. They *are given* special care because they are very fragile. If the packages *aren't handled* carefully, the computers *can be damaged*. Computers that *are damaged* must be sent back to the United States.

Passive: The computer *is sent by* the company.
The computers *are needed by* the customers.
Active: The company *sends* the computer.
The customers *need* the computers.

Rewrite the sentences. Use the passive.
■ 1. Estelle sells computers. *Computers are sold by Estelle.*
2. The customer needs the computer.
The computer _____ by _____ .
3. The customer must pay for the computer.
The computer must _____ .

Figure 1: *English Alpha: 4*

Some language textbook series begin introducing short *narrative* or *expository* passages by the third or fourth book. Often these passages build on topics or themes previously used in the unit or chapter.

But learners need considerably more material which concentrates on reading for reading's sake than can be found in a language-centered textbook. (See Chapter 3/Stoller, for examples of low-level materials.) Reading narratives probably serves as the best bridge between the typically short passages in a language textbook and natural or unchanged texts. For one reason, the story form seems to be known by all people everywhere. Also, a story is more apt to hold the reader's interest since it holds out the question: What happens next?

READ AND UNDERSTAND

Did you hear about Pat's week in the United States? She wrote the winning poem in a contest. Her prize was a trip to San Francisco! She left on the tenth at 9:30 in the evening. She got to San Francisco at 8:40 a.m. on the eleventh. One night in a first-class hotel was part of the prize, so she went straight there. She was so tired that she slept the whole day.

At eight that night she got up for dinner. She ate in the hotel dining room, and the bill was so expensive that she went straight back to bed. The next morning Pat counted her money. She found she hadn't brought nearly enough. She found a cheaper hotel and paid her bill in advance. Then she counted her cash again. She thought she would have enough for five days—as long as she ate only one meal a day! She spent most of her cash on museums, theater tickets, and a bus tour of Napa Valley.

When she caught the plane home, she was tired, broke, and hungry! But she told me that she had enjoyed herself anyway.

1. What did Pat write?
2. What did she win?
3. What did she do her first day in San Francisco?
4. Where did she eat dinner?
5. What did she do the next day?
6. Did she have enough money for seven days?
7. What did she spend most of her money on?
8. How did she feel when she caught the plane home?

Figure 2: Narrative Passage: *New Horizons, Book 3*

READ AND UNDERSTAND

Buying By Mail

You have probably seen ads in newspapers or on TV for mail-order houses. Perhaps you have been sent a catalogue and have bought something by mail. Why do people buy things they have not seen in person? One of the main reasons might be that some people believe that things can be bought more cheaply by mail. Another advantage of mail-order shopping is that it is more comfortable to sit at home and look through a catalogue than to rush around the stores. With a catalogue from a large firm, you have your own shop window for almost everything you might want to buy.

The mail-order business is very wide-spread. Some companies have agents who show merchandise from the catalogues to likely customers. Perhaps you have had one of these agents call you or come by your home. They are paid a commission for every order they take.

Buying from a catalogue is so easy. It saves the shopper time and trouble. Sometimes, it saves the shopper money on one item. But people often buy more than they can really afford, since they can buy on time, or credit. Some companies allow a customer to pay for an item over a long period of time if they have a charge account. People can also pay a certain percent of the total price. This is called a down payment. Then the customer pays a certain amount of money every month until the merchandise is completely paid for. Mail-order houses sell just about everything—furniture, tools, household goods—even heavy machinery and vehicles.

1. How do mail-order houses advertise?
2. What are the advantages of buying by mail?
3. What are the disadvantages of buying by mail?
4. What is the difference between charging an item and paying for it on time?

Figure 3: Expository Passage: *New Horizons, Book 4*

Altering source scripts

For most teachers, it is probably easier to either abridge or alter a source script into a form which makes it more comprehensible for learners than to create an engaging story. Everyone who has tried writing an original story which uses limited grammatical elements and selected vocabulary understands the problem. Moreover, many reading teachers feel that while it is too time consuming to produce all of their own classroom materials, having an understanding of techniques for writing altered versions of original scripts is a vital skill.

Some years ago, when the language teaching profession was chiefly concerned with structural elements, Earl Stevick (1963) offered techniques to teachers for adapting anecdotes, or mini-narratives, to make them understandable by learners at various stages of competence. Stevick advised, find a short anecdote made up of no more than one or two cleverly complex sentences. Reduce it to a list (Version A) which includes each detail of action and description separately. If the anecdote includes dialogue, list each utterance as a separate item, too. After you have completed Version A, notice how much lexical redundancy it includes. For beginning level students, this is an important feature which aids comprehension.

Next, write an intermediate version (B), by combining two or three of the items in the list in a single sentence using introductory phrases. A third version (C), should go even further by introducing more modification, dependent clauses, and sentence embedding when possible. Below, in Figure 4, are three versions offered by Stevick.

A more sophisticated version would include further deletions, more sentence embedding, connective elements between sentences, as well as attention to more realistic register than appeared in Stevick's Versions B or C. Of course, the original anecdote should be selected because it contains some meaningful connection to the experience of a particular group of learners. For example, the fact that a member of the class had been stopped by a traffic officer and came to class with a share-and-tell tale could motivate a teacher to offer the group a short anecdote for reading which relates to this particular topic. To help learners become more sensitive to the complexities of English anecdote style, all three versions (B, C, and D) could be read and then discussed.

Ambulance, Version A

1. An ambulance was traveling down a highway.
2. The ambulance was traveling at 80 m.p.h.
3. The siren of the ambulance was wailing.
4. A state policeman was on a motorcycle.
5. The state policeman overtook the ambulance.
6. The state policeman stopped the ambulance.
7. The driver said, "I was speeding."
8. "I know that."
9. "Ambulances carry sick people."
10. "The state allows ambulances to speed."
11. "Why did you stop me?"
12. The policeman replied, "I was trying to tell you something."
13. "There is no patient in your ambulance."
14. "You left your patient's home."
15. "You were in a hurry."
16. "You forgot your patient."

Ambulance, Version B

An ambulance was traveling down a highway at 80 m.p.h. Its siren was wailing. A state policeman on a motorcycle overtook the ambulance and stopped it.

The driver of the ambulance said, "I know that I was speeding, but the state allows ambulances to speed because they carry sick people. Why did you stop me?"

The policeman replied, "I was trying to tell you that there is no patient in your ambulance. You were in a hurry when you left your patient's home, and you forgot him."

Ambulance, Version C

An ambulance was traveling down an open highway at 80 m.p.h., with its siren wailing, when a state policeman on a motorcycle overtook it and stopped it.

The driver of the ambulance protested, "I know I was speeding, but ambulances carrying patients are allowed to speed. Why did you stop me?"

The policeman replied, "That's what I was trying to tell you. You were in such a hurry when you left your patient's home that you forgot him!"

Figure 4: *The Ambulance:* Versions A, B, and C

Version D

"What's wrong with you? I know I was speeding," the protesting ambulance driver shouted at the policeman. "Are you crazy? You know as well as I do that ambulance drivers are allowed to speed."

"Lay off," the policeman replied. "You're in such a hurry you left your patient's home without him. Just take a look in the back."

Reconstituting source scripts

With students who are more advanced, teachers can use unedited source scipts without simplifying lexical items or altering grammatical construction through application of a process of modification. Lying somewhere between specially created and completely natural texts, such reconstituted materials are still altered for pedagogical purposes even though the original writing remains intact.

The example of a teacher-prepared reading lesson ("It's a Geep") taken from *Time* illustrates many of the elements which a teacher can apply to turn an interesting clipping into more understandable form for L2 learners. Notice that care has been taken to include not only the heading of the original article but the section title (Science) as well. The one-page handout has been designed to simulate the look of the original magazine while still aiding comprehension through adding other features. The paragraphs are numbered on the left-hand margin; the lines are indicated on the right-hand margin. These letter/number designations are important for ease of reference during class and small group discussions of the material. Glossing of key words, terms which are central to overall meaning, is another prominent feature of reconstituting. In teacher-prepared materials, the "new words" are usually selected because the teacher is aware of the vocabulary stock that a specific group of learners has studied.[2] After reading the article, learners discuss the implications of the ideas contained in it; they are not asked "comprehension" questions which would only test their understanding of literal information (see Jensen, this volume).

Another technique for reconstituting original articles is the practice of reproducing the original with more white space around each paragraph. This is particularly helpful for L2 learner-readers when using items taken from newspapers in which the print is set quite tightly.

Science

From the picture below, can you guess what the article is about?

Cambridge's hybrid creature

Horns, long hair and four parents.

It's a Geep

Crossbreeding goats and sheep

Key Words

Use your dictionary to find the meanings of these key words which are repeated frequently in the article:

    crossbreed   embryo
    hybrids   blood protein

New Words

Paragraph A

prank	1. 1	a joke or trick
angora	1. 2	a variety of goat with long, silky hair . . . the thread is used to make sweaters
dubbed	1. 7	called

Paragraph B

manipulate	1. 10	to change, adapt
surrogate	1. 16	substitute
mingle	1. 12	to mix together

A   t looks like a zookeeper's prank: a goat 1 dressed in a sweater of angora. But the odd-looking creature that appeared on the cover of the journal *Nature* last week is no joke. The animal is a crossbreed of two en- 5 tirely different species, a goat and a sheep. Inevitably, it has been dubbed a geep.

B   Now 18 months old and thriving, the geep was produced by the latest tricks of embryo manipulation. Scientists at the 10 Institute of Animal Physiology in Cambridge, England, mingled new embryos from both sheep and goats when each consisted of no more than four to eight cells. Ultimately, these were placed in the 15 wombs of surrogate sheep or goat mothers and allowed to grow to term. Such hybrids are called chimeras (after the mythic monster with a lion's head, goat's body and serpent's tail).   20

C   Because each embryo came originally
from the fertilized eggs of both a goat and
a sheep, the animals had four parents.
The Cambridge experimenters produced
a total of six animals with characteristics 25
of both sheep and goats. Only one of
them, however, had blood proteins from
both species. That animal behaves like a
goat and has even tried mating with fe-
male goats, but like another hybrid, the 30
mule, its sperm are defective. At Justus-
Liebig University in Giessen, West Ger-
many, other embryo manipulators also reported producing goat-sheep.

D   Though such experimenting is sure to 35
trigger debate, scientists point to practical
benefits: it should make it easier to rear embryos of endangered species in the wombs
of other species or even create hybrids as
valuable as the indomitable mule.   ■

Paragraph D
trigger	1. 36	to start
an endangered species	1. 38	a species in danger of becoming extinct
indominatable	1. 40	cannot be subdued, overcome

To Talk About

1. Why will experiments like this one trigger debates?

2. What kinds of beliefs might be represented on the two sides of the question about embryo manipulation?

Figure 5: *It's a Geep*

Natural texts

Current methodology in L2 instruction places emphasis on using natural materials, or examples of the target language as used by native speakers for authentic, communicative goals. Becoming a successful mature reader by definition means being able to read unedited texts produced by writers who make no accommodation to readers who are less than fully competent. Moreover, if fluency is to be achieved, L2 learners need ample practice reading natural texts. The activity of reading must extend beyond the L2 classroom and into the individual learner's study and recreational time.

Fortunately, the goal of reading fluently is more achievable than is that of becoming a near-native or native-like speaker in a foreign or second language, particularly for people who do not have access to models of the spoken language. In a foreign language context, becoming a successful reader is probably the only skill which can be realistically achieved within the context of an ordinary classroom. The role played by the L2 teacher in the accomplishment of this goal is crucial.

The responsibility of selecting the necessary natural reading materials for classroom use as well as guiding learners to additional resources for reading materials is probably the teacher's primary function. Since the range is so broad, some guidelines may be helpful. Natural materials for reading consist of just about everything which exists in print in the target language. Obviously, that takes in a universe of possibilities which needs to be reduced to some manageable list.

Unchanged texts

There are many types of natural texts which can be understood by L2 learners without any editing because they are written in fairly simple, straightforward style (Davies and Widdowson 1974; Davies 1984).[3] Teachers who work with intermediate and advanced learners and so look to natural texts as sources for selections can make use of the whole continuum of stylistic text types ranging from popular to academic writing. At one end, popular writing is probably more readily accessible by virtue of containing shorter sentences, less specialized vocabulary, and greater use of accompanying illustrations and typographical features which aid comprehension. Academic, or professional writing, at the other end, is more information-dense since it usually has fewer expanded examples. As for vocabulary, it contains more Latin-based words and expressions.

Even though a learner's educational goal is to study subjects necessary for obtaining a higher education degree, it may turn out to be a better strategy in an ESL reading course to utilize texts for intensive classroom work which are nonspecialized in nature as preparation for plunging into reading more specialized academic material (van Naerssen 1985). A reading teacher looking for natural texts should not overlook obvious possibilities that are close at hand: *Dear Abby* letters from the newspaper, the news digests prepared for native speaker secondary school students, and selections from general audience popular magazines. Often, these sources can provide important background information to familiarize learners with social issues and current topics. From a practical point of view, an important criterion to keep in mind is that of brevity. If the teacher expects to photocopy the material for classroom use, an editorial from a newspaper is usually easier to handle than a news feature. Yet, even more important is the topic and its relevance to the interests of a particular learner audience.

Textbooks for native speaker students

Another source of natural text materials, lying somewhere between popular writing and academic sources, is the textbooks prepared in all subject content areas for native-speaking students, either at the high school or first-year college level. It is usually the case that topics covered in liberal arts college curricula, basic concepts from economics, political science, sociology, anthropology, geography, science and ecology, among others, are presented in simple language with ample graphic material such as maps, illustrations, graphs, charts, etc. Those sources are valuable since they introduce L2 learners to the basic vocabulary of educated discourse.

Academic subject area textbooks for native speakers also give L2 learner-readers greater exposure to expository writing, the kind which presents ideas or information by developing explanations—hence the term expository. Since this mode is used throughout higher education for term papers, reports, and essay examinations, it is important for L2 learners to gain a great deal of experience reading such material, even before they must produce it themselves in written format.

In fact, some ESL teachers have turned to college freshman composition texts, the kind which present reading passages as examples of good writing. These books frequently organize the selections for reading by the rhetorical features contained within them, or under headings such as analyzing through classification, illustrating ideas by using examples, explaining by means of comparison and contrast, expanding ideas through analogy, explaining through process analysis, proving a point by analyzing cause and effect relationships and explaining ideas through using definitions.

While selections in texts for college freshman composition courses have already passed an anthologist's test of interesting topics for American students, still the ESL teacher needs to carry the selection procedure a step further by assessing their cross-cultural implications. For example, how much information about life in the United States do learners need in order to understand the selections? The ESL teacher must be alert, too, to the genre of reading texts intended for native-speaker students in American high schools and community colleges. Often, these texts are carefully prepared for academically low achieving students who need remedial help in basic literacy skills. Since they often focus on topics concerned with self-worth and interpersonal relations, they may be misunderstood by people from cultures where quite different modes of living prevail.

Anthologies for L2 learners

But the quest for interesting, motivating yet still digestible reading materials for use in the L2 classroom may simply take too much of the teacher's time. A commercial textbook is the obvious answer. Because of the growing realization in recent years of the importance of reading in second language courses, a number of reader-anthologies have been produced to meet the needs of L2 learner-readers. If a reading textbook contains lively selections as well as exercise material which gets at the skills necessary for mature reading, it can serve the teacher well. Such a text can be utilized for extensive, out-of-class, or individualized reading. Moreover, an anthology always has the built-in possibility that through it a reluctant reader will begin to browse a bit and become caught up with reading for pleasure. The teacher can still augment the reading textbook with selections which build and expand on its contents. These supplementary handouts may also have the advantage of presenting more timely, up-to-the-minute accounts of a particular topic contained in the reading book.

Unanticipated texts

There will always be some learners who are not motivated by a textbook since the very look of it produces feelings of anxiety, frustration, boredom—or all three—the result of previous negative experiences. In these instances the use of unanticipated texts, or materials for reading which learners didn't expect to find in a language classroom, is called for. Beyond all other approaches, this one requires ingenuity and creative collecting on the teacher's part. Unanticipated materials could be copies of a novel upon which a currently popular film or TV miniseries is based, or a book version of a film—the movie-to-book phenomenon of today's publishing world. Or, they might be sources for quite utilitarian reading such as college and university brochures and catalogs, consumer guides, mail-order catalogs, and the campus newspaper, literary, or humor magazine.

Special purpose courses

Along with emphasizing natural texts, current L2 methodology also has stressed designing courses to meet the needs of specific learners and their short and long term objectives for learning English. As indicated through careful needs analyses, such L2 courses take into account the actual situations, tasks, and skills which learners require in their jobs and professions. English for special purposes (ESP) programs frequently specify reading skills as a primary objective.

Teachers who have an assignment whether as a classroom facilitator, a course designer, or a materials developer in an ESP program might be faced with a conflict: should they narrow the focus of reading to the particular types of materials learners will require in job or professionally related situations, or should they encourage the students to read as widely as possible by dipping into many types of books, magazines and journals? Can the course focus on the subject area content of learners' special interest yet still introduce the topic through the medium of various types of reading materials?

In the following sections, this dilemma is discussed from two points of view: first, in terms of the background knowledge needed for reading with comprehension (informational-cultural background), and second, in terms of the specific knowledge needed to read particular types of texts.

6.3 THE LEARNER'S BACKGROUND KNOWLEDGE IN RELATION TO TEXTS

In straightforward terms, reading with comprehension comes about when the reader's previous experience and knowledge connects with the author's content as it appears in the text. This idea, extended to other facets of human comprehension, is studied more abstractly by social scientists under various titles such as "schema theory," "frame analysis," and "scripts." The notion is easy enough to understand if one thinks of reading about an entirely new subject area in one's mother tongue. Most of the words, certainly the organization of the words into sentences, and the division of ideas into paragraphs conveys meaning. But real comprehension is elusive if one has no previous background of experience with the subject. For example, try reading this passage (Figure 6) from a secondary school physics textbook; if, of course, you've never taken up the subject. (If you happen to be a physics enthusiast, substitute a text on a topic about which you have seldom, if ever, read or studied.) How much meaning is there in the selection for you?

11

MODELS for MATTER

We know that matter is made of atoms and molecules. Even the simplest molecule in nature is a complicated system. While an exact equation describing the behavior of molecules *is* known, it is too mathematically complex to be solved in any exact way. Without an exact solution for the real system, we have to invent model systems to try to explain the properties of matter we observe. No one model can usually explain all the properties of any kind of matter. We have to use one model for one property and another for a different property. In this chapter, we are concerned with several models we use to explain a few of the important properties of matter. This chapter does not tell the whole story, but at least it clarifies some of the rules in the game of model-making for complicated systems.

11.1 MOLECULAR BONDS

The simplest act an atom can do is to move. The next simplest act is to join with other atoms to form molecules. Just about all atoms can join with others to form molecules of one sort or another. The only exceptions are the atoms of the noble gases—helium, neon, argon, krypton, xenon, and radon. Sometimes the noble gases do get tied up into molecules, but only weakly. The molecules separate into atoms very easily. Why don't the noble gases form molecules very well? Their atoms are pretty much like any others—they have nuclei with positive charges surrounded by electrons. The only difference between the atoms of the noble gases and other atoms lies in the arrangement of their outside electrons, which we shall discuss later in Chapter 17.

This fact tells us that the important basic force —the **molecular bond**—that holds atoms together in molecules must be some kind of electric force between the outer electrons of atoms. If molecular bonds resulted from any other kinds of forces—nuclear or gravitational forces, or electromagnetic forces between nuclei—a noble gas should form

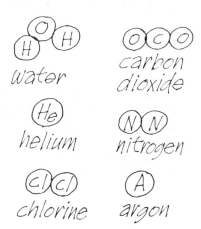

water

carbon dioxide

helium

nitrogen

chlorine

argon

Figure 6: *The World of Physics,* Hulsizer/Lazarus

The need for previous knowledge in order to understand what one is reading goes beyond the reading of material in textbooks. Have you ever been on a long trip and then returned home to find that the items about local events in the newspaper seem strange and a bit foreign? Understanding a daily newspaper requires keeping up with what is happening in the community, the nation, and the world. Even daily reading calls for background knowledge. The headline from a newspaper, shown below, would only be understood if the reader knows two terms as used in the context of college student affairs: minorities, Greek control. If one gave these terms other meanings, the entire sense of the headline is lost. Of course, other words in the headline establish the particular context of meaning. But then, headlines are meant to be read rapidly.

MINORITIES WIN UCLA COUNCIL SEATS
Record Student Vote Seen as Ending Era of Greek Control

The discussion in this section considers three implications of background knowledge in dealing with texts for L2 courses: (1) the place of reading in-depth, or how a teacher can manage texts to help learners utilize their prior knowledge; (2) strategies for learning new material, or what to do when there is no previous knowledge of the text's content; and (3) a teacher-made lesson which combines attention to background knowledge and techniques for analyzing texts.

Techniques for reading-in-depth to provide background knowledge

Reading-in-depth is a term which describes a variety of techniques for activating learners' experience with and knowledge about a topic. In L2 reading instruction, one of the teacher's chief concerns is to provide the element of reading-in-depth. The teacher achieves this objective by selecting, arranging, and orchestrating texts. Attention to reading-in-depth can come about in many ways. It occurs, for example, when the teacher provides materials for extensive reading which deal with each learner's own country—in English. Or, when a teacher assigns a library task in which students use the card catalog to find books about his/her own country. In this section, a number of other suggestions are made for implementing reading-in-depth through the materials used for intensive reading lessons.

The reading-in-depth element in anthologies

A conventional table of contents found in some published reading programs for L2 is a smorgasbord or potpourri of selections resulting in a bill of fare built on a list of quite separate topics. On the surface the approach appears logical since it gets at motivation by offering something for everyone. Considering that materials preparers for wide audiences must try to meet the tastes and interests of so many, how else could they proceed?

The smorgasbord approach, however, because it does not link topics or themes in any meaningful way, fails to take reading-in-depth into account. Of course, the teacher can supplement topics in the book with additional ones which are connected with it; but in selecting a smorgasbord text to begin with, the teacher should realize its limitations.

Another approach in anthology construction is the thematic table of contents. It moves along a bit on the scale in the direction of more attention to reading-in-depth by including selections built around a particular theme, typically one based on external facts — information, or on personal moods and feelings. Even more attention to reading-in-depth occurs in texts which have thematically organized units. In these types, all the selections in a particular unit or chapter contain a unifying thread by virtue of a common core of meaning.

Attention to reading-in-depth can occur as well in the exercise material accompanying the selections in an anthology. One such technique is recapitulation in which the main reading selection is followed with a paraphrase version: many of the words and sentences are rephrased but the content is the same as in the original (Markstein and Hirasawa 1982). So reading-in-depth is activated when learners read the same content in a new form.

Dividing longer texts into shorter sections

There are many advantages in utilizing longer texts because they give students experience reading sustained passages rather than short, truncated selections. Thus, they offer the possibility for real reading to take place. In addition, the reading of longer passages affords reading-in-depth since as one progresses into the text, comprehension is increased through the background one has just acquired.

It becomes the teacher's responsibility when utilizing longer texts to arrange them in ways which provide for the fullest use of the reading-in-depth principle. Some texts lend themselves to being divided into more manageable length by adding sub-headings which give section or part numbers. Then, exercise material can follow each section (Dubin and Olshtain 1984). By breaking up a longer text into shorter segments, individuals are able to move ahead at their own pace, yet everyone in the class is still reading on the same topic. Narratives, in particular, lend themselves to being segmented into shorter segments for use in L2 classrooms, but the technique can be applied to nonfiction writing as well.

Reintroducing topics

Whether the teacher selects materials for intensive reading practice from natural sources exclusively, uses one anthology or a few, or draws on a combination of selections from both teacher-prepared and commercial texts, topics can be reintroduced to afford the maximum attention to reading-in-depth. If the textbook contains an appealing selection in terms of content, the teacher can bring in an extension of the same content-theme, yet utilize a different type of source. For example, if the selection from the anthology is taken from a popular magazine source, the teacher could augment that material with a selection from a textbook for native speakers, or from a magazine aimed at readers with college background. In addition, the experience of reading similar or related content matter from a variety of sources is an important strategy which should be included in programs which provide instruction in reading-to-learn (see below).

In a somewhat different context, academic L2 programs, learners usually need to work on the kinds of critical thinking skills necessary for doing college-level reading and writing. A valuable reading-in-depth technique in these programs is to include selections which present a critique or a critical review of a text. For example, students might read a selection from a nonfiction book then read reviews of it; or, they can read a selection which comments on a controversial, contemporary topic, then read another selection which looks at the same body of information from a different point-of-view. Current political, environmental and economic issues offer plentiful possibilities for incorporation into lessons which present a statement of the points under discussion followed by the reading of opinion articles.

The running story

Frequently, teachers may employ reading-in-depth by utilizing selections of current news stories. As developments build in the story, the learner-reader acquires more and more background knowledge about the particular topic. Items from newspapers, popular, or professional magazines can be introduced over a period of time for intensive reading practice. Or, news items can be posted on a bulletin board. Interest in the topic usually increases as learners become more and more familiar with the details surrounding the event.[4]

The display of headlines shown on the next page (Figure 7) illustrates one such running story developed by a teacher around the theme of a space shuttle voyage of a few years ago. As technical problems occurred, interest in the delayed launch date increased. By the time the spacecraft had been successfully launched, the learners had become aware of a number of the semi-technical details with which news stories are filled.

A few weeks after the launching and successful completion of the craft's mission, the teacher introduced an additional story, this time an extended article from *The New Yorker* magazine. Because of its length, many students would have found it too difficult to read earlier in the course. But with previous knowledge which had been built up over a period of time by reading about the space shuttle in other accounts, they were able to read the more sophisticated version of the same event with almost complete comprehension.

Hopes of NASA to Ride on Shuttle in April
Agency Shows Enthusiasm for Often-Delayed $15-Billion Project

Space Shuttle Functions Perfectly . . . on Paper

Heat Shield, Engine 'Bugs' Spoil Plans

Officials Jubilant as Space Shuttle's Engines Pass Test

Countdown on Shuttle Test Begins

A REPORTER AT LARGE
SHUTTLE-1

Figure 7: Headlines/Text

Strategies for reading-to-learn

Despite the importance of background knowledge in reading comprehension, everyone at times must read texts for the purpose of learning from them. Indeed, most reading assignments given in college and university undergraduate classes call for students to read new information with understanding. Thus, the nature of college reading is for the purpose of reading-to-learn, an activity which calls for specific strategies for dealing with the text at hand.

A vital component of L2 reading instruction for college/university students should be to provide specific strategies for learning new material, whether it is from a required textbook, collateral reading, a professional journal, or any other type of printed source. At this point, L2 reading courses and those intended for native speakers often coincide; in fact, the study skills which L2 learners need tend to be the same as those which are sometimes presented in learning skills centers on university campuses.

Conscious learning

A key strategy for this purpose of reading, one which is integrally connected with reading-in-depth, involves reading the same material from various sources, practically at the same time. It is an important tool for learning new subject matter which is frequently utilized by people studying law and medicine, fields in which the learning involves remembering a great many details, and understanding specialized terms and vocabulary.

The L2 teacher can incorporate this strategy by having learners read about the same topic from a variety of sources. In demonstrating how the technique works, the teacher should take pains to provide reading sources from different types of texts, including material which is information-dense along with additional material which is written in a more expansive style.

An example of the technique is familiar to many language teachers who have taken courses in theoretical linguistics. Reading about transformational-generative grammar in the writings of Noam Chomsky the first time through requires a background of specialized knowledge which many humanities majors do not possess. After a first attempt with the original source, it is helpful to read the same ideas as interpreted by another author, particularly one whose objective is to address a nonspecialized audience of people who want to understand the broad picture rather than to work their way through tangles of technical terms and oblique references. This purpose is often the function of any elementary textbook in a subject area. But reading from a few books at the same time involves more than just reading one introduction to the field. Moreover, it enables a reader to return to the original, information-dense source—often the "required" reading—with a residue of built-up background information.

A number of other strategies for learning new material are variations on a central theme, all designed for coping with texts written in an information-dense style. These are all or any of the following: (1) underlining the important terms, ideas; (2) writing notes to oneself in the margin as reminders of where the key points can be located; (3) writing brief paraphrase statements of key ideas in the margin; (4) talking about the material with a fellow student after reading by asking each other questions, clarifying misunderstandings, and in general, making the material one's own.

The SQ3R technique

Well-known to study skills specialists who are concerned with instruction for native-speaker students, the SQ3R approach was formulated more than twenty years ago by Francis Robinson (1962:31-32). It was designed to deal with the informational material typically found in textbooks. The title stands for the abbreviation of the steps in the procedure: survey, question, read, recite, review.

1. **Survey**   Glance over the headings in the chapter to see the main points which will be developed. Also read the final summary paragraph if the chapter has one. This survey should not take more than a minute and will show the three to six core ideas around which the discussion will cluster. This orientation will help you organize the ideas as you read them later.

2. **Question**   Now begin to work. Turn the first heading into a question. This will arouse your curiosity and so increase comprehension. It will bring to mind information already known, thus helping you to understand that section more quickly. And the question will make important points stand out while explanatory detail is recognized as such. Turning a heading into a question can be done instantly upon reading the heading, but it demands a conscious effort on the part of the reader to make this a query for which he must read to find the answer.

3. **Read**   Read to answer that question, i.e., to the end of the first headed section. This is not a passive plodding along each line, but an active search for the answer.

4. **Recite**   Having read the first section, look away from the book and try briefly to recite the answer to your question. Use your own words and include an example. If you can do this you know what is in the book; if you can't, glance over the section again. An excellent way to do this reciting from memory is to jot down cue phrases in outline form on a sheet of paper. Make these notes very brief. Now repeat steps 2, 3, and 4 on each subsequent headed section.

That is, turn the next heading into a question, read to answer that question, and recite the answer by jotting down cue phrases in your outline. Read in this way until the entire lesson is completed.

5. **Review** When the lesson has thus been completely read, look over your notes to get a bird's-eye view of the points and their relationship and check your memory as to the content by reciting on the major subpoints under each heading. This checking of memory can be done by covering up the notes and trying to recall the main points. Then expose each major point and try to recall the subpoints listed under it.

6.4 A SAMPLE TEACHER-MADE READING LESSON WHICH ACTIVATES BACKGROUND KNOWLEDGE AND UTILIZES TECHNIQUES OF TEXT ANALYSIS

The article shown below was taken from the opinion-editorial page of a daily newspaper (see Figure 8). Using it as material for an intensive reading lesson would be appropriate with a class of intermediate-advanced students in an academic English course. It is presupposed, too, that the learners had already been introduced to the broad topic of genetic engineering through reading the selection from *Time*, "It's a GEEP" (see Figure 5). Although the subject matter draws on various related fields in the biological sciences, the issues which both selections raise are of concern to most educated adults in today's world. Thus, introducing it once more furthers learners' store of general information, or emphasizes reading-in-depth.

The L2 teacher who wants to make use of such natural selections has the responsibility to carry the task a step beyond clipping and reproducing the article by creating the exercises and activities which will help learners grasp the author's plan together with the author's purposes. But in order to write exercise material which goes beyond testing comprehension, the teacher must first analyze the text.

Constructing exercises to accompany a selection also involves judging the degree of detailed analysis which a particular group of learners might profit from. Too much nit-picking in the exercises might only create confusion and cause students to overlook the main ideas in the selection. Essentially, the teacher should try to discover the author's plan in terms of the function of the paragraphs, the cohesion markers which link the main ideas of paragraphs together, and the elements which provide overall unity in the text, or coherence. This information becomes the basis for writing comprehension, discussion, and follow-up questions. Each text, however, is unique. So it is difficult to set out an exact list of instructions. Illustrated below is how a teacher has marked the significant parts of the text for later inclusion in classroom materials: Realize, of course, that the text has been marked for the teacher's use, not for the learners.'

Genetic Engineering
By Lee Dembart

¶   line

A   The debate over genetic engineering research is ex-   1   *establishes the analogy*
actly analogous to the debate over commercial nu-
clear power.

B   In each case, the majority of scientists consider the   5
technology safe, but a vocal group of citizens says the
experts are biased by potential economic gain and should
not be trusted.

C   In each case, opponents correctly claim that no one   10   *repeated element*
can guarantee 100% safety and that the consequences of
an accident would be so catastrophic that the technology
should be abandoned.

D   In each case, proponents contend that the potential   15
benefits for humanity vastly outweigh the minuscule
risks.

E   Now genetic engineering has reached the courts,   *tie-in to current news issue*
where Federal Judge John J. Sirica recently issued an in-   20
junction to prevent a University of California researcher
from intentionally releasing altered organisms into the
environment as a test of their effectiveness in shielding
potato plants from frost damage.   25

F   Sirica's ruling was made on procedural grounds—the
government, which approved the experiment, had not
prepared a satisfactory environmental impact statement—but the decision sent shock waves through the   30
genetic engineering community. Will experiments in
this promising field be mired in endless litigation?   *need previous info.*
Should biologists expect biotechnology to follow the
course of <u>Diablo Canyon</u>?   35

G   It is not surprising that things are working out this
way. The specter of the atomic scientists, who created   *develops n. power analogy*
the nuclear age and then lived to regret it, has haunted
biologists since they first began manipulating the chem-   40
istry of life a decade ago.

H   At the time, the biologists themselves were the first
to sound the alarm. At the Asilomar Conference in 1975,
they called for a worldwide moratorium on genetic engineering research until the risks could be better under-   45
stood, the first time in history that scientists agreed to
forgo the quest for new knowledge.

I Subsequently, the National Institutes of Health set 50 up a Recombinant DNA Advisory Committee, which set guidelines for research that were mandatory in federally supported investigations and voluntarily adhered to throughout industry. 55

note cohesion markers

J At every stage of review, the advisory committee found that the hazards of a new form of life escaping from the laboratory and wreaking havoc on the world were substantially less than first feared. Genetically en- 60 gineering organisms are weaker than natural ones, and there is no evidence that they could survive and multi- ply and alter the environment. As a result, the controls on research have been continually reduced. 65

K Nonetheless, the question remains: What if?

L In most of the biotechnology work so far the goal 70 has been to turn a common microorganism into a living factory to manufacture, say, insulin or interferon or a hepatitis vaccine. The altered organisms are kept in large vats, and their products are skimmed off the top. If they got out, it would be by accident. But the proposed exper- 75 iment of Steven E. Lindow of UC Berkeley involves the intentional release of genetically engineered organisms into the environment, a very different situation and a forerunner of much biotechnology to come. 80

signals: here comes other side of the argument

M For several years, scientists have predicted that ge- netic engineering of plants will have much greater im- 85 portance than genetic engineering of microorganisms. But altered plants will be worthless unless they can be planted on a large scale, which requires putting them in- to the world.

N Lindow has altered a microorganism so that it pre- 90 vents the formation of ice crystals until the temperature drops well below freezing. By spraying this new organ- ism on potato plants in a remote area of Northern Cali- 95 fornia, he thinks the plants will be able to survive longer, increasing the crop and the yield.

develops case for p. engineering

O Biologists say that meeting the world's growing de- mand for food hinges on the continued development of genetic technology, just as nuclear physicists say that 100 meeting the world's growing demand for energy re- quires nuclear power. But many citizens remain con- vinced that the scientists don't know as much as they claim to, and they are frightened that one small mistake 105 will be disastrous.

analogy again

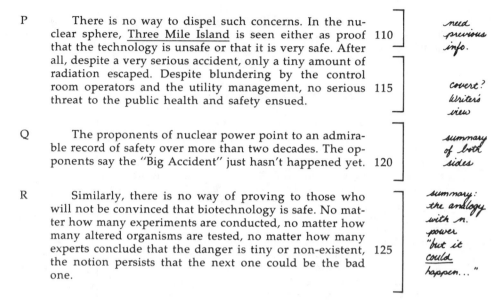

P   There is no way to dispel such concerns. In the nuclear sphere, <u>Three Mile Island</u> is seen either as proof 110 that the technology is unsafe or that it is very safe. After all, despite a very serious accident, only a tiny amount of radiation escaped. Despite blundering by the control room operators and the utility management, no serious 115 threat to the public health and safety ensued.

need previous info.

covert? Writer's view

Q   The proponents of nuclear power point to an admirable record of safety over more than two decades. The opponents say the "Big Accident" just hasn't happened yet. 120

summary of both sides

R   Similarly, there is no way of proving to those who will not be convinced that biotechnology is safe. No matter how many experiments are conducted, no matter how many altered organisms are tested, no matter how many experts conclude that the danger is tiny or non-existent, 125 the notion persists that the next one could be the bad one.

summary: the analogy with n. power "but it could happen..."

Figure 8: Genetic Engineering

Creating exercises

The next step is to use the analysis of the text in writing various types of pre- and post-reading questions. Rather than to find out what the students know after reading the selection, the questions should help them to better understand it by leading them to see the author's plan and main purpose.[5]

    1. For brainstorming, before reading the selection: What are the arguments for and against the use of nuclear power?

    2. How could these arguments be used in the debate over genetic engineering?

    3. After a first reading of the article: Paragraphs B, C, and D develop the author's main point. What is it?

    4. Since this article appeared in the editorial pages of a daily newspaper, it is not surprising that it builds on a particular news item. What is that piece of news? (Paragraphs E, F)

    5. How does the issue of genetic engineering differ from that of nuclear power? (Paragraphs G, H)

6. Paragraphs H, I, J all begin with a word or phrase which signals a sequence of time. Why did the author use these time signals with which to begin each of the paragraphs?

7. What does the word *nonetheless* (Paragraph K) signal to the reader?

8. How do Paragraphs M, N, and O develop the case in favor of genetic engineering?

9. In Paragraph P, the author makes a statement which:

   a. _____ establishes the author's own point of view on the issue of genetic engineering

   or

   b. _____ develops the case in favor of nuclear power.

   Which statement above do you think is the author's reason for including the section in Paragraph P beginning "After all . . ."

10. In Paragraph Q, the main ideas of the two sides are both summed up in a single sentence each. With a partner, try to state the proponents' and the opponents' ideas—without looking at the text.

"Genetic Engineering" could also be used as the basis for small group discussions around the central issues contained in it as well as for writing assignments. It is up to the sensitivity of the teacher to gage the interest shown by a group of learners in the particular selection in order to decide what further activities might be warranted.

6.5 TAKING IN THE WHOLE CONTEXT

To be a successful reader involves deriving meaning from the entire context of a selection. One aspect of using the whole context implies knowing the characteristics of the particular text-type one is reading. ESL/EFL reading teachers who want to use natural texts with intermediate-advanced students need to be concerned with the important characteristics of those types of source materials which L2 academic purpose courses typically draw from. At the same time, the utilization of such reading materials should be augmented by providing L2 learners with techniques for whole context reading, or utilizing the entire selection as a means for comprehending it as fully as possible.

Attention to the characteristics of particular text-types is generally associated with the efforts of literary critics who study literary genres: the novel, essay, poem, etc. Language specialists, on the other hand, are apt to pay little regard to such matters. But in dealing with texts for the purpose of providing instruction for advancing L2 learner-readers, it is vital to look closely at expository text-types, for there is meaning in the type, just as there is in a single paragraph, page, or chapter. Further, the kind of meaning inherent in a particular text-type is inextricably bound up with one's general cultural knowledge—it is the background which educated readers of English bring to most texts they might pick up.

If you are a regular reader of weekly newsmagazines such as *Time*, *Newsweek*, or *Business Week*, you possess a store of background information which you bring to your reading almost unconsciously. In fact, you could probably guess the source of an item correctly if you were given a so-called "blindfold" test in which you read about the same news event as it appeared in two, or even three of these sources. To be successful at the "blindfold" test requires considerable previous reading experience since these three magazines, on the surface at least, are similar.

A greater contrast might be found between *Time* and *The New Republic*. Further, an intelligent reader of any of these four weekly magazines approaches it with a complex background of expectations built up through previous experience. The sophisticated reader expects, for example, to find topics treated from a particular viewpoint, to find certain kinds of advertisements, to find a particular range of vocabulary or register, etc.

Knowledge about the whole context of a text is vital for reading comprehension. Unfortunately, too often in ESL/EFL courses reading selections are taken from sources without maintaining enough of the contextual clues from the whole to give the learner-reader a sense of the original. Since effective reading calls for using the total context for understanding, this practice reduces the students' access to meaning. Indeed, part of the basic thrust behind advocating the use of natural or authentic text materials for L2 reading emphasizes the same point. An important principle in this approach is that the teacher-editor should not clip away text-type information in the copies provided to learners.

For example, in Section I, the heading "Science" from the *Time* article "It's a Geep" was preserved. That *Time*-style typeface itself is a hidden clue to meaning. The educated reader "knows" the source from seeing the heading. To know the source is to activate an entire range of background information, for example, the writer/reader relationship, the point of view of the writer as displayed in the text, the register of the text, the format of the text—to mention a few salient but crucial features.

Lack of attention to text-type characteristics in ESL/EFL reading courses could result in giving learners only a fragment of the knowledge they require both for mature reading and for their special needs in reading-to-learn. Sometimes it is the case that ESL/EFL teachers who come from a background in humanities or social sciences are unfamiliar with scholarly or nonacademic/nonfiction sources beyond their own areas of specialization. However, their intermediate-advanced level students frequently major in sub-fields of science and engineering. In their search for relevant science-related articles, these ESL/EFL teachers might solely utilize the sources from which they themselves can learn. More often than not, these are popular culture magazines intended to acquaint non-specialist audiences with new advances in science from a lay person's perspective. But these popular sources for science topics are quite different from scholarly or even nonacademic/nonfiction sources in terms of their textual features. Moreover, it is the latter types which appear on "required" reading lists for academic courses.

In the following section, characteristics of all three types of sources are outlined—scholarly, nonacademic/nonfiction, and popular culture articles. Then, in the final section, further pedagogical suggestions are presented for whole context reading.

A brief outline of some natural sources for L2 reading

In this section, some significant characteristics of three distinct sources of reading material are presented in relation to four features contained in each: (1) the writer/reader relationship; (2) the writer's overall point of view; (3) the level of usage or register contained in the writing; and (4) the format.

Dividing all of expository writing into three categories at first seems to be a simplistic approach. Obviously, any number of sub-categories could be pointed out based on a variety of criteria. However, in terms of selecting materials for use with L2 learner-readers, this three-way classification is useful because it highlights a crucial variable: the relation between the writer and the reader. This relationship is embodied in the answer to questions such as:

1. Who is the writer?
2. Who is the audience to whom the writing is directed?
3. Who is the reader?
4. Why has the reader turned to this writer's work?

Identifying the writer/reader relationship is fundamental. Other characteristics of text-types follow from it and to a large extent are determined by it.

Academic sources

1. Generally, a scholar-researcher is addressing his/her peers. There is an assumption of thorough pre-knowledge based on what is considered axiomatic as opposed to what is open to discussion.
2. The intention is to persuade the reader to accept a more advanced concept or further statement involving a known issue within the

field. The tone is factual, objective, and descriptive. Argumentation takes place through presentation of findings, logic, and reasoned refutation.

3. Extensive use of professional and/or specialized terms is evidenced, along with a conscious use of the language of claim, assertion, qualification, possibility, likelihood, suggestion, etc. There is avoidance of absolute statements.

4. Published in books as collections of papers, but more likely found in professional journals, anthologies, monographs, and proceedings. Use of abstracts, subheadings, footnotes, and references. Inclusion of tables, charts, illustrations, photographs. Tendency to be non-columnar in layout. No decorative artwork or graphics.

Nonacademic/nonfiction sources

1. Typically, a specialist or highly informed generalist writes to a non-specialist audience. If the writer is treating his/her own original investigation, the tone adopted must switch to accommodate non-specialist readers.

2. The purpose is to inform and to simplify high-level knowledge. The writer often engages the reader's interest through using a narrative or even by delaying the main idea until the end to sustain interest through the entire article.

3. There is use of educated vocabulary, but without the jargon of an academic field. The writer may identify him/herself by using first person. There are short paragraphs, frequent expansive examples which illustrate a main theme or idea.

4. Sometimes found in textbooks which introduce a field of knowledge to people who have had no previous background, for example, secondary school students; also, popular specialty magazines, for example: *Psychology Today, The New Yorker*, nonfiction books; and long articles in news weeklies and newspaper magazine sections. Usually, there is columnar layout and ample use of artwork. Often, displays of inserted bold-face key sentences taken from the article are used to break up long columns.[6]

Popular culture sources

1. The writer is usually a journalist-author who is not involved professionally in the topic; in fact, the writer expects that the reader's purpose in selecting the piece is primarily that of recreation/enjoyment.

2. Beyond the basic journalistic constraint of accuracy, there is no intention to give thorough background. Statements are broad, all inclusive. The main idea probably appears in the lead with contributing details following. Statements are apt not to be attributed to sources. Opinions and facts tend to become blurred. There are many sub-categories of popular cultures articles which divide this text-type: features, news items, reviews, interviews, editorials, etc.

3. Use of short sentences, brief paragraphs. The register is considered closer to spoken language than is found in either scholarly or non-academic/nonfiction writing.

4. Columnar layout in peridicals. This text-type is also frequently found in popular, nonfiction books. Extensive use is made of illustrative matter: photos, artwork, graphics, etc.

6.6 PEDAGOGICAL IMPLICATIONS FOR WHOLE-CONTEXT READING

1. Provide learners with enough of the whole context of a selection so that significant clues to meaning are not overlooked.

2. Point out important, in-print features which answer the question: what can we guess about the content of this book/article before reading it? For example, clues from the title page, date and place of publication, organization of and details in the table of contents, information about the author(s), inclusion of back matter such as notes, bibliography, appendix, index, etc.

3. Point out stylistic features incorporated in the vocabulary, sentences, and paragraphs which indicate a particular register of language: for example: formal-academic, elaborative, or journalistic registers.

4. Encourage L2 learner-readers to always ask these questions: "What is the source of the selection I am reading? Who is the author? For what audience is the selection intended?"

NOTES

1. It is not the perspective in this chapter to focus on second language reading materials prepared for a wide audience. Two examples of specially written commercial texts are Dubin and Olshtain 1984; and Drayton and Skidmore 1985.

2. A classic source for word lists is West's General Service List of English Words (West 1953). For a discussion of the limitation of such lists see Widdowson (1983).

3. Other terms which have been used to point out the contrast between changed or altered texts and unchanged texts which L2 learners can read with comprehension are "simplified" and "simple" (Widdowson 1978). But since "simple" in American English conveys the idea of childishness, it seems an unfortunate term.

4. A similar technique was demonstrated by Taylor (1985) in relation to the skill of listening comprehension through the use of video-taped segments of TV news programs.

5. For further discussion of creating reading skills exercises using natural texts see Dubin and Olshtain (in press).

6. Classifying magazines under these three types presents problems. For example, nonacademic/nonfiction sources can include both writing by specialists to a non-specialist audience as well as journalists reporting on a subject about which they have had relatively recent, although extensive experience. Actually, The New Yorker and Psychology Today are examples of magazines which could be listed under both nonacademic/nonfiction sources and popular culture sources. Then, too, magazines tend to come and go quickly. They also change their editorial policies. For these reasons, further examples have not been listed.

FOR STUDY AND DISCUSSION

1. Discuss the pros and cons of the following statement:
   A reading program in an English for academic purpose course should be built around materials which are exclusively in the area of the learners' subject of specialization.

2. How might a teacher maintain a reading-in-depth focus concerning the selection of materials yet still manage to introduce the students to a variety of text-types? Try to illustrate your answer by finding a few selections from different types of publications which, at the same time, deal with the same subject matter.

3. Select a particular academic discipline or some sub-area of it in which L2 learners are apt to be interested. What are some suitable sources for reading materials? Try to suggest a few in each of these three categories: a) scholarly, b) nonacademic/nonfiction, and c) popular culture.

4. Find a selection from either a newspaper or newsmagazine which you believe would be suitable for an intensive reading lesson with a particular group of L2 learners. The selection must fit on a single piece of 8 1/2 x 11 paper. Photocopy the selection so that each person in the group can receive a copy. Take pains to follow the suggestions in this chapter regarding a) the numbering of the lines and paragraphs, b) leaving white space on the paper, and c) retaining some typographical features of the source in which the article appeared.

5. Prepare a one-page handout for L2 learners which will aid them in understanding the key words in the selection you chose in No. 4. What other words or expressions in the article do you believe should be glossed in order to make sure that the learner-readers understand the main point of the selection during the first reading? (See "It's a Geep," Figure 5, as a model.)

6. Study the article you have selected carefully for its textual features. For example: try to find the main function of each paragraph; look for words that link sentences and paragraphs together, or cohesion markers; look for elements that give the piece unity, or coherence elements.

7. Use the results of your analysis of the article to write 3-5 exercises which will help L2 learners use the features which you have located in the text as aids in reading with fuller comprehension (See Creating Exercises, in section 6.2, as a model).

FOR FURTHER READING

The issue of specialized or generalized texts in second language reading courses is discussed at some length in Widdowson (1983).

This chapter implies that teachers who want to write exercise materials to accompany reading selections need to be concerned with analyzing such texts. However, the term "discourse analysis" tends to be confusing since it is used for both natural, spoken language, or spoken discourse, as well as for written language, at times called text analysis. A good place to begin reading about both types is Stubbs (1983) who helps to make the distinction clear in the Introduction. A very thorough textbook, intended primarily for use in linguistics courses, is Brown and Yule (1983), in which both spoken and written texts are considered. A more difficult book is deBeaugrande and Dressler (1981), however its focus is entirely with written language.

Implications of schema theory and text organization for purposes of L2 reading instruction are discussed by Carrell and Eisterhold (1983) and Carrell (1984a, 1984b).

For further examples of writing exercise material for L2 learners which makes use of the features found in natural, written texts see Dubin and Olshtain (in press).

Chapter 7

Reading Assessment

Sharon Allerson
University of Southern California
and

William Grabe
Northern Arizona University

7.1 INTRODUCTION

At many stages in a reading curriculum it becomes necessary to evaluate students' reading abilities, their problems and weaknesses, their progress, and their final achievement in relation to the specific objectives of the program. A reading program must also develop a viable means for placement in a reading curriculum; one that is not simply the reflection of a more general placement procedure which may not include a reading assessment component at all.

It has often been the case that reading programs are not viewed as important independent components of more general second language English curricula. Rather, they are typically considered the means toward other teaching ends, whether that be grammatical structure, discourse grammar, vocabulary study, information for writing assignments, etc. In almost all cases, the implication is that students already know how to read, though some students, admittedly, have difficulty. It should be evident, however, that many students have reading difficulties which can only be identified through careful assessment. As Grabe (this volume and Eskey 1973:169) have argued, reading may well be the single most important language skill required by students for academic success.

There are a number of reasons why students' reading abilities must be assessed. First, it will demonstrate that reading skills require focused attention in the curriculum. Student difficulties with reading tests will show that they need instruction in reading. Since the tests will identify deficiencies, it will no longer be possible to ignore reading skills. Second, initial placement testing of reading may influence administrators to include reading programs in the curriculum; they might otherwise support a differently structured curriculum. This aspect of assessment must not be overlooked as studies have consistently shown that an active, interested administrator is a major factor in successful reading programs (Samuels 1981; Hoffman and Rutherford 1984). Third, initial assessment of reading skills will invariably demonstrate that students placed in a program level based on general proficiency cannot be assumed to possess the same reading abilities. This sort of knowledge is the first step to more careful and appropriate curricular development.

Apart from the above three initial assessment needs, there are the more standard, though no less important reasons for reading assessment: to determine a student's progress, to isolate particular skill weaknesses, to motivate and provide constructive feedback, to alter and improve ongoing instruction, and to provide a realistic final evaluation. While this list might be extended further, the point is that reading assessment is an essential part of any successful reading program.

7.2 WHAT IS ASSESSMENT?

Reading assessment, as a general term, covers a range of testing and evaluation procedures. A test is typically a sample of student behavior on a task or set of tasks which allows ready comparison with other student performances. This definition holds for the formal testing procedures employed in reading, the most obvious of which are the standardized commercial tests. In first language contexts, a wide range of such tests exist. In second language contexts, there are also a number of examples: some are sub-parts of larger proficiency tests; a few others, specifically for reading, have only recently begun to appear.

Reading assessment, however, is much more than the use of standardized tests. Assessment covers placement tests set up by language programs to establish initial student placement. Standardized tests have only limited utility for general student placement and even less for placing students in particular reading curricula. In almost all language program contexts, an internal placement procedure is needed. If the placement procedure is well-designed it may also be used for diagnostic purposes. Diagnostic testing, another aspect of assessment, is used primarily as a way to determine a student's particular strengths and weaknesses in reading. Diagnostic tests should include a battery of tasks to isolate possible student deficiencies. Such information is important as a way to inform teachers of students' need. It also provides a way to determine the content of a reading program, particularly for a reading lab which includes individualized instruction.

Even when students have been placed in a reading program, assessment does not stop. Many of the reading skills developed in the course of a reading program require frequent and systematic feedback for both students and teacher. A good part of this assessment should be done informally through teacher observation, attitude questionnaires, and teacher-student interviews. In the course of the reading program, informal assessment should be combined with achievement tests, progress charts and homework assignments. Assessment must also involve some measure of achievement whereby the students can be evaluated in their reading development by the end of the curriculum. Final evaluation is not only needed to define course expectations and establish norms for student success, it also becomes an important means for reassessing program goals, materials effectiveness and instructional design. In summary, reading assessment should pervade a well-designed reading program.

7.3 FURTHER CONSIDERATIONS IN THE ASSESSMENT PROCESS

Reading assessment is not simply a matter of deciding which assessment strategy to employ. There are a number of factors that necessarily interact with the kinds of assessment discussed above. First, there is the issue of a reading theory to support assessment objectives and test design. Naturally, theory shapes assessment. Given the recent development of interactive theories of reading, and their ability to provide a more compelling account of various results of reading research, we will present our discussion of assessment in relation to the major tenets of such a theory (see Grabe 1985 and Eskey and Grabe, this volume). Stated briefly, interactive models suggest a need to test skills at many levels, since all of these skills are assumed to play a significant role in the reading process. They include everything from the rapid identification of vocabulary and syntactic structures, to the interpretation of larger discourse patterns, the making of inferences, etc. In addition, since interactive models are defined by the interaction of various sub-skills, ideal assessment strategies would involve combining skills. The full implications of interactive models for assessment are yet to be determined, but that should not deter us from working with a theory which best captures current thinking on the nature of reading.

Second, reading assessment must be considered also by various procedural considerations, including selection/construction, administration, scoring, interpretation and record keeping of assessment tasks. Selection most typically means choosing among standardized tests. These choices will often be determined not by needs for reading assessment alone, but also by general admissions and placement considerations. The choice of a standardized test may also be influenced by ease of administration, ease of scoring, ease of interpretation, accessibility, and cost. These are further reasons for constructing more specific placement exams as part of program placement. It is also possible to select placement tests from among those developed by other programs. However, most programs recognize the need to construct their own placement tests to match the specific context constraints which any program operates under (i.e., particular types of students, number of students, etc.). Therefore, assessment frequently requires test construction rather than the selection of tests. Discussion of this aspect of assessment goes well beyond the scope of this paper (for an introduction to test construction, see Heaton 1975; Madsen 1983). What is essential is that persons involved in reading assessment be informed in both reading theory and in test construction.

Assessment scoring, interpretation, and record keeping may also involve complexities which must be foreseen in an effective reading program. Apart from the need for personnel with some background in testing (to score appropriately standard commercial tests, cloze tests, placement tests and final exams) there are further questions of how to rate and weight in-class achievement tests, informal observation, one-on-one tasks and interviews, homework assignments, reading rate improvement and improvement in various other specific skills. No simple advice can be offered on this issue beyond the need to plan appropriately according to the specific circumstances of any particular program. It should be stressed, however, that the purpose for any particular assessment strategy or task must be clear at all times, including the overall motivation for such procedures from reading theory, and individual program needs and specifications.

7.4 THE ROLE OF TEXTS IN READING ASSESSMENT

Unlike those aspects of reading assessment which are covered in a number of testing courses and textbooks, the matter of choosing appropriate texts is one area that is typically ignored. Unfortunately, this issue is very important not only for materials development but also for assessment purposes. Among the major concerns are: (1) whether more but shorter texts are better than fewer but longer texts; (2) whether texts should be on topics of wide familiarity or on topics that few students would be likely to have knowledge of; (3) whether texts should be of a general topical nature or devoted to specific topics that represent students' majors. In fact, one reason this issue of text choice is often passed over is that there is no clear consensus on these questions (see Flahive 1978; Widdowson 1983; Johnston 1984; Dubin this volume).

A further complexity in the choice of appropriate texts is that different programs have different objectives, and the objectives should determine the kinds of texts used for assessment. No small set of all-purpose texts will be appropriate for all assessment needs. Thus, if the goal of the program is to assess reading rate, long texts on more general topics may be more appropriate. The same considerations might apply if the goal is scanning or skimming. However, if the purpose is simply to state the main idea, then a number of shorter passages will provide the appropriate number of task items. If the purpose is for careful reading of a text, a more specific academic genre of intermediate length would be more appropriate. A simple perspective on text choice can be outlined as in Figure 1.

Text Analysis

1. Determine the purpose of the test and appropriate topics according to students' academic needs and interests.
2. Determine text difficulty by estimating the complexity of syntax, vocabulary, discourse structure, required background knowledge, and genre type.
3. Field test the text on a similar group of students.
4. Determine the appropriateness of the text for the reading tasks to be required. These tasks could include the following:

    a) understanding main ideas

    b) understanding vocabulary in context.

    c) understanding inferential information

    d) recalling details (careful reading)

    e) understanding logical organization

    f) understanding rhetorical devices (i.e., reference).

    g) scanning

    h) skimming

    i) evaluating author's arguments
5. Decide to use the text or continue searching for other texts.

Figure 1: Text and Task Analysis

To this point we have reviewed types of assessment procedures and various factors involved in determining the choice and format of specific procedures. This is summarized in Figure 2.

Assessment Instruments	**Factors Influencing Choice**
standardized commercial tests	
placement tests	test selection/construction
diagnostic procedures	test administration
teacher observation	test scoring
one-on-one interviews	test interpretation
homework	text choice
progress charts	
in-class achievement tests	
final achievement test/exit test	

Figure 2: Assessment Instruments

The remainder of this paper will examine in some detail the various assessment procedures outlined above, what options are available for use in a reading program, and various issues debated with respect to each procedure.

7.5 STANDARDIZED TESTS

Standardized second language tests are those that are commercially available, ranging from the reading sub-section of the TOEFL examination to recent, less well established commercially available tests such as the ELSA test (Ilyin, Doherty, Lee, and Levy 1981). In actual fact, there are relatively few standardized L2 reading tests, thus a basic issue to raise with respect to standardized tests is whether first language reading tests offer particular benefits for second language reading assessment.

In first language reading assessment, Harris and Sipay (1980, 1985) note that standardized silent reading tests may be developed for three functions, including survey tests, analytic tests (diagnostic), and tests of a single function such as vocabulary level. Survey tests are the type of reading tests most relevant to issues of second language reading assessment. As Harris and Sipay (1980) note:

> The major purpose of a survey reading test is to give a fairly
> accurate measure of a pupil's general level of silent reading abili-
> ty compared with that of others who take the test . . . . Most sur-
> vey tests have two parts, vocabulary and comprehension, the
> latter includes sentences or paragraph meaning, depending on
> the grade level for which the test is intended. (p. 192)

Other sub-skills are tested in various survey tests depending on the purpose of the test and the grade levels at which it is used. These sub-skills include measures of labeled phonic analysis, word-study skills, letter recognition, letter sound, reading rate, and directed reading (skimming, scanning) (Harris and Sipay 1980, 1985). By and large, most L1 reading survey tests center around vocabulary and comprehension questions. Thus they are not very different from a number of the standard second language reading tests.

Whether L1 tests are appropriate for second language reading assessment is an open question. Actual choices will depend on how the test results are used, how well it discriminated in pre-testing, and how appropriate it is in terms of culture specific background knowledge. As Johnston (1984) notes, even when test bias exists, the test may be justified if it provides useful information, and if discriminatory decisions are not made as a result of the test scores obtained. Where instructional needs are well served by an L1 test, then the students and the program benefit. Where L1 tests provide reading measures not found in second language tests, their use may also be worth the pre-testing effort.

L1 reading tests are designed for either secondary or elementary level students. Secondary level tests may be more cultural bound, and often include a literary bias. Such tests would probably frustrate even the best students (information on secondary level tests may be reviewed in Blanton *et al.* 1972; Harris and Sipay 1980, 1985; Perkins and Pharis 1980; Gordon 1983).

Elementary level L1 reading tests typically employ a somewhat different set of skills measures apart from vocabulary and comprehension. A number of these, like letter recognition and phonics, may not be appropriate to second language reading assessment needs. The texts used in these tests also tend to be quite short; thus, they do not provide sufficient context for the testing of mature second language students. There is also the problem of reading material which may not interest more mature students.

In sum, the use of L1 tests appears to be problematic, but possible. If L1 assessment instruments are field-tested on groups of students typical of the target population, test data could be analysed, and, in particular, be compared with other sources of information about students' reading abilities (e.g., teacher evaluation, other test scores, interviews). Ultimately, whether an L1 test should be included depends on the usefulness of the information it provides (see Harris and Sipay 1980, 1985 for an extensive review of L1 tests).

Overall, however, reviews from both first language and second language perspectives indicate that many of the L1 standardized reading measures offer little for second language testing beyond test format options. Within L1 reading itself, reviews by Wanat (1977) and Johnston (1984) argue that standardized reading tests may be seriously inadequate. Gagne (1972) notes the same about commercially available reading achievement and diagnostic tests. From the second language perspective, Thonis (1983) argues that L1 reading tests are constructed with different assumptions, and draw on different sorts of information than would be relevant in the second language context. Stevenson (1982) raises further issues for the second language testing context, some of which equally refer to the inappropriateness of L1 testing for second language students. It would seem that, in general, L1 standardized tests provide us with few assessment and evaluation tools not already available in second language standardized reading tests.

At the same time, research in L1 reading assessment has raised issues of importance for any attempt at reading assessment. Thus, Harris and Sipay (1980, 1985) and Johnston (1984) both note that informal reading assessment, oral interview techniques, the extent of background knowledge allowed for, the need to distinguish norm-referenced and criterion-referenced testing—and their appropriateness, and the need to consider what makes a reading test valid, are all issues deserving careful treatment in any discussion of reading assessment. These issues, however, require treatment which extends far beyond the scope of this chapter. Sources on these topics in the L1 context include Burns and Roe (1980); Schell (1981); Pikulski and Shanahan (1982); Lesiak and Bradley-Johnson (1983); Rakes, Choate and Waller (1983); and Johnston (1984).

Standardized second language reading tests are few in number and, until recently, have all been of the silent reading plus multiple choice question format. Currently available second language reading tests include subsections of the TOEFL, the Michigan test and the CELT test (vocabulary). A separate reading test, the King-Campbell Reading test (ELS 1982), is also available. None of these tests goes beyond vocabulary and passage comprehension. Certainly they do not access all aspects of the reading process. If one accepts an interactive view of reading, then these tests do not adequately reflect the full range of skills that students employ. As Johnston (1984) notes:

> Hierarchical models of reading have found little support in the literature, . . . which tends to give more support to inter-active models. Reading . . . involves the integration of a variety of declarative, procedural, and strategic knowledge in different ways, depending on the state of the comprehending system and the information available to it from various sources.
>
> The dynamic interactive nature of the reading process does not lend itself well to specification in terms of discrete objectives with simple criterion. (p. 160)

Reading assessment of some sort, however, is necessary, and commercial standardized tests can play a role. What must be recognized is that standardized test results should be considered only a part of the information needed to assess students' overall reading abilities.

7.6 CLOZE TESTING

A second type of commercial reading test is now becoming available for widespread use based on variations of cloze procedures (the ELSA test, Ilyin et al. 1981). Generally, the cloze procedure has been considered a good assessment technique for reading in L1 for the last 30 years. Recently, however, cloze, as a valid measure of reading ability, has come under serious questioning. In L1 reading, articles by Kibby (1980); Shanahan, Kamil, and Tobin (1982); Cziko (1983); and Shanahan (1983) argue that standardized nth word random deletion cloze exercises do not provide a reliable measure of reading abilities. Further, Stanovich (1981) points out that interactive models of reading, in which rapid word perceptual abilities are as important if not more important than larger contextual strategies for reading, may undermine the construct validity (underlying assumptions) of cloze as a measure of reading ability.

Performance on the cloze task is dependent on the ability to generate consciously a word consistent with the sentence . . . . If, as has been argued, the conscious attention process is less implicated in contextual facilitation as reading proficiency develops, then performance on cloze tasks may be less indicative of actual context usage at higher reading levels. Thus, the correlation between between reading proficiency and cloze performance (e.g., Ruddell 1965) may not be indicative of a causal relation. Older and better readers may respond more accurately on cloze tasks because of their larger mental store of linguistic and general knowledge. (Stanovich 1981:263)

If cloze tasks measure a student's ability to consciously guess a form based on the context, and this skill is only a secondary reading strategy in the actual reading of good students, then the claim that cloze measures actual reading abilities is open to question. Again, the issue is not whether we take an extreme position and totally ignore the potential of cloze as a measure of reading, but that we have a healthy skepticism of any statement where cloze is claimed to be *the* measure of reading ability.

Over the last five years, cloze has similarly been the object of extensive critical review in second language assessment, both as a measure of language proficiency and as a measure of reading ability. Alderson (1979); Klein-Braley (1983); Stevenson (1982); Johnson (1982); and Levenston *et al.* (1984) have all noted problems with the classic random deletion approach to cloze testing as a measure of language proficiency. Given this recent scrutiny, it is not clear to anyone exactly what is being measured by cloze tests. (Cf. Oller, 1979) Although cloze still retains its status as a reading measure in second language testing, this use of cloze is equally suspect, as Stevenson (1982) notes.

What is most interesting in the continuing discussion of the cloze as a possible reading test is that what test users would like to have, or want to believe, is obviously at odds with what some research would seem to indicate. (p. 273)

The use of modified cloze involving rational deletions, that is, the deletion of items not randomly but according to a principle, creates a different set of issues. Recent research suggests that these tests may provide better measures of certain reading skills. Flahive (1978); Chapman (1981); Bachman (1982); and Levenston *et al.* (1984) all indicate ways that rational cloze deletion may lead to better testing reliability and validity. But rational cloze testing has by no means been thoroughly enough explored to allow for more than tentative acceptance. It is one of a range of testing procedures that will probably have to be used in conjunction with other methods to derive a more valid overall assessment.

What can be concluded with respect to standardized tests of reading, and to cloze procedures generally, is that they may provide a first indication of a student's reading ability, but perhaps not much more. Administrators, looking for ways to place students appropriately in terms of reading abilities, will have to use some sort of internal placement test to verify students' entering reading levels. If we are to pursue the assumptions of an interactive model of reading as the basis for construct validity, an internal placement test would have to account for the range of skills predicted by such a model. It would also conceivably have to account for the interaction of these skills. The first of these two objectives is approachable, the second, less so. A final reason for using a placement test is that major standardized tests are often only used for admissions purposes. Teachers may not have access to the actual tests, and scores alone may not provide adequate information regarding students' reading abilities in English.

7.7 PLACEMENT TESTING FOR A READING PROGRAM

An internal placement examination for reading may be set up to account for perceptual identification skills, reading rate skills, general comprehension skills, and for lexical/syntactic knowledge. A sample outline of such a placement test might be:

Five sections

1. 150 simple recognition items.	(5 minutes)
2. 75 synonymy/antonymy items.	(5 minutes)
3. 20 words from context or a 30 blank rational cloze test.	(20 minutes)
4. 40 completion—vocabulary and passage comprehension.	(20 minutes)
5. Reading rate passage (1000 words in five minutes). 10 multiple choice comprehension.	(10 minutes)

This reading test could easily be combined with an essay, dictation, grammar, and oral interview battery to form a rather thorough placement procedure. The five parts for the reading test can be set up to match the goals of the program. Recognition items are illustrated in Harris (1966), Miller (1984) and Stoller (this volume). Vocabulary in context items are discussed in Haynes (1984) and in Jensen (this volume). Setting up a reading rate passage is explained in both Mahon and Jensen (this volume).

For most programs, the placement test will provide an accurate indication of reading abilities and provide for appropriate level placement. In some programs, especially those with some amount of individual or small group instruction, a diagnostic testing time during the first week might also be called for. Parts of placement tests may sometimes be used for diagnostic purposes, in particular the recognition, reading rate and rational cloze procedures. However, diagnostic testing allows for more extensive exploration of the individual student's particular needs. It also allows the program to maintain test security for the placement test.

7.8 DIAGNOSTIC ASSESSMENT

Whereas standardized tests give broad, often global assessments of students' reading abilities, the initial diagnostic assessment can include activities which focus on particular component processes. They usually involve administering a series of reading experiences which utilize classroom materials.

The purposes of diagnostic assessment are numerous: (1) Diagnostic testing can act as a check on the placement procedure. Any problem in placement will be discovered and adjustments made. (2) Diagnostic procedures will provide more detailed examinations of students' particular strengths and weaknesses. Because diagnostic testing is done in individual classes by the teachers themselves, one-on-one procedures may be employed. This can include reading and questions, interviews, oral reading, and retelling tasks. (3) These diagnostic procedures also have the additional advantage of indicating when a student may have more general learning disabilities, which can then be dealt with appropriately. (4) Diagnostic procedures can include questionnaires which may also be used for consciousness raising activities. Questions about amounts and types of reading, attitudes toward reading, self-assessment of reading abilities, and understanding of the reading process all will lead to better student awareness, a better focus on objectives, and better motivation. (5) Diagnostic assessment and the close relations created between teacher and student allow the teacher a way to approach disappointed students and get them to work productively. (6) Diagnostic procedures allow the teacher to match the resources of the curriculum to the needs of the students. (7) The collection of data via the diagnostic measures functions as a type of pre-test against which post-instructional assessment can provide a more accurate estimate of actual progress made during the course. Overall, a program can respond to students' individual needs only to the degree that diagnostic assessment provides appropriate feedback.

In order to conduct the initial diagnostic assessment appropriately, the teacher should be clear about the goals of the course. The diagnostic test provides data about students' abilities in relation to those goals so that class time is focused on actual instructional needs, not needs that were presumed when the course curriculum was first designed. To illustrate this point, the goal of the course may be to develop students' abilities to draw conclusions, but when students' abilities to draw conclusions are assessed only a few students may demonstrate difficulty (perhaps the younger ones who have less life experience to draw on). In contrast, all students might demonstrate difficulty in skimming for the main idea. If strengths and weaknesses are ascertained, teachers will have a better idea of what students need to work on, both as a group and individually.

Dishner and Readance (1977), in the L1 reading literature, suggest a reading guide that looks as if it might be simple yet effective if adapted to second language reading material. The reading guide asks students to refer to their textbook and complete several reading tasks. In a second language context, the format can be used with a reading whose primary purpose is for some other language task. Figure 3 presents a version of their guide. Note that the goal is to assess a number of skills quickly; there are only a few questions for each skill.

This exercise is similar to those in intermediate and advanced EST courses. The difference lies in the emphasis on obtaining information about students' abilities to answer different types of questions quickly. Furthermore, the reading inventory indicates to the students what skill is being assessed so that they also become aware of their reading strengths and weaknesses. Similar exercises could be developed for other levels. The key factor is that the teacher initially attempts to get a broad overview of students' abilities to cope with the demand of the materials.

Specific Reading Skills

Directions: Read the text on man's use of energy, then answer the following questions based on what you have read.

A. Understanding vocabulary.

1. Define "fusion."

2. Explain the following statement in your own words: "Electricity is man's most versatile form of energy."

3. What does "hydroelectric" mean?

B. Noting main ideas.

1. To date, what has been the main use of atomic energy?

2. What is our main source of secondary power?

C. Noting details.

1. Name the three top producers of electricity in the world.

2. Name one isotope of uranium.

D. Drawing conclusions.

1. Compare the principles of fission and fusion.

2. Why might nuclear energy become a major source of power for some countries?

3. How will the development of nuclear energy affect other sources of energy in the future?

E. Noting organization.

1. What is the main topic (thesis) of this article?

2. How does the author divide his topic?

Figure 3: Group Informal Reading Inventory
(Adapted from Dishner and Readance 1977:42-43)

Another initial diagnostic procedure might be the use of a short cloze passage from a text believed to be appropriate. However, all the qualifications noted earlier for cloze apply as well. While we are not sure what the cloze is telling us about a student's overall reading ability, a number of deletion patterns (i.e., conjunctions, pronouns) are relevant to diagnostic uses, particularly with rational cloze deletions. Results of cloze tests of this type can be discussed in group and individual conferences. This combination (cloze and conference) is likely to provide the teacher with the best student profiles. The assessment of reading rate, recognition skills and other processes that are practiced in the reading lab also begins in the initial diagnostic assessment, as does record-keeping.

With reference to the different charts that students keep of their progress in reading lab activities (see Stoller, Mahon, Jensen, this volume), it seems advisable that many of the reading activities be monitored on progress charts rather than in the teacher's grade book entirely. Student progress charts should keep track of students' work on vocabulary exercises, outside readings, in-class reading quizzes, cloze test exercises, etc. Each chart could have room for both quantitative information and qualitative commentary on the student's strengths and weaknesses. There are, however, some progress charts that the teacher alone keeps (analysis of formal tests for which security is important, data collected in focused observations, or the results of reading conferences, for example). The teacher and student can share record-keeping responsibilities. This reduces the burden on the teacher and increases the student's awareness of his progress. Figure 4 is an example of a reading progress chart for reading comprehension quizzes.

Finally, the initial diagnostic procedures should include the administration of surveys which bring to light students' reading interests and attitudes (like the one in Figure 5; for further examples, see the Mahon chapter, this volume). The information that these questionnaires provide is valuable in that they allow the teacher to individualize the course more productively. The teacher can also get to know individual students better and relate group reading tasks to individual interests. For example, if the class is reading a text on communication skills, the teacher can ask students how such skills are important in their field of specialization.

Name_____

Quizzes (Record the date)

% correct	1	2	3	4	5	6	7	8	9	10	11	12	13	14
100														
90														
80														
70														
60														
50														
40														
30														
20														
10														
0														

Problem areas to work on:

Quiz 1:_____

_____

_____

Quiz 2:_____

(etc.)

Figure 4: Reading Comprehension Quizzes
(Note: in a 16 week term, with three reading quizzes every two weeks, the form should be designed for 20 quizzes.)

General Reading Interest Survey

Directions: Complete the following open-ended questions about personal interests.

1. My major is . . . . .
2. I like this subject because . . . . .
3. The subject I liked least in school is . . . . .
4. The reason I dislike this subject is . . . . .
5. The kinds of books I enjoy reading most (in any language) are . . . . .
6. The magazines I enjoy reading most (in any language) are . . . . .
7. My favorite place to read or study is . . . . .
8. When I read I feel . . . . .
9. My favorite TV show is . . . . .
10. My favorite pasttimes are . . . . .

Figure 5: Reading Habits Survey
(Adapted from Rakes, Choate, and Waller 1983)

7.9 ONGOING ASSESSMENT
DURING THE COURSE

Formal tests which yield quantitative data are designed to be reliable, that is, produce consistent results; however, it is difficult to determine what these tests actually say about a student's reading abilities because there are so many variables involved in test taking (Wanat 1977). Informal in-class assessment strategies are more task specific and thus may be more valid for feedback. Johnston (1981) believes that such validity should be emphasized because it will improve our interpretation of student skills in relation to course instruction and objectives. Moreover, the assessment of students' reading abilities will be strengthened if we have several different measures of reading skills. To this end, the following informal assessment strategies will be discussed: reading quizzes, cloze tests, questionnaires, focused observations, and reading conferences.

In-class tests

Reading quizzes may take a variety of shapes and sizes. The purpose here is not to specify what should be quizzed, or exactly how. Each program will have its own focus of instruction and its own objectives. The essential point is that quizzes be given regularly. Students must feel that there is a consistent plan for classroom assessment and feedback. The expectations of regular assessment and feedback in class indicate to students that the reading program is well thought-out and that the teacher is serious about the work demands placed on students. Quizzes should not be taken casually, and the grades should always be entered in record books. The point is not to make the quizzes overly important but to indicate that they are worth the students' time. (See Heaton 1975 and Madsen 1983 for in-class test construction.)

Variations of cloze tests have been developed for class use where certain types of function words are deleted. For example, one may delete all auxiliary verbs, adverbs of time, articles, prepositions, conjunctions, relativizers, subordinators, etc. The decision is in part constrained by the text selected. Content words may also be deleted in a number of circumstances, to review difficult but important vocabulary, to test command of adjectives, etc. One particularly interesting type of content word rational cloze is topic deletion wherein a key word or words are omitted throughout the text. The reader must integrate information presented in the text in order to ascertain the topic. This type of cloze works well with texts which define a concept. The functional restatements and synonyms provide valuable information about the topic.

A final use of the cloze procedure, developed by Martin (1980), is a discourse cloze exercise in which a sentence from a text is deleted. Students are asked to select the appropriate sentence from several response choices, one of which is the actual sentence from the text. Martin used this procedure to assess ESL students' understanding of hierarchical organization within a text. Sentence deletion could focus on many kinds of textual relationships (e.g., cause and effect, examples, etc.) as well as the understanding of main ideas or supporting ideas. For all of the above cloze procedures the scoring of the deletions depends on the type and purpose of the test. Correct responses in a cloze often include semantically and syntactically appropriate responses; with certain cloze exercises, the exact word may be required due to textual or grammatical constraints.

When using a cloze procedure in the classroom, it is important to find texts of the appropriate difficulty level. One way to estimate the difficulty of a text is given in Figure 6 below, adapted from discussions in Jones and Pikulski (1974), Oller (1979) and Harris and Sipay (1980, 1985). The percentages are for exact response passages. Teachers should revise these upward approximately 15% for semantically appropriate response scoring, or find a suitable level through student feedback. Similar efforts to scale functional levels of student abilities can be defined for comprehension and word recognition exercises. Harris and Sipay (1980:182-183, 1985), for example, note 90-75-50% for comprehension exercises and 99-95-90% for word recognition exercises.

Errors made during cloze exercises may be analyzed to help the teacher understand certain reading strategies of students. Teachers could use this sort of analysis with the students present, soliciting their feedback. Involving students in the analysis will make the resulting student profiles more valid, and students will become more aware of the reading process. Finally, we should recognize that the use of cloze, though somewhat controversial, may play a role in providing useful information on students' reading abilities.

Guidelines for Assessing Difficulty of a Text Using Cloze

Above 50% correct   Independent Reading Level

(The student should be able to read the text with ease.)

35% to 50%   Instructional Reading Level

(The teacher should design appropriate instructional material to help students deal with the difficulties this text presents).

Below 35%   Frustration Level

(The text may prove quite difficult for the student although interest and motivation may enable the reader to overcome difficulties.)

Figure 6: A Scale for Assessing Text Difficulty

Questionnaires

Questionnaires provide an important means for obtaining information about students' reading attitudes and may be used for more than initial diagnostic purposes. They provide a more structured way to gather attitudinal and behavioral information than through casual questioning. They can be developed to probe a variety of instructional problems pertaining to ongoing progress, attitudes to certain exercises, changes in reading patterns during the course of the reading program, recommendations for different reading material, etc.

In designing a questionnaire, the teacher should first consider the area of interest and create initial questions to address this area. If the questionnaire appears reasonable, she should give the questionnaire to other teachers and to groups of students for field testing. Questionnaires may be open-ended, or closed (the possible responses are listed for the students to choose from). Closed questionnaires are faster to fill out and less dependent on students' writing abilities. They overcome the potential problem of non-responses from students. On the other hand, closed responses may limit the type and variety of information students might provide; thus, the teacher may only obtain information she already knew in the first place. Choices in questionnaire construction ultimately rest with the teacher and the context in which the questionnaire is to be used.

Observations/conferences

Perhaps the strongest informal assessment procedure in reading programs is the focused observation. Frager (1984) has argued strongly for the validity of teachers' assessments through observation. In this study, content area teachers in U.S. secondary schools were found to reproduce the assessments made by reading diagnosticians quite accurately just by observing students on a videotape. The teacher's assessments were made with relatively little observational input, while the reading diagnosticians' were made after administering an entire battery of tests. If teachers' observations are valid, then it follows that they can provide teachers with useful information about reading instruction.

Focused observation by teachers may be raised to a conscious level of assessment when teachers actually formulate evaluation questions; e.g., Does the student read fluently? The teacher should then consider possible behaviors which might indicate that a student does or does not read fluently—observing a student's progress reading through a text with a pencil or his finger, seeing students subvocalize, making constant reference to a dictionary, asking classmates for help, etc. The question posed, and the relevant observed behavior, can be recorded for later reference. The teacher's perceptions can be clarified by talking with students or by other formal or informal assessment strategies. Observations made by the teacher should be important to students as well. Thus, the results of focused observations should be discussed with students, possibly at scheduled reading conferences.

A reading conference between the teacher and a student is an assessment procedure that should not be overlooked. It is quite common for a teacher to have a conference with a student about a grammar or writing problem, and the same should be so for a reading problem. Unfortunately, reading is not a skill which creates external products for teachers to respond to. There is no reading product, like a written essay, upon which to focus. However, a reading experience can be generated in the course of a brief conference. This reading experience can telescopically focus on a student's reading skills because of the one-on-one contact and the fact that there are fewer distractions and demands made on the teacher's attention compared to the classroom environment.

An individualized reading experience could consist of a silent or oral reading of a text from classroom materials, possibly one with which the student had some difficulty. The literature and assessment procedures for oral assessment of this type are extensive. Good reviews may be found in Harris and Sipay (1980, 1985) and Johnston (1984). Our preference is for silent reading, as oral reading can make students very nervous, and poor pronounciation can interfere with the fluency of the reading.

For conferences employing silent reading, Kucer (1983) suggests that students read the text with a highlighter, marking the trouble spots they encounter as they continue to read. When the student has finished reading, the teacher should ask him to summarize orally what he has read. This summary can be recorded for future reference, leaving the teacher free to focus on the student's reading behavior and comprehension abilities. When the student has finished summarizing the text, the teacher may probe with further questions. Extending the interview in this manner ensures that summary responses, if limited, are due to comprehension problems and not an unwillingness to perform. (Oral summaries do add spoken production factors to the analysis, but these are less likely to be limiting than written summaries.)

After the summary, the teacher and student should focus on the problem spots which the student highlighted in the text. The teacher and student together can analyze the problems and how they may be handled. This strategy raises the student's awareness of those skills and strategies which he needs to work on. The joint effort also involves the student in the assessment process, making the reading problems encountered more immediate (see Hosenfeld 1984, for retrospective and thinking aloud reading analyses).

In addition, the student and teacher should discuss the reading itself and the student's feelings about it. This discussion will provide the teacher with useful information on the attitudes of the student towards reading. Such attitudes may explain the student's development and progress throughout the course of the reading program. Relevant information and observations made by the teacher should be noted much as any evaluation measure would be.

Alternative strategies for reading conferences include focusing on other recent material that a student may have read, analyzing responses to a cloze test given at an earlier time, or discussing earlier observations by the teacher on the student's reading problems. Central to all strategies is that conferences are a valuable part of reading assessment; they should be held on a regular basis as time permits. Reading conferences also motivate students, making them more likely to seek out the teacher's help in the future, and making them more likely to communicate their progress.

7.10 THE FINAL EVALUATION

The final evaluation should reflect as much as possible the activities included in the initial needs assessment, although the same materials need not be used. When assessing reading, a pre-test/post-test situation may be set up, though such approaches, if they represent the only basis of final evaluation, can be misleading. Progress in pre-/post-test evaluations may be attributable to many extraneous variables. If careful records have been kept, as suggested here, and if records of ongoing informal assessments have been included in students' files, then the final evaluation will not be reduced to a single formal test battery, but will follow from ongoing evaluations of the student's progress in many reading skills. The final evaluation that a teacher makes under these circumstances is more likely to be a valid indication of skills development in the reading program. It will amount to as accurate an estimate as possible given the constraints of time and practicality.

Student and teacher evaluations of the course should also be sought. The information that these questionnaires provide, combined with the assessment of individual student progress throughout the course, will make it possible to evaluate effectively the reading course itself, including the materials, instructional practices and balance of tasks on different reading skills and strategies.

7.11 CONCLUSION

The field of second language reading assessment is still in the developmental stages. Suggestions have been made in this chapter for a reading assessment repertoire with which teachers may respond to the varied evaluation situations encountered in second language reading instruction. Teachers should explore these and other possible assessment strategies, improving the resources to which ESL teachers currently have access. With efforts to improve second language reading assessment, teachers will also increase their understanding of the reading process, their students' needs, and the close relationship between ongoing assessment and effective reading instruction. Reading assessment is not of necessity sterile and remote procedures which impose themselves on the classroom environment; it can be an integral part of the learning process.

FOR STUDY AND DISCUSSION

1. Why is reading assessment an essential part of the learning experience?

2. What types of assessment are possible and in what contexts is each most suitable?

3. Why should a program include both a reading placement test and a set of diagnostic procedures?

4. Describe a class in a second language program. Include student proficiency level, purpose of the class, and the general context of the language program itself. Based on this information, which assessment procedures would you recommend as most appropriate? What types of assessment would be least appropriate for the particular situation you have described?

5. How would you summarize the use of cloze procedures for second language reading assessment purposes? Would you disagree with any of the conclusions of the authors on this issue?

6. Figure 6 provides a scale for assessing text difficulty. How can you determine the usefulness of this kind of scale?

7. What complications might arise when trying to use questionnaires? When might they be inappropriate for use?

8. What sorts of activities can the teacher use as ways to examine students' reading during individual conferences? What problems might arise when using conferences for assessment purposes?

9. Why is the appropriate choice of texts for assessment purposes a serious problem? What guidelines and procedures might help in text choice (you may want to refer to Dubin, this volume)?

FOR FURTHER READING

There are few sources on second language reading assessment which present concise overviews of either standardized testing or informal assessment procedures. The interested reader can, however, explore a number of issues raised in this chapter by turning to sources on particular topics. Overviews of standardized reading assessment, and theoretical concerns such as norm vs. criterion referenced testing, are given in Harris and Sipay (1980, 1985) and Johnston (1984). In addition, these sources provide extensive reviews of oral assessment. Good sources for the debate on cloze testing include Cziko (1983) and Shanahan (1983) for first language issues, and Stevenson (1982); Alderson (1983); Klein-Braley (1983); and Brown (1984) for second language issues.

First language in-class assessment, both formal and informal, are discussed in Schell (1981); Pikulski and Shanahan (1982); and Lesiak and Bradley-Johnson (1983). Practical advice on constructing in-class tests will be found in Heaton (1975) and Madsen (1983). There is little information on assessing texts for in-class assessment purposes. Klare (1984) reviews readability and may be the best source for the problems in using readability formulas to assess text difficulty.

Readers should also be aware of two journals, *Reading in a Second Language*, and *Language Testing*, for articles related to reading assessment, both standardized and in-class. Second language reading assessment is one area in which the need for information far exceeds the available literature.

Chapter 8

Computer Assisted Reading Instruction (CARI)

Susan Young Dever
University of Southern California

8.1 INTRODUCTION

The birth of Computer Assisted Reading Instruction (CARI) occurred during the early days of Computer Assisted Instruction research in the 1950s at Stanford University. It followed a generally slow pace of development until the spread of the microcomputer in education throughout the late 70s and 80s. The wider availability of hardware for student use has resulted in expanded production of reading instruction software, the more ambitious of which attempts to teach a wider range of skills and levels than have been dealt with before. The question most educators face today has progressed from "should we use computers?" to "which software provides the best instruction?"

In this chapter we will view CARI software from three perspectives (which should prove to be helpful in the evaluation process). Part I will discuss CARI software from the perspective of its content, namely in terms of the reading knowledge and skills used, particularly as suggested by various reading models. Part II will view CARI software from the perspective of the complexity of the instructional task through which the student learns the reading skills described in Part I. Part III will discuss computer/learner interaction and CARI software. It will review findings in the area of artificial intelligence and how they affect the computer's ability to communicate in natural language with the student. Program-learner control, and how it has been incorporated into CARI, will also be discussed.

This chapter is not designed to serve as a specific checklist for software selection. (For examples of such guides see Bradley 1983-84; Geoffrion & Geoffrion 1983; and Strei 1983). Rather, it is intended to provide a preliminary conceptual framework of what is possible in CARI. Using this framework, the author will discuss the range of CARI materials that are currently available and what are not, but could and perhaps should be.

Why use computer assisted instruction?

There has been a great stir within the educational community regarding the adoption of the computer as a widespread medium of instruction. Claims and counter-claims of the wonders of computer assisted instruction (CAI) that incorporates multi-colored animation, digitalized sound reproduction, and branching cinema via video disk (to name but a few) are flying in all directions. Meanwhile, the majority of educators sit on the sidelines unsure of exactly what the computer is capable of and how it can be used by a student or in a class (Baum 1983; Jamieson and Chappelle 1984).

Several years of experience with computers in the classroom now allow us to state confidently that the computer does have a number of broad capabilities that make it an acceptable mode of instruction. Furthermore, it seems certain that the ongoing evolution of computer software (and hardware to a lesser degree) will soon bring us to the point that the computer will not only be an acceptable alternative medium of instruction, but will in fact be preferable to many other media. This is because the computer can combine various capabilities (sound, graphics, interaction, evaluation, adaptive instruction, etc.) ordinarily found scattered among other media (projectors, tape recorders, textbooks, etc.) but combined as a rule only in the human teacher. In addition, widespread usage will result in CAI being delivered at a potentially lower cost per student-use hour than equivalent instruction delivered by a teacher.

Capabilities of computer assisted instruction that are advantageous to student learning fall into two very broad areas. The first is that CAI makes possible extensive individualized instruction of an interactive nature (Underwood 1984). Traditionally, education has depended on the textbook for widespread individualized instruction. The textbook is incomparable in its ability to disperse inexpensively a specific body of information to a very large number of individuals. However, in spite of attempts by authors to the contrary (as in this book the inclusion of questions for discussion at the end of each chapter), the textbook is a non-interactive medium of instruction.

The teacher in the classroom, on the other hand, is the medium of instruction that has been traditionally relied upon to bring interaction to student learning. But the amount of interaction is directly proportional to the number of students in the class. Those of us in language teaching are unhappily aware of this fact when we are assigned to teach conversational skills to classes of 30 and 40 students. It is probably not too wide of the mark to estimate that an average student in an average public school class spends less than 5 minutes of a 50 minute period actually interacting with the instructor or other students on the instructional topic.[1]

Although there are examples of computer assisted instruction being used very effectively in small group work among students (Baltra 1984; Higgins and Johns 1984; Wyatt 1984) and teacher-led class activities (Geoffrion and Geoffrion 1983; Higgins and Johns 1984), CAI is most commonly presented as a one-on-one mode of instruction. A student interacts with the computer by typing in answers to CAI questions. He then receives some sort of response (the form of both questions and answers being pre-determined by the author of the CAI lesson) as to the correctness of his answer. He progresses at his own speed through the instruction and never has to worry about the computer becoming impatient or reacting negatively to him because of the errors he makes.

The individualized interaction of CAI also results in benefits to students similar to those found in individualized teacher-student interaction. Research has shown (Kulik, Kulik, and Cohen 1980) that all students learn through computer assisted instruction, but that students of lower ability learn more due to their need for additional individualized interaction being met.[2] The class-wide effect of CAI is that scores are truncated on the lower end and that the spread of scores clusters more closely around the higher norm (Kulik, Kulik, and Cohen 1980).

A second general capability of the computer that can be utilized to great advantage in instruction is its ability to keep records to an extent that is impractical if not impossible in other instructional settings. The computer is capable of recording non-intrusively every interaction with the student and, if desired, in a manner totally invisible to him. In addition to creating gradebook-style records familiar to classroom teachers, the computer can use this information to evaluate each student's on-going performance and to direct future instruction. Such record-keeping capabilities also offer great potential in studying student learning styles, the effectiveness of instructional design, and different subject matters' best order of presentation, to suggest but a few. In the long term, we as educators may discover that the greatest benefit to come out of the use of computer assisted instruction is in what we are able to learn about learning itself (Leach and Beale 1984).

What makes good instruction?

Instruction, whether presented via a traditional medium such as the teacher or textbook or through a newer medium such as the computer, must be assessed fundamentally on two criteria: (1) just exactly what does it teach? and (2) how does it go about teaching?

The first of these refers to the content of instruction. In some subjects, instructional content consists predominantly of a compilation of facts and figures which the student does his best to memorize. However, in most subjects the content of instruction is a combination of information and the skills to interpret or manipulate this information. Reading falls into this latter category. For example, successful reading students learn, whether in a reading class or other language class, information such as vocabulary (together with its phonetic and morphological components) or the typical rhetorical structure of a paragraph or longer reading passage. In a reading class, they also learn skills that directly utilize this information, such as skimming for the overall content of a passage or scanning for specific information.

The second question, how does it go about teaching?, refers to the design and construction of specific instructional tasks. These tasks (exercises, games, quizzes, etc.) teach the information and skills that make up instructional content and can be viewed quite independently of the content.

The human teacher has the capability of adjusting the complexity of instruction consciously, or perhaps more importantly unconsciously, to the needs of his students as the instruction is taking place. He does this in a myriad of ways which educational researchers are still struggling to identify. One way the teacher has been shown to adjust instruction is by regulating the content of the instruction being presented to the student. When the student seems unable to perform as expected in the reading class the teacher may determine that extra work on a prerequisite skill such as letter recognition or vocabulary building is required. Likewise, when the student becomes impatient or bored the teacher can challenge the student with more difficult reading activities or engage his attention with subject matter that the student finds more interesting.

Another way in which the teacher can adjust instruction (to the needs of the learner) is by regulating the complexity of the task that the student performs in order to learn the particular target skill. When it appears that the student is not able to perform an entire learning activity alone, the teacher figuratively if not literally can take the student by the hand and lead him through the learning task. The reading teacher might, for example, do this by first pointing out to the student examples of vocabulary that indicate the author's opinion, then by asking the student to find examples of such vocabulary and interpret them, and finally by giving him an entire

	Low Level of Complexity	Mid Level of Complexity	High Level of Complexity
Bottom-up Skills Vocabulary Building (Discrete Items)	The student should find the words in the maze that describe the main character in the passage he has just read. (This activity might be presented in a game format, the student racing against time to finish, for example, before the glass overflows or the whachamacallit eats the whole thingemajig or bells and whistles sound and the screen bursts into color.)	If the student cannot guess the meaning of an unfamiliar word, or he determines from further reading that his guess was incorrect, he should study the word for morphemic similarity to other words that he knows. (The computer might respond to the student's first request for assistance by listing words with the same root and affixes and asking him to identify them, and to additional requests by helping the student graphically pull the word apart, define root and affixes, identify examples of their use in a randomly selected listing of words, etc.)	The student should define words selected from a reading passage he has just finished reading. (The computer might run a key-word search through the student definition and match words found in the student answer with keywords in the program glossary. When discrepancies occur, the computer can query the student using an expanded Eliza-type interaction until words in the student definition match keywords in the program glossary.)
Top-down Skills Vocabulary Building (Vocabulary in Context)	The student should utilize context to define specific words and phrases from a reading passage. (The computer might present the student with optional definitions or synonyms down the left side of the screen. A graphical or textual representation occurs on the right that reflects or logically follows from the student's choice. After the student selects one of the options, he views or reads the resulting representation on the right and compares it with the original passage. He may request a "grade" on the accuracy of his definition.)	The student should try to guess the meaning of a word or phrase from its context and check his comprehension against future reading. (The computer might present a reading passage to the student. After he has read the passage the computer might offer the student the choice of selecting the correct definition immediately or continuing to read the passage, this time with contextual clues highlighted. The student may ask for further assistance which will come in the form of further contextual clues being highlighted and in the form of notes on how he can use the highlighted forms to arrive at a more complete comprehension.)	The student should work a crossword puzzle with a synonym (or antonym, definition, paraphrase) of the underlined word (or phrase). All hints are sentences from the reading passage he has just read. (The computer may respond to student request or response with hints or contextual clues from the reading passage that he may have overlooked. The student may also request morphological clues. The game aspect of crossword puzzles might be enhanced by scoring most heavily for the use of contextual information.)

Figure 1: Examples of CARI Activities for Particular Reading Skills across Levels of Task Complexity

passage to read and discuss. Similarly, the teacher can challenge the student by withholding guidance when it appears that the student is able to perform adequately without it.

It is important to make clear the distinction between the complexity of instructional content and the cognitive complexity of instructional tasks. We as teachers and students are accustomed to thinking of instructional complexity in terms of how content is sequenced. That is, learning vocabulary seems to be easier than learning to draw inferences from a reading passage since learning vocabulary is ordinarily considered prerequisite to learning to infer. However, the instructional tasks aimed at developing any one reading skill may themselves be assessed as being more or less complex in a cognitive sense. For example, in a lesson on vocabulary development, different tasks may require students to recognize words and their meanings, to manipulate them within a given context, or to produce them in a problem solving context, activities that range from the cognitively very simple to the very complex (see Figure 1).

Although some correspondence may occur between the task's level of complexity and the reading skill level in which it provides instruction, the apparent degree of correspondence in computer assisted reading instructional software is exaggerated by the limited numbers of programs yet available (see Figure 2). Low-level reading skills (comprising the bulk of bottom-up instruction) are paired almost exclusively with instructional tasks of low cognitive complexity and high-level reading skills (similarly addressed by top-down instruction) with highly complex learning tasks. This imbalance may result from many educators not distinguishing clearly between the complexity of the reading skills being taught and the cognitive skills being required of the student in the learning activities.

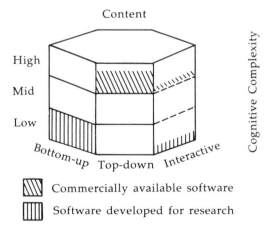

Figure 2: Relative Amounts of Different Software Types

In fact, instruction presented through any medium can and should be viewed from the perspective of the complexity of its instructional tasks as well as its content. However, it is particularly valuable to do so with computer assisted instruction. CAI, more than all other instructional media with the possible exception of the human teacher, is designed to serve as a stand-alone system. It works with students exhibiting the wide variance normally found within entry level skills, aptitude, and learning styles just as the teacher in the classroom does.

It may be that the teacher is able to make adjustments in instructional content and task complexity because he can relate the student's learning processes to his own experiences in learning and is thus able to mentally process simultaneously a wide range of sometimes vague feedback from the student. Until more software becomes available that allows the computer to learn from student input, a major drawback to using the computer in instruction will be that it has no learning experience comparable to the teacher's. It is currently only able to react to pre-defined student responses. Thus, it is the responsibility of the instructional software designer to include in the program the capability of adapting instructional content and task complexity to student needs. One of the fundamental elements of this adaptive capability is the provision of optional tasks at varying levels of complexity for each reading skill. This range of task complexity for low to high level reading skills is lacking in almost all commercially available CARI software and its absence serves currently to cripple the computer as a stand-alone medium of reading instruction.

8.2 THE CONTENT OF INSTRUCTION[3]

Reading theory has followed a chronological progression of bottom-up to top-down (in the 60s and 70s) to (most recently) interactive models. Curiously enough, much of the Computer Assisted Language Learning (CALL) software currently on the market, most of which has been written within the past five years, consists entirely of bottom-up type activities. Computer Assisted Reading Instruction (CARI) software, likewise, is mostly comprised of instruction in bottom-up reading skills. Following are examples of specific skills in which CARI is available. They are discussed in the order of the instructional approach they emphasize—bottom-up, top-down, and interactive.

Bottom-up reading skills

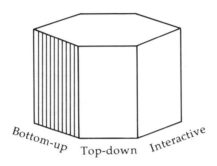

Bottom-up   Top-down   Interactive

Letter / word / phrase recognition

There must be some means of initially connecting the written form with meaning. To this end, low-level recognition exercises, particularly in letter recognition work, are sometimes presented in conjunction with an audio component: voice synthesizer, computer-controlled audio tape or disk recording, or human tutor. Software without an additional audio component seems most useful with very young native speakers who already have a large spoken repertoire, but seems of limited use with ESL students, especially adults.

Another method of associating writing with sound is through the use of graphics, both still and animated. Programs such as *Reading Instruction for Beginners* go one step farther by mixing sound, graphics, and animation for the combined purposes of tying the written and spoken forms together, of capturing and retaining the interest of the student, and of giving comprehensible directions to the student.

Other recognition exercises require the student to locate letters or letter groupings within words. Similar exercises can be constructed using words or larger chunks of text.

Recognition activities are more often than not combined with a timer (see Stoller, this volume). The computer can serve as a tachistoscope that presents a learner-determined number of characters on the screen for a learner-determined length of time.[4] Students can produce sounds orally or can be asked to write the letters on a piece of paper or type them back into the computer. A timer is also often included with recognition activities in a game format. The student can compete against himself, the computer, or other students.

Rate building

A bottom-up type of activity widely found in CARI that uses a timer as an integral element is rate building. Rate building exercises, at their lowest level, are the letter and word level tachistoscopic exercises mentioned in the previous section. More commonly, though, CARI rate building exercises are composed of words or phrases presented in a meaningful sequence on the screen. The student or teacher sets the reading rate at the beginning of the exercise, usually by choosing from among optional speeds offered, such as "slow," "medium," or "fast" (see Stoller, this volume).

One drawback to setting the speed in advance in most CARI that is currently available seems to be that once the student has begun an exercise, he is 'locked into' the pre-set presentation speed. It would seem that for instruction using pre-set speeds to be most effective, accurate evaluation and placement is essential as is the capability of setting the speed at small increments.

Although several of the large-scale courses of computer assisted reading instruction attempt relatively comprehensive evaluation of the student's entering ability, shorter instructional packages which comprise the bulk of software currently on the market make only limited attempts to do so. Most often, the responsibility for accurate evaluation of both student and program level falls upon the teacher. The lack of computer administered entry level evaluation seems a particularly serious issue yet to be carefully addressed by CARI software designers.

An interactive medium like the computer can be used for continuous evaluation of student performance throughout the instruction. A simple alternative method for setting the reading rate of a CARI activity might be to combine on-line evaluation with pre-setting speed. The student can be instructed to read the passage displayed on the screen and, when he is finished, type any key. The computer will calculate the student's speed based on the length of the passage and the length of time it takes him to complete it. The computer might then continue the passage or move into another, presenting the text at a slightly faster or slower speed. Regular assessment of the student's comprehension by means of multiple choice or cloze items, for example, could also be used to re-set presentation speed within an exercise. *Young English Software* combines elements of this type into a score re-setting function which operates continuously throughout the program's use. It also records rate and accuracy into the "Hall of Fame," a score display routine that ranks the current student's score with the last half-dozen program users.

Having the student take the responsibility of pre-setting and re-setting his own level of instructional difficulty within a program has further advantages. This control of choice seems to be one of the major reasons for the overall popularity of CAI among students who have used it. See Part 3 for more discussion of Learner Control.

Aside from the lack of accurate student evaluation, a second drawback to many CARI reading rate exercises exists. In many of the instructional programs items are presented one by one in a "window" on the screen, that is, on one line surrounded by blank screen, a fixed image, or text (see Figure 3). In some of these packages, each item is centered within the window, and it is impossible to anticipate where the first letter of the next item will appear on that line. As a result, the eye is forced to flicker back and forth horizontally every few seconds just before each new item appears. This is not only very tiring visually but also very questionable pedagogically. Such movements seem counterproductive to the development of efficient eye movements for reading and the centered placement of text is not representative of the reading field observed by the eye in normal reading (Rayner 1981; Taylor and Taylor 1983).

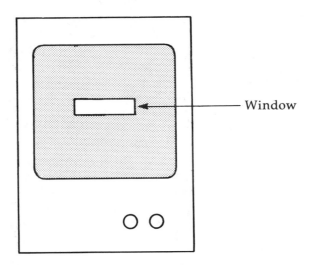

Figure 3: "Window" Display Commonly Found in CARI Programs

Most item-by-item reading rate software displays a word or phrase in isolation on the screen for a pre-specified length of time. When that time is up, the item disappears and is immediately replaced by the succeeding item in the text. Even when the text is left-justified within the window, it might be argued that the student is not acquiring appropriate eye movement habits for scanning because the new text "pops" into view in exactly the same location as the old. He has no opportunity of utilizing regression, a rapid visual cycling back over words or phrases already read, as a natural aid to speed and comprehension.

Other reading rate materials, providing a more natural format, display the text in an additive manner until the entire passage is visible on the screen. In this type of presentation, the student is encouraged to read at the rate of presentation but is able to read at a more natural, and varying, pace since he is able to utilize the visual context of the word or phrase. If the student displays excessive use of regression, appropriate regression behavior can be encouraged by progressively erasing previously read text. Or he might be cued in the use of more efficient eye movement, for example, by the presentation of text in meaningful units, or by highlighting key words or concepts (Grinols 1984) (see Figure 4).

The item-by-item rate building format may be suitable for instruction if adequate prior evaluation of the student's reading rate is available and if the instructional software allows the selection of a presentation rate appropriate to the student's level. The additive presentation type, on the other hand, does not require such precise matching of student and pre-set presentation rate and might thus be more widely applicable in most instructional settings.

 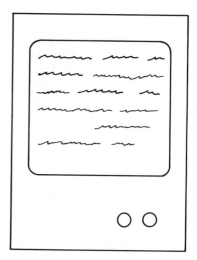

Figure 4: Example of Additive Presentation Format

Reading comprehension

Just as "all roads lead to Rome," so we might say that all language skills lead to reading comprehension. Much of the CARI software commercially available takes advantage of this fact by advertising itself as instruction in reading comprehension. However, few of these programs are of the scope to focus on more than two or three sub-skills. In fact, many of them are limited solely to text presentation followed by multiple choice comprehension questions, thus appearing more like quizzes than instruction. They take little or no advantage of the dynamic capabilities of the computer and can therefore be argued to be more suitable to textbooks than CARI (Baker 1984).

Instruction in the broad area of reading comprehension can be found in some large scale "courses" of instruction. One example of software designed to teach the general skill of reading comprehension is one part of the PLATO Corrections Project *Reading Comprehension Program* under development in 1983 (Higgins and Johns 1984). This program consists of lessons in: (1) finding information in text, (2) paraphrasing text and answering paraphrase questions about the text, (3) identifying the main idea and themes of text, (4) making inferences from text, (5) dealing with logical relationships, (6) vocabulary development, (7) following directions from text, (8) skills for taking reading comprehension tests, and (9) self-monitoring of comprehension (Higgins and Johns 1984).

The scarcity of reading comprehension software which incorporates instruction in several skill areas results in part from a heretofore limited production effort in the area; it also reflects, however, one of the most serious limitations of the computer in reading instruction, that of text presentation (England 1983). Most computers (for example, almost all Apples as originally supplied) in classroom use today can display clearly a maximum of some 100 words on the screen at one time. This figure is particularly small for reading comprehension work, since many comprehension activities are constructed around reading passages long enough to permit content development, generally several paragraphs or longer in length.

A 100-word passage covers the entire screen with single spaced text except for a narrow border around all sides. Reading such a condensed body of text displayed at a resolution considerably lower than that of print (especially on color monitors) becomes tiring to the eyes in a very short time. A more comfortable text display is double-spaced with wider margins, but this limits the passage length to approximately 50 words, an even less desirable number. As a result, comprehension activities based on passages that exceed this length require the student to "page" through the text from one end to the other. When comprehension questions follow the reading passage, they often require additional pages, thereby causing comprehension exercises to devolve into memory activities.

Due to the limited text presentation capacity of the average computer monitor, it seems preferable to concentrate on other instructional activities that capitalize upon the strengths of the computer medium. Reading comprehension instruction constructed around lengthy texts, for example, might present pre- and post-reading activities on-line, referring the student to a textbook for the passage itself. These pre- and post-reading activities on computer might well include recognition and rate-building exercises using short excerpts from the original passage and other exercises that take advantage of the dynamic and interactive capabilities of the computer. In fact, this is a relatively common procedure in non-CARI; while shorter passages are presented integrated with learning activities, longer passages, like books and articles, are typically separate.

Paging through computer text presents a more subtle problem to the reader. When paging through a book, we usually have at least a rough idea of where we are currently in relation to how much we have already read and how much we have to go. We can keep track, at the least, by comparing the thickness between our left thumb and fore-finger and our right thumb and fore-finger. When paging through text on the display monitor, it is much more difficult to gauge our position relative to the beginning and end. Some software producers, such as those of *Whole Brain Spelling*, have attempted to solve this problem by placing the current page number and total number of pages at the top or bottom of each screen. Others include some sort of graphic representation of location, such as a thermometer that fills up as one progresses through the program. For the inexperienced reader, these cues may prove to be adequate for locating himself within a passage. However, for the experienced reader, none of these props seems to work as well as the thumb and forefinger.

Top-down skills

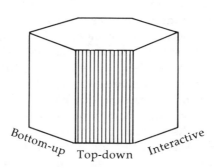

While concentration on bottom-up reading sub-skills dominates the CARI software currently available, stirrings of interest in top-down instruction are beginning to be felt. As will be recalled, top-down activities are constructed in such a way as to make it possible for the student to relate what he is learning to what he already knows. There is then the fundamental requirement that we recognize what the student knows and is able to attach new knowledge to. We, thus, have two choices: to identify the student's prior knowledge, or if he is lacking that knowledge, to provide him with what he needs.

We can attempt to elicit the student's prior knowledge by asking him what he knows. However, it is rarely if ever that simple; we will ordinarily have to elicit from the student knowledge that he isn't aware he has. Additionally, for this knowledge to be of any use in future instruction, we must see to it that he arranges it in a form, or schema (Geoffrion and Geoffrion 1983), within which he can appropriately integrate new information. Ausubel proposes that the student be given this content structure in advance in the form of a pre-organizer (Snelbecker 1974).

Blohm (1982) reports on his work in CARI with "graphic pre- and post-organizers," diagramatic representations of the concepts and key terms of a text's content. The student uses pre-organizers to preview the relationships and contrasts among the concepts and key terms. He also uses pre-organizers to consolidate and organize his previous knowledge on the subject. After he reads the passage, he views the post-organizer in order "to reorganize, consolidate, and review (when necessary) the text content just read" (p. 10). He is asked to fill in the missing key concepts and vocabulary on the partially complete post-organizer. When he has finished, the computer checks his accuracy, marking correct answers and suggesting paragraphs and lines to read in order to correct inappropriate answers.

An example of commercially available software that in a different way addresses top-down skills, providing the student with both information and structure, is *M-ss-ng L-nks*. This program begins by presenting a reading passage to the student. After he finishes reading it, each letter in the passage is replaced by a hyphen, and the student begins supplying the missing letters. As the student supplies a correct letter, that letter also appears wherever else it occurs in the passage. The object is to rewrite the passage. In this case, the student acquires a schema of the subject matter as he first reads the passage; he then, quite literally, fills the blanks.

The student's schema may relate to various skills and information other than the subject matter of the passage that contribute to reading proficiency, such as discourse structure, paragraph organization, and grammatical forms. As an example, the student may know little or nothing about personnel management. However, he does know that formally structured paragraphs commonly have a topic sentence and supporting sentences. Therefore, while reading a passage from a management text he is able to use this knowledge of paragraph organization to assist him in comprehending the subject matter of the passage.

Similarly, the student working with *M-ss-ng L-nks* might also be able to use his knowledge of vocabulary usage to assist him in discovering the missing words. For example, he might be aware of how frequently certain words appear in the typical written passage. He might try to replace "---" with "the" and "-" with "a" simply playing the odds. He might then try the same with helping verbs such as "are," "have," and so forth. Later he might relate his subject matter schema and grammatical schema to that of word frequency in order to discover the location and identity of compound verbs throughout the passage. *Cloze Call*, another program very similar to *M-ss-ng L-nks* in design, comes closer to being capable of indicating the relationships between schemata. It permits the teacher (while entering new text material) to key each deleted item by defining its function in the sentence (Schripsema 1985).

Interactive skill development

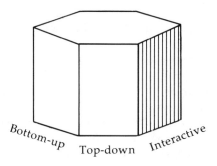

Bottom-up   Top-down   Interactive

There are very few if any CARI software packages commercially available that require the use of several reading skills simultaneously, a goal for reading instruction based on an Interactive Reading Model. Producing a software package with the structural complexity of a multiple skill CARI package has proved to be beyond the resources (financial or skill) of the majority of instructional software developers to date. However, the increased attention being paid now to top-down and Interactive materials development and production is resulting in an increasing number of programs focusing on two or more sub-skills. Such a development can be considered a first step toward interactive reading skills instruction.

Most of these programs actually focus on one or two skills sequentially, but closely relate their activities. *Gapper* (Morrison 1984), a learning game, does this through a sequence of five phases. The first phase gives the students an opportunity to preview the five multiple choice comprehension questions to be asked later. They use these questions to focus their attention on the main themes of the passage.

The second phase is the timed reading in which the total time is calculated. The third phase is a comprehension quiz using the questions previewed in Phase I with immediate feedback given to the students for each incorrect answer. The fourth phase is a cloze passage with each letter of the missing words replaced by an asterisk. The students may ask for hints or may guess. Each wrong guess will replace an asterisk with a letter, simplifying the task. Phase V consists of replacing all words of the passage with asterisks and having the students recreate the entire passage. In this phase, each occurrence in the passage of the students' guess will appear as he first guesses it.

Sequentially, *Gapper* provides learning activities in the following bottom-up and top-down skills: determining objectives and main themes of the passage in the pre-reading activity, scanning/speed reading, reading comprehension, utilizing contextual clues and schemata to replace missing cloze items, and utilizing linguistic clues and schemata to rewrite the entire passage. Since the learner is using the same text throughout all five phases, we can argue that *Gapper* comes very close to an application of an interactive model approach to CARI, although it does not focus on the skills simultaneously.

In the PLATO Correctional Program in Reading Comprehension referred to earlier, distinctions among some tasks, particularly the higher level ones, become blurred as the various tasks integrate different reading skills. Blohm (1982) also allows for some interaction among reading skills and information by allowing the student to request computer supplied glossing in either a definition or paraphrase format when and only when he determines that to be necessary for comprehension.

With very careful design, materials can be designed which branch into instruction in a number of skills based upon each student response. At the moment, such a program requires more extensive computer memory and more sophisticated evaluation algorithms to correctly select the computer response than is possible with most microcomputers in educational use.

8.3 THE DESIGN OF INSTRUCTION

In the previous section we talked about how instruction can be organized according to its content, that is, the reading skill focused upon in the exercise. In this section we will continue our discussion by talking about how instruction in the various skills contributing to reading proficiency can be viewed according to the cognitive complexity of the task the learner undertakes to learn them. Gagne (1977) expands Bloom's hierarchy of cognitive complexity (for a brief description, see Romiszowski 1984) into a hierarchy of learning. A fundamental assumption of Gagne's learning hierarchy is that each body of knowledge is acquired at each cognitive level in the order of complexity (Gagne 1977).

In the following discussion of computer assisted reading instruction, tasks will be described as belonging to one of three levels of instructional task complexity, low, mid, and high.[5] In the lowest level, the student must identify the correct answer among the options supplied. Any exercise that requires the student to choose the correct answer from a list or grouping of alternatives falls into this group. This includes true-false and multiple choice format exercises which are quite easy to program and have been widely used since the earliest days of CALL.

Activities of the second, or mid-, level of complexity guide the student through the performance of a skill by presenting him with strategies or rules. Tasks at this level are relatively rare in CARI instruction today. At the third level, activities that are cognitively highly complex, in contrast to those at lower levels, require the student not only to perform a skill but also to figure out how best to perform it. Most programs that include activities of this type are products of non-commercial program development for research purposes. This author knows of only one instructional program (PLATO Corrections Project) that attempts to present instruction over the entire range of instructional task complexity.

It is important to remember that CARI software can be viewed both from the perspective of its content as discussed in Section 8.2 of this chapter and from the perspective of its instructional task design as discussed here. Therefore it should come as no surprise to find that a number of the software packages referred to in Section 8.2 to demonstrate specific content levels will also be referred to in this section to demonstrate levels of task complexity.

Tasks of low-level complexity

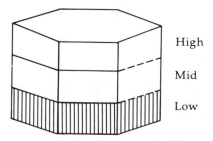

High

Mid

Low

Most of the CARI software currently available contains only activities at the lowest level of complexity. One type of low-level exercises is that of tachistoscopic exercises that give the student practice in word discrimination in a timed format. The student is presented a word on the screen for approximately a second and then asked to choose the word from among several distractors.

Focusing on letter discrimination is a game called *Window Letters* in the PLATO Early Reading Curriculum. In this game, the student moves a window around the screen to allow him to see various parts of a letter. He tries to guess as quickly as possible what the letter is.

Another example of low-level activities is that of word search puzzles. A screen-full of random letters is presented with words scattered throughout, vertically, horizontally, or diagonally. The student's task is to find the words in the matrix (Geoffrion and Geoffrion 1983). A number of programs are available to create word search activities, although most are designed as teacher aids to produce printed puzzles rather than to be used on-line by the student.

It is possible to design exercises of low task complexity for top-down reading skills comparable to those for bottom up skills. Graphic pre- and post-organizers such as those produced by Blohm (described in the previous section) could be altered to become tasks of low level complexity by adding optional answers for the student to select from. Geoffrion and Geoffrion (1983) suggest, as another example, a treasure hunt-style game in which the student races against time to locate key words and phrases in a paragraph, thus identifying and discriminating among such concepts as paragraph structure and its constituent topic sentences and conclusions.

Similarly, it is possible to introduce skills such as inferencing through tasks of low complexity. The critical reading component strand of the *Pal Reading Curriculum* presents practice in inferencing through multiple choice question and answer exercises (also see Jensen, this volume). When the student answers incorrectly, he is told by the computer why he is wrong.

Tasks of mid-level complexity

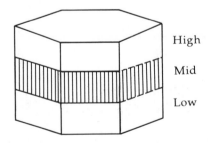

High

Mid

Low

Activities of mid-level complexity might be described as presenting the student with the pieces to a puzzle and the strategies for its solution. The manipulation of spelling rules is an example of a mid-level activity that can be used to give instruction in a bottom-up reading skill. The student might be given a rule that states that words ending with the sound -er in a stressed syllable will double the final -r when adding -ed or -ing. He then might be given a paragraph in which occur some words with the double -r and others with a single -r. He finally relates the correct pronunciation and stress to each.[6]

Reading strategies can also be introduced through activities of mid-level complexity. The *Pal Reading Curriculum* lessons on identifying the main idea of a passage instruct the student in the difference between main ideas and details and in where each is most likely to be found in a paragraph. Then the process of finding the key ideas is demonstrated by highlighting the appropriate portions of a sample passage.

Guiding a student through a learning task seems simple enough, even keeping in mind the limited memory that seriously restricts program size for most microcomputers. However, there are almost no examples of mid-level tasks available in CARI software today.

Tasks of high-level complexity

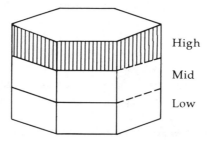

High

Mid

Low

In highly complex activities, the student on his own must select from a repertoire of previously learned reading strategies, linguistic information, and world knowledge the necessary tools to perform the tasks. Activities of high-level complexity may even require the student to modify previously learned strategies in order to produce new ones more appropriate to the problem in hand.

Currently, much effort is being expended on the development of a wide variety of high-level CARI activities. The bulk of this growth is in instruction on reading sentences, and paragraphs, and in developing reading strategies, although there is considerable potential for the use of highly complex activities with all reading skills. There are, for example, a number of crossword puzzle activities available that can be utilized for vocabulary building purposes.

Jumbler, by Higgins and Johns, having versions focusing on words, phrases, and paragraphs, requires the student to reorder jumbled elements in the correct sequence. Similarly, *Textman* (Geoffrion and Geoffrion 1983:189) in a "hangman" type game format, has the student reorder sentences in a paragraph. For each error the student makes in *Textman*, the "man" comes closer to being hanged.

Geoffrion and Geoffrion (pp. 132-3) also suggest that computers might serve as a vehicle for the teaching of note-taking. They feel that the organizational abilities called into play in the setting up of files and file structures in a computer system might serve as a model for the organizational abilities in producing clear and comprehensive notes and, by implication, recognizing the organization of texts when they are read.[7]

Practice in relating new information to current schemata, techniques of employing and producing pre- and post-reading activities, these and other reading skills are equally learnable through the use of activities at each of the three levels of complexity.

Programs combining tasks of different complexity levels

In a few of the instructional programs described above, activities, each of a different level of complexity, are combined to produce a more comprehensive learning program. This makes the instruction more effective for a wider number of students. In fact, much of the criticism of early computer assisted language learning was due to the fact that the instruction was of a single type of task, almost always of very low complexity and thus too limited for widespread application. More recent criticism (Wyatt 1983) notes the continued overwhelming preponderance among commercially available software of low-level tasks which make little reference to more complex cognitive activities. Therefore, it should come as no surprise that programs combining instruction over a range of reading content with instructional tasks over the three levels of cognitive complexity are virtually nonexistent. It is likely, however, that the extensive production of new materials now underway will lead to more comprehensive and balanced CARI instruction.

8.4 COMPUTER LEARNER INTERACTION

This section views CARI from the perspective of type and means of communication between the computer and the learner during instruction. We will discuss here that interaction in the light of the language used, both the language used in the reading activities and the language of the interaction itself. We will also discuss how computer-learner interaction can be used to modify the instructional task. These are subjects that lie in the forefront of the computer assisted language learning field.

The one characteristic of computer assisted instruction that sets it apart most dramatically from all other non-human mediated instruction is its potential for immediate one-on-one interaction with the student. This characteristic is one of the slowest to be taken full advantage of on a wide scale, perhaps due to the newness of nonhuman/human linguistic interaction. It has taken time to explore the many potential forms of interaction between man and machine (punched cards, keyboards, touch-screen monitors; text, graphics, voice synthesis; numbers, letters, commands, conversations) and even more time to figure out how best to implement them. In some cases there is still little agreement on how these different forms of interaction will affect instruction, and whether they will ultimately prove to be worth the effort of being implemented. Nonetheless, the overwhelming trend within the CAI field is toward expanding the capability of the computer to communicate with the student in a more natural language-like mode and toward expanding the role of the student in the adaptation of instruction to fit his particular needs (England 1983).

Artificial intelligence - intelligent computer systems

One direction in which the field of artificial intelligence (AI) is moving is toward the development of what is called an "intelligent" computer system, that is, one that comes as close as possible to simulating the processing capabilities of the human mind. The implications of this for computer learner interaction are numerous. To suggest but a few, there would be less demand on the learner to adapt to the limited communicative capabilities of the computer and thus more opportunity to concentrate on the instruction at hand. The computer's ability to match instruction to the individual aptitudes and knowledge of the student would also be greatly enhanced. And of particular interest to the language learner, the computer would become a vehicle for much more extensive language skill development than is now possible.

However, there are a number of problem areas that must be addressed by AI researchers and that are of particular interest to those of us in the language learning field. One of these is the computer's limited ability to communicate using natural language. A second problem lies in the vast difference in memory and processing capacity between the human brain and computers, especially the microcomputers in widespread educational use. A third problem is our limited understanding of exactly how the mind progresses from beginning to end in solving a problem.

The computer's limited ability to communicate in natural language exists partly because most computer languages are characterized by a relatively rigid linear structure. These artificial languages were intentionally developed with such a structure to minimize ambiguity so that they would be able to express logical structures efficiently. Unfortunately, that nonambiguous linearity makes the translation to natural language difficult at best.[8] One physical result of the computer's inability to easily manipulate natural language structures and ambiguities is the need for a large memory, since it must store linguistic items in a less than ideally efficient manner.

The difficulty with natural language communication is not only that the computer must store vast amounts of language structures and vocabulary. It is also that the computer must be "taught" information about the world about which it is communicating in order for it to communicate in a form approaching natural language (Waldrop 1984). Higgins (1983; see also Eskey, Chapter 1) uses the following interchange to illustrate the extent of the problem.

> First Person: "You're late." (spoken in some heat)

> Second Person's Reply: "It was raining this afternoon."

From this simple interchange we can guess the status of one person in relation to the other. We can assume that being late caused the first person some difficulty or anxiety. We might also assume that the second person had to walk outside and did not have an umbrella, or perhaps got caught in a traffic jam. Covering all possible interpretations in this as in any similar passage of natural language discourse can prove to be an endless task. The sheer quantity of data and the memory required to store it increases exponentially with the addition of more discourse (Waldrop 1984).

In fact, memory and processing limitations, particularly when using microcomputers, mean that extensive natural language communication is unfeasible within the current state of the technology. A compromise must be made between the scope of linguistic interaction around a single subject and the number of different subjects about which communication between student and computer can take place. We may, in other words, communicate at great length in quite natural language about a single subject, or we may conduct a very limited interaction in very restricted language about a large number of subjects.

A number of educational programs have been designed to permit extensive interaction between the student and the computer by limiting the "world" that serves as the subject of that interaction (Higgins and Johns 1984).[9] One well-known program of this type, *John & Mary*, accepts natural language from the user about objects or people seen on the monitor. As the user gives commands to John or Mary to do something or go somewhere else within the two rooms, the graphic images on the monitor change position in response. When the user asks the computer a question about them, he receives a short written response. If he presses the enter key with no command or question he can watch the machine hold a question/answer dialogue with itself about the two figures.

Programs of a micro-world design that require larger amounts of reading are text-based adventure games, along the lines of the popular *Zork*. The user undergoes a series of adventures while working his way through a maze. Each step of the way is described in text by the program and is followed by the user's natural language response to the demand for a decision. For the user to escape from the maze, he must read each passage carefully to comprehend fully both the description of each step of the maze and to infer the underlying strategies required to escape. By limiting the dimensions of the world to the maze and the scope of interaction to that demanded by the program, the computer is capable of responding appropriately to most language entered by the user. For many users, the progressively unfolding storyline of adventure games provides a drawing power rarely found in instructional materials.

A recent variation on the adventure game to appear is called "interactive fiction." Whereas the adventure game is essentially a puzzle solving activity for the user, the interactive fiction program depends upon the user playing a role, or more accurately, becoming a character in the story. In *Cutthroats*, the user must converse with the crew in order to discover which of them is a traitor and to locate the sunken treasure without losing his own life. Some of these conversations are initiated by story characters sharing secrets or asking his advice about what they should do next. Other programs soon to be released will allow the user to ask hypothetical questions to story characters and receive responses that also react to the tone of the question in, for example, an aggressive or friendly manner (Addams 1985).

Some interactive fiction programs are also of immediate interest to the field of reading instruction because of their subject matter. Already on the market are programs based upon popular science fiction works by authors such as Isaac Asimov *(Robots of Dawn)*, Ray Bradbury *(Fahrenheit 451)*, Anne McAffrey *(Dragonriders of Pern)*, and Douglas Adams *(The Hitchhiker's Guide to the Galaxy)*.

Most text-based interactive fiction and adventure games commercially available today are probably too complex and lengthy to be directly useable in the reading classroom. However, such programming carries great potential for future reading instruction. Interactive fiction and adventure games could be made prime candidates for effective and entertaining CARI programming by including convenient stopping points or the capacity to stop and resume at any point throughout the story to conform to the requirements of a class period. Traditional elements of reading instruction such as vocabulary building and reading strategies could be incorporated as well into the design of conversation between characters and user and into the design of maze-escape strategies necessary to the successful completion of the game.

Due to the immense complexity of programming necessary for the computer to approach true comprehension of natural language, many software packages try to simulate natural language communication by using a simpler key-word search technique. The computer searches the student's response for a word or phrase that has been stored in its internal lexicon along with cues for its use.

In *Eliza*, a program featuring a simulated conversation between a counselor and patient, the computer searches each student response for an item it recognizes (Dewdney 1985). The computer then either incorporates it into its next question ("My mother hates me." "Is it because your mother hates you that you came to see me?") or gives a stock response (on every occurence of the word "machine" the computer will respond with "Are you afraid of computers?"). While this interaction is not true communication in a natural language sense, each interplay is meaningful, at least to the user.[10]

The use of a key-word search is enhanced in other programs by combining it with "learning" from the student. In a game called *Animals*, designed along the lines of the game "20 Questions," the computer asks the student yes/no questions to determine the identity of an animal he is thinking of. At the beginning of the game the computer starts with "elephant," "cow," and the question to distinguish them "Does it live on a farm?" loaded in its memory. If, for example, the student answers that his animal lives on a farm but is not a cow the computer will ask the student to name his animal and create a question that will distinguish it from a cow. As the game progresses and students add animals and questions to the computer's memory the demands made on the student's reading and writing skills expand. Another version of *Animals* has been written to include the categories of Animals, Objects, Cities, and People (Higgins and Johns 1984).

The potential of computer-learner interaction of the type found in programs such as *Eliza* and *Animals* has been largely untapped in CARI. A larger body of text than is currently used in these two programs might be presented in an *Eliza*-type format. The student could be instructed to skim or scan the text and a timer could be used to encourage faster reading or to keep track of the student's speed. The text might be built around increasingly difficult vocabulary based upon the appropriateness of the student's response, or it might include questions that elicit the student's making inferences. These might all apply to a text whose development is guided by the response of the student much like a series of letters. The similarity of this type of interchange to personal correspondence can be enhanced by adding the computer's capability to learn information overtly and covertly from the student and retain it for later use.

Program/learner control

Inherently, different media permit the student different degrees of control over the instruction they carry. For example, the book, or any other regular text format, usually allows the student very little control over his instruction. He does have the option of going back, if he knows where to look for what he needs. And he also has the option of skipping forward, but he runs the very real risk of missing something that he needs in order to comprehend the chapter he skips to.

The instructional medium with the potential for allowing the most learner control is the teacher. Some teachers, of course, use a teaching style that prohibits any but directed student activity. However, in the ESL classroom for academically oriented students, we often find students participating, even directing, class activities as part of their language learning experience.

The computer has two capabilities normally found only in a teacher that allow the student to modify the instruction he receives. The first of these characteristics is the ability to interact meaningfully with the student. This is a main focus of the field of Artificial Intelligence which we have just been discussing.

The second capability that the computer shares with the teacher is the ability to respond appropriately to different student input (Chapelle and Jamieson 1983). In computer programming, this is referred to as branching. The student does not have to be locked into step-by-step, or linear, instruction as he does in film. However, we must note here that even though the computer, like the teacher, is capable of adapting instruction to fit the student's needs, it doesn't always do so. Software can be written to permit or, often by default, to prohibit learner control.

In language learning it is often found advisable to encourage the student to play an active role in the selection and shaping of his instruction. When playing a more active role the student usually exhibits greater and longer concentration and more enthusiasm for the activities he participates in. He also practices a role he will have to play in his real-world language experience outside the classroom. Referring to this characteristic of CALL, Higgins and Johns state, "In this respect, as in many others, it may be that the crucial advantage of the computer as a medium for training is the opportunity to involve the trainee in the important decisions as to how the training will be carried out" (Higgins and Johns 1984:43).

Two areas in which the student may exercise control over his instruction are in selecting the content of the instruction and in selecting the design of his instruction.

Learner control of instructional content

Many programs regularly present the student with some sort of menu or list of selections when signing onto the program. The menu requires him to choose the lesson or exercise he wishes to work on. A typical CARI reading package offering instruction in a number of different skills presents the student with the choice, for example, of vocabulary building or speed reading exercises. At the end of the instructional activity he is returned to the same table of selections at which point he may then select an exercise on another skill.

Many programs also give the student a choice of textual content within a particular activity. For example, one version of *M-ss-ng L-nks* allows the student to select from a menu of nine different children's classics. Similarly, in *Quizit*, a vocabulary building game, the student may choose vocabulary from any of several different vocabulary sets organized according to topics (for example, Foods).

Another version of student input into text presentation permits the student to participate in the story-line development of the text. In *Story-Maker*, a student reads the initial segment of a story. He then chooses among several offerings of segments to follow. The story branches to a continuing segment based on the student's selection. Additionally, at some points the student is given the option of inserting his own story element. Text-based adventure games designed for reading instruction in which the student instructs the computer in its next move provide similar opportunities for the student to modify the textual content. The adventure games and interactive fiction found in the entertainment software market and described earlier are even more complex versions of this type.

Textual simulations of real life problems requiring solutions fall into a third type of program design utilizing student input to determine the development of the reading passage subject matter. *Action Mazes*, designed to be used by small groups of students, presents a problem together with optional courses of action. The group together selects an option, discovers what comes of it, and makes further selections, until it has worked its way toward a successful outcome.

Learner control of instructional design

In a previous part of this chapter we discussed instructional designs based upon differing levels of cognitive complexity. The student may be invited to choose which design at which level he feels is most appropriate to his individual learning needs. *Ticcit*, a CAI system developed at Brigham Young University in the 1970s, was designed to allow the student to select instruction according to a more detailed but similar hierarchy of instructional design types (Reigeluth 1979; Merrill 1984a, 1980). Experience with

Ticcit and other research in this area has suggested that a student can learn to improve his learning strategies by the selection of instructional designs (Merrill 1983). However, learner control over instructional design leads to most effective learning when the student is regularly given information about how much he has learned in relation to what he has yet to learn (Tennyson 1981-82).

Relatively little development in overt learner control of instructional design has yet occurred in CARI. To a certain extent, this reflects the limited development of CARI software with activities representative of more than one design type.

The most common example of activity including learner control that can be found in CARI software is the gloss function available in some programs. Blohm (1982) has developed a rather sophisticated glossing routine that allows the student to request either definitions or paraphrases of the reading text. Blohm suggests that this reading program contributes to the effectiveness of student learning by providing feedback on the strategies the student has used as indicated by the number and types of glossing he requested, in addition to his reading speed.

It is interesting to speculate on how learner control might be incorporated into a program like *M-ss-ng L-nks* in which the student selects the instructional format for the text: all vowels omitted, only first letters printed, every other word, the last letter of each word, the first word of each sentence, and so forth. In the first format, one might characterize the replacement of single vowels as an activity of low-level complexity since the students simply choose from among five possibilities. The other formats, however, which require the replacement of other combinations of letters, even entire words, are highly complex tasks. They require the student to select and use various reading strategies and types of information to complete the exercise. The difference in task complexity between the two formats could be pointed out to the student along with the fact that he could select one over the other based upon his learning needs; he would then be able to exercise conscious control over the design of his instruction.

Just as desirable from an instructional perspective would be to include in *M-ss-ng L-nks* instruction in strategies for identifying the missing elements. These might include strategies such as relating the word in question to the overall subject matter structure of the passage, relating the word to the probable grammatical structure of the sentence it occurs in, or relating a missing letter to the letters surrounding it. In addition, this instruction could be presented through a discovery learning mode, similar to what currently exists in *M-ss-ng L-nks*, or through a "teacher-" (in this case, read "program-") directed mode.[11]

There is much to be learned about learner control in CARI. Before it can be widely implemented there must be extensive development of instructional programming that includes rapid and accurate assessment of student learning processes, as attempted by Blohm's reading program. Effective use of learner control depends upon the student being aware of the level of his learning.

Additional effort must be devoted to identifying which learners benefit most from active learner control. Some students prefer a passive learning style in which the teacher or computer plays a more authoritarian role in instruction. These students may find CARI with significant learner control less desirable. This preference for a passive learning style may prove to be less widespread in a native speaking English student classroom than in a multi-cultural second language student class. In the academically-oriented ESL class, instruction is often designed to encourage students to take a more active part in order to introduce them to classroom strategies commonly expected of students in American higher education. Producers of ESL software may soon follow in designing programs, one of whose aims will be to teach students to exercise a greater amount of control over the instruction they receive.

8.5 CONCLUSION

We have discussed here the application of computer assisted instruction to reading instruction. Although we have made occasional references to the computer hardware that may be used in CARI, our emphasis has been primarily on software, that is, the instructional programming. Computer assisted learning, like all other learning, depends not so much on the medium of instruction as on the quality of the instruction presented through the medium (Kulik, Kulik, and Cohen 1980).

CARI software has been viewed from three perspectives: the Content of Instruction, the Design of Instruction, and the Computer/Learner Interaction. These are clearly not the only ways CARI software can be viewed, but together they form a structure for assessing the overall instructional capability of a particular program in the light of what is known to be possible in CAI.

It seems certain that computer assisted reading instruction will continue to expand in importance in language education. Its capability to present instruction adapted to the individual student sets it apart from all other nonhuman media. Whether or not that capability is utilized is the challenge that we as instructional designers and users all face.

NOTES

1. It is not my intention to state that no learning takes place in large classes. Students do, for example, learn conversational skills by observing highly interactive conversations between others without participating actively themselves.

2. These results showing student learning are, of course, predicated on the instruction being "good" instruction. CAI is no different from any other educational medium, including the teacher, in that students learn from good instruction and do not learn from poor instruction. Much of CAI's "bad press" early on was due to the quality of some of the instructional software available.

3. In this chapter, the word "content" will refer to the subject being taught; in CARI, "content" thus refers to the particular reading skill under instruction. To avoid confusion, when referring to the content of a reading passage used in a CARI exercise the terms "subject matter" or "textual content" will be used.

4. A tachistoscope is a device that is capable of projecting text for precise periods of time less than one second in duration. Tachistocopes have been used in instruction aimed at increasing reading speed.

5. Educational researchers have posited widely varying numbers of levels of cognitive complexity. Gagne (Aronson and Briggs 1983), for example, proposes five general types of learning which are further divided into more specific categories, all of which are arranged hierarchically in order of complexity. For the sake of simplicity in this discussion, I have limited the number to three.

6. It should be noted that there is some controversy over the importance of phonological rule mediation for reading comprehension, particularly in light of the constraints specific to L2 reading (see Grabe, this volume), although the issue is unresolved at present (Beck 1981; Smith 1982). Several "CARI" programs on the market include the topic; thus it has been addressed here as a possible source of reading instruction depending on the teacher's view of this practice.

7. Notetaking is occasionally referred to as a reading skill (Geoffrion and Geoffrion 1983), although the overt connection between them may not be obvious.

8. Several computer languages have been developed with the recursive structure found in natural language. One of these, LISP, is used extensively in AI research, but the only widespread use of it in education is LOGO, a dialect whose primary application to date has been in teaching non-language concepts (Loritz 1984).

9. *Shrdlu*, by Terry Winograd, was the forerunner of programming of this type and is still a model for "intelligent" conversation between computer and user (Dewdney 1985). *Shrdlu* "enables a person to communicate with a computer in English about a simulated world of blocks on a tabletop. The program analyzes requests, commands and statements made by the user and responds with appropriate words or with actions performed in the simulated scene" (Winograd 1984:142).

10. *Eliza*, like *Shrdlu*, was not created to be an instructional program, but rather was designed to demonstrate the capability of the computer to conduct meaningful communication with a user. However, a version of *Eliza* that can be adapted for instruction is available. At the moment, I am aware of German language instruction based on *Eliza*, though to my knowledge, it is yet to be used for English or ESL instruction.

11. Most producers of commercially available software go to great lengths to prevent others from making changes in their software. You may, however, tamper as much as you like with any software in the Public Domain. If you are interested in trying out some of the suggestions described here also see Higgins and Johns (1984) for a description of a forerunner to *M-ss-ng L-nks*.

FOR STUDY AND DISCUSSION

1. Discuss the strengths and weaknesses of several instructional media that you regularly use (textbooks, film, audiotape, blackboard, photographs, and, yes, even teacher). Be sure to include their suitability to class, small group, and individualized instruction. Also consider to what degree each can be used independently of the others.

2. What distinction is the author making between content and instructional design?

3. What are the different levels of cognitive complexity proposed by the author? Give examples of each. Discuss the suitability of these levels to CARI. Do you feel that the number should be reduced, increased, or remain the same?

4. Select one Bottom-up and one Top-down reading skill. How would you design learning activities of high, mid, and low cognitive complexity for each?

5. What is Artificial Intelligence? Discuss how it might be incorporated into CARI.

6. Discuss different potential roles for the teacher and other students in CARI.

7. Discuss advantages and disadvantages of allowing the learner control over the content and level of cognitive complexity of his learning task. How might these vary with students of different age, sex, or cultural background?

FOR FURTHER READING

It is difficult to keep up with the rapidly growing body of literature on computers in education. Following are suggestions for reading at the time this book goes to press. However, by the time you read this there will certainly be several new works well worth reading. Professional journal and newsletter editors have become aware of this interest, and reviews in these publications seems to be one of the most efficient means of 'keeping up.'

1. Computer Assisted Reading Instruction
    Geoffrion and Geoffrion (1983) provides a very readable and informative account of Computer Assisted Reading Instruction and how to use particular software packages with native speakers. Any of the books and articles by Wyatt are similarly informative regarding CARI in the ESL field.

2. Computer Assisted Language Instruction
    Both Higgins and Johns (1984) and Underwood (1984) are excellent resources for ideas on what the computer CAN do in language learning. I also recommend *CALICO Journal* for reports on current work in CALL research and development.

3. Artificial Intelligence and Learner Control
    Waldrop (1984) and Winograd (1984) serve as excellent introductions to the field of Artificial Intelligence. Papert's *Mindstorms* (1980) is a delightful journey into the potential of computers in learning.

4. Instructional Design
    Books and articles on instructional design are often rather heavy going for the noninstructional design specialist. Snelbecker (1974) and Reigeluth (1983) offer broad overviews of the field in a relatively digestible format.

5. Software Production
    Walker and Hess (1984) provides a wealth of information on all steps of CAI software from theoretical issues to production techniques. Kenning and Kenning (1983) is a short course in BASIC for the language teacher. It includes a very useful appendix that presents an extensive list of familiar language learning exercise types that are easy to "computerize." Higgins and Johns (1984) includes a discussion of software planning and production and extensive sample program listings.

SOFTWARE MENTIONED IN THIS CHAPTER

Most software that is referred to by name in this chapter is listed below. Those programs commercially available are listed with addresses to which you may write for further information. Those which are not commercially available are listed with reference to a bibliographical listing in which further description can be found.

Action Mazes
See Higgins and Johns 1984.

Animals
See Higgins and Johns 1984.

Cloze Call and *Text Write*
See Schripsema 1985.

Cutthroats — Infocom Inc., 55 Wheeler St., Cambridge, MA 02138
Also see Addams 1985.

Dragonriders of Pern — Epyx Inc., 1043 Kiel Ct., Sunnyvale, CA 94089
Also see Addams 1985.

Eliza — Artificial Intelligence Research Group, 921 N. La Jolla Ave., Los Angeles, CA 90046.
Also see Dewdney 1984; Higgins and Johns 1984.

Fahrenheit 451 — Trillium Corp., One Kendall Square, Cambridge, MA 02139.
Also see Addams 1985.

Gapper
See Morrison 1984.

Hitchhiker's Guide to the Galaxy — Infocom Inc., 55 Wheeler St., Cambridge, MA 02138.
Also see Navas 1985, and Schulz 1985.

Jumbler
See Higgins and Johns 1984.

John & Mary
See Higgins and Johns 1984.

Logo. Many, many versions. For partial listing see Watt 1984. Public domain version also available called *Ladybug* by David N. Smith, 44 Ole Musket Lane, Danbury, CT 06810.

M-ss-ng L-nks — Sunburst Communications, Room N 1, 39 Washington Ave., Pleasantville, NY 10570. Various versions in English and foreign languages.

Pal Reading Curriculum — Universal Systems for Education, 2120 Academy Circle, Suite E, Colorado Springs, CO 80909.
Also see Geoffrion and Geoffrion 1983.

Quizit — The Regents/ALA Company, Two Park Avenue, New York, NY 10016.

Reading Curriculum — CCC (Computer Curriculum Corporation), Palo Alto, CA.
Also see Geoffrion and Geoffrion 1983.

Reading Comprehension Program — PLATO Corrections Project
See Higgins and Johns 1984.

Reading Instruction for Beginners — Microteacher, Inc., 12760 High Bluff Drive, San Diego, CA 92130. Available with or without voice systhesizer.

Robots of Dawn — Epyx Inc., 1043 Kiel Ct., Sunnyvale, CA 94089.
Also see Addams 1985.

Shrdlu
See Dewdney 1984; Higgins and Johns 1984; Winograd 1984.

Story-Maker — Andee Rubin, Bolt Beranek and Newman, Inc., 50 Moulton Rd., Cambridge, MA 02138.
Also see Geoffrion and Geoffrion 1983; Higgins and Johns 1984.

Textman
See Geoffrion and Geoffrion 1983.

Ticcit — Brigham Young University, Provo, UT.
Also see Reigeluth 1979; Merrill 1983a, 1983b, 1984.

Whole Brain Spelling — Sublogic Communications Corp., 713 Edgebrook Dr., Champaign, IL 61820.

Window Letters — PLATO Early Reading Curriculum
See Geoffrion and Geoffrion 1983.

Young English Software — Addison-Wesley Publishing Company, Reading, MA 01867.

Zork I, II, & III. Infocom, Inc. 55 Wheeler St. Cambridge, MA 02138.

Bibliography

Bibliography

Adams, Marilyn J., and Allan Collins. 1979. A schematheoretic view of reading. In *New directions in discourse processing*, Roy O. Freedle (Ed.), 1–22. Norwood, N.J.: Ablex Publishing Corporation.

Adams, W. Royce. 1969. *Increasing reading speed.* London: Macmillan Company.

———. 1980. *Prep for better reading.* New York: Holt, Rinehart and Winston.

———. 1981. *Developing reading versatility.* New York: Holt, Rinehart and Winston.

Addams, Shay. 1985. Interactive fiction. *Popular Computing* 4(5):96–99, 180–2.

Akst, Geoffrey, Ruth Davis, and Virginia Slaughter (Eds.). 1984. *Microcomputers and basic skills in college: applications in reading, writing, English as a second language, and mathematics* (Spring, 1984). New York: Instructional Resources Center, Office of Academic Affairs, The City University of New York.

Alderson, C. 1979. The cloze procedure and proficiency in English as a foreign language. *TESOL Quarterly* 13(2):219–228.

———. 1983. Commentary on 'Alderson, 1979'. In *Issues in language testing research*, John Oller (Ed.), 213–217. Rowley, Mass.: Newbury House.

———. 1984. Reading in a foreign language: a reading problem or a language problem? In *Reading in a foreign language*, J. C. Alderson and A. H. Urquhart (Eds.), 1–24. New York: Longman.

Alderson, J. C. and A. H. Urquhart (Eds.). 1984. *Reading in a foreign language.* New York: Longman.

Al Rufai, M. H. 1976. Ability transfer and the teaching of reading. *English Language Teaching Journal* 30(3):236–241.

Anderson, Henning. 1973. Abductive and deductive change. *Language* 49(4): 765–793.

Anderson, Jonathan. 1972. The development of a reading laboratory for second language learners. *RELC Journal* 3(1 and 2):50–59. June-December 1972.

Anderson, Richard C. and P. David Pearson. 1984. A schematheoretic view of basic processes in reading. In *Handbook of reading research*, Pearson, P. David (Ed.), 255–292. New York: Longman.

Asimov, Issac. 1971. The eureka phenomenon. In *The left hand of the electron.* New York: Mercury Press. Reprinted in A. Eastman *et al. The Norton reader: an anthology of expository prose*, 4th ed., 97–107, 1977. New York: W. W. Norton & Co., Inc.

Bachman, L. 1982. The trait structure of cloze test scores. *TESOL Quarterly* 16(1):61–70.

Baker, Robert L. 1984. Foreign-language software: the state of the art or pick a card, any (flash) card. *CALICO Journal* 1(2):6–10.

Baltra, Armando. 1984. *Computer assisted language learning: L1 software for L2 students.* Sao Paulo, Brazil: Centro Eletronico de Linguas — CEL-LEP.

Bateson, G. 1979. *Mind and nature.* New York: Ballantine.

Baudoin, E. Margaret et al. 1977. *Reader's choice.* Ann Arbor: University of Michigan Press.

Baum, Joan. 1983. *Computers in the English class with particular attention to the City University of New York, Research monograph series, report no. 6* (October, 1983). New York: Instructional Resources Center, Office of Academic Affairs, The City University of New York.

Beck, Isabel. 1981. Reading problems and instructional practice. In G. Mackinnon and T. Waller (Eds.), 53–95. *Reading Research*, Vol. 2. New York: Academic Press.

Been, Sheila. 1975. Reading in the foreign language teaching program. *TESOL Quarterly* 9(3):233–242.

Berliner, David. 1981. Academic learning time and reading achievement. In *Comprehension and teaching: research review*, John Guthrie (Ed.). New York: Holt, Rinehart and Winston.

Berman, R. 1984. Syntactic components of the foreign language reading process. In *Reading in a foreign language.* J. C. Alderson and A. H. Urquhart (Eds.), 139–156. New York: Longman.

Bettelheim, Bruno, and Karen Zalen. 1981. *On learning to read: the child's fascination with meaning.* New York: A. Knopf.

Bever, T. G., and T. G. Bower. 1970. How to read without listening. In *Readings in applied transformational grammar*, Mark Lester (Ed.). New York: Holt, Rinehart and Winston.

Blanton, William E., and J. J. Tuinman (Eds.) 1972. *Reading: process and pedagogy.* Bloomington, Ind.: School of Education, Indiana University.

Blau, S. 1983. Invisible writing: investigating cognitive processes in writing. *College composition and communication* 34(3):297–312.

Blohm, P. J. 1982. I use the computer to ADVANCE advances in comprehension-strategy research. ERIC document ED 216 330.

Bradley, Virginia N. 1983-84. The surface features of four microcomputer reading programs. *Journal of Educational Technology Systems* 12(3):221–232.

Brown, Bruce, L. Dillon, K. Inouye, K. Barrus and D. Housen. 1981. An analysis of the rapid reading controversy. In *The social psychology of reading*, John Edwards (Ed.). Silver Spring, Md: Institute of Modern Languages, Inc.

Brown, Gillian, and George Yule. 1983. *Discourse analysis.* New York: Cambridge University Press.

Brown, J. D. 1984. A cloze is a cloze is a cloze? In *On TESOL 83*, J. Handscombe, R. Orem, and B. Taylor (Eds.), 109–119. Washington, D. C.: TESOL.

Brown, P. J. and S. B. Hirst. 1983. Writing reading courses: the interrelationship of theory and practice. In *Language teaching projects for the third world*, C. Brumfit (Ed.), 135–150. New York: Pergamon Press.

Brumfit, C. J. 1977. The teaching of advanced reading skills in foreign languages, with particular reference to English as a foreign language. In *Language teaching and linguistics: surveys*, 1978, Valerie Kinsella (Ed.). Cambridge: Cambridge University Press.

Burns, Paul, and Betty Roe. 1980. *Informal reading assessment*. Chicago: Rand McNally College Publishing Co.

Calfee, Robert, and Dorothy Pointkowski. 1981. The reading diary: acquisition of decoding. *Reading Research Quarterly* 16(3):346–373.

Carrell, Patricia L. 1984a. Evidence of a formal schema in second language comprehension. *Language Learning* 34(2):87–112.

———. 1984b. The effects of rhetorical organization in ESL readers. *TESOL Quarterly* 18(3):441–469.

———. 1984c. Some causes of text-boundedness and schema interface in ESL reading. Paper presented at the 18th Annual TESOL Convention, Houston, March, 1984.

Carrell, Patricia L., and Joan C. Eisterhold. 1983. Schema theory and ESL reading pedagogy. *TESOL Quarterly* 17(4):553–573.

Chabot, Robert J.; H. David Zehr; Olga V. Prinzo; and Thomas V. Petros. 1984. The speed of word recognition subprocesses and reading achievement in college students. *Reading Research Quarterly* 19(2):147–161.

Chapelle, Carol, and Joan Jamieson. 1983. Recognition of student input in computer-assisted language learning. *CALICO Journal* 1(2):11–13.

Chapman, L. J. 1981. The perception of language cohesion during fluent reading. In *Processing of visible language,* Vol. 1. P. Koleis, M. Wrolstad, and H. Bauma (Eds.). New York: Plenum Press.

Chastain, Kenneth. 1976. *Developing second language skills: Theory to practice.* 2nd ed. Chicago: Rand McNally College Publishing Co.

Clarke, Mark. A. 1978. Reading in Spanish and English: evidence from adult ESL student. *Language Learning* 29(1):121–150.

Clarke, Mark A., and Sandra Silberstein. 1977. Toward a realization of psycholinguistic principles in the ESL reading class. *Language Learning* 27(1):135–154.

Coady, James. 1979. A psycholinguistic model of the ESL reader. In *Reading in a second language,* R. Mackay, B. Barkman and R. R. Jordan (Eds.). Rowley, Mass.: Newbury House.

Coates, Richard. 1982. State of the art: phonology. *Language Teaching* 15(1):2–18.

Cohen, Andrew; H. Glassman; P. R. Rosenbaum-Cohen; J. Ferrara; and J. Fine. 1980. Reading English for special purposes: discourse analysis and the use of English informants. *TESOL Quarterly 13(4):551–564.*

Cohen, Andrew, and Carol Hosenfeld. 1981. Some uses of mentalistic data in second language research. *Language Learning* 31(2):285–313.

Cooper, M. 1984. Linguistic competence of practiced and unpracticed non-mature readers of English. In *Reading in a foreign language*. J. C. Alderson and A. H. Urquhart (Eds.), 122–135. New York: Longman.

Croft, Kenneth (Ed.). 1980. *Readings on English as a second language*. Cambridge, Mass.: Winthrop.

Cziko, G. 1983. Another response to Shanahan, Kamil and Tobin: Further reasons to keep the cloze case open. *Reading Research Quarterly* 18(3):361–365.

Davies, Alan. 1984. Simple, simplified, and simplification: what is authentic? In *Reading in a foreign language*, J. Charles Alderson and A. H. Urquhart (Eds.), 181–196. London and New York: Longman.

Davies, A., and H. Widdowson. 1974. The teaching of reading and writing. In *Techniques in applied linguistics*, Vol. 3, J. P. B. Allen and S. P. Corder (Eds.), 155–200. Oxford: Oxford University Press.

deBeaugrande, Robert. 1980. *Text, discourse, and process*. Norwood, N.J.: Ablex.

———. 1984a. *Text production: toward a science of composition*. Norwood, N.J.: Ablex.

———. 1984b. Learning to read vs. learning to learn: a discourse processing approach. In *Learning and comprehension of text*, H. Mandl, N. Stein, and T. Trabasso (Eds.), 159–191. Hillsdale, N.J.: Lawrence Erlbaum Associates, Publishers.

deBeaugrande, Robert, and Wolfgang Dressler. 1981. *Introduction to text linguistics*. Harlow: Longman Group.

Dewdney, A. K. 1985. Artificial insanity: when a schizophrenic program meets a computerized analyst. *Scientific American* 252(1):14–20.

Dishner, E. K., and J. E. Readence. 1977. Getting started: using the textbook diagnostically. *Reading World* 17(1):36–49.

Downing, John. 1979. *Reading and reasoning*. New York: Springer-Verlag.

Drayton, Anne Marie, and Charles Skidmore. 1985. *In good company: a skill-building reader*. Reading, Mass.: Addison-Wesley Publishing Co.

Dubin, Fraida, and Elite Olshtain. 1980. The interface of writing and reading. *TESOL Quarterly* 14(3):353–363.

———. 1981. *Reading by all means*. Reading, Mass.: Addison-Wesley Publishing Co.

———. 1984. *Three easy pieces: reading for fluency and enjoyment*. Reading, Mass.: Addison-Wesley Publishing Co.

———. In press. *Course design: developing programs and materials for language learning*. Cambridge: Cambridge University Press.

Edwards, John R. (Ed.) 1981. *The social psychology of reading*, Vol 1. Silver Spring, Md.: Institute of Modern Languages.

Eisenmann, Carol. B. 1984. Learner control and simulation: a review of the literature. Unpublished paper. University of Southern California.

Elias, Jo Anne. 1975. Predicting your way through written English: an approach to teaching advanced reading to ESL students. In *On TESOL '75*, M. Burt and H. Dulay (Eds.). Washington, D.C.: TESOL.

Elley and Mangubhai. 1983. The impact of reading on second language learning. *Reading Research Quarterly* 19(1):53–67.

ELS (English Language Services). 1982. *An English Reading Test*. (Harold King and Russell Campbell).

England, Elaine. 1983. Design and evaluation issues on CAL materials. *CALICO Journal* 2(1):11–13.

Eskey, David E. 1973. A model program for teaching advanced reading to students of English as a foreign language. *Language Learning* 23(2):169–184.

———. 1983. Learning to read versus reading to learn: Resolving the instructional paradox. *English Language Teaching Forum* XXI(3):2–4.

Ferguson, Charles. 1959. Diglossia. *Word* 15:325–340. Reprinted in *Language and social context*, P. P. Giglioli (Ed.), 232–251. New York: Penguin Books.

Ferguson, Nicolas. 1973. Some aspects of the reading process. *English Language Teaching* 28(1):29–34.

Flahive, D. 1982. The use of the URI in the measurement of reading proficiency. In *Proceedings of the second annual international conference on frontiers of language proficiency and dominance testing. Occasional papers on Linguistics, Number 3*, 37–45. Carbondale, Ill. Dept. of Linguistics, Southern Illinois University.

Frager, A. M. 1984. How good are content teachers' judgments of the reading abilities of secondary school students? *Journal of Reading* 27:402–406.

Fry, Edward. 1975. *Reading drills for speed and comprehension*, 2nd ed. Providence, R.I.: Jamestown Publishers.

Gagne, R. 1977. *The conditions of learning*, 3rd ed. New York: Holt, Rinehart and Winston.

———. 1978. Reading achievement and diagnostic testing. In *Proceedings of the second annual international conference on frontiers of language proficiency and dominance testing. Occasional papers on Linguistics, Number 3*, 1–15. Carbondale, Ill.: Dept. of Linguistics, Southern Illinois University.

Galinski, C. 1982. Information and documentation in science and technology in Japan. *Journal of Information Science* 5:63–77.

Gaskill, William H. 1979. The teaching of intermediate reading in the ESL classroom. In *Teaching English as a second or foreign language*, M. Celce-Murcia and Lois McIntosh (Eds.), Rowley, Mass.: Newbury House.

Geoffrion, Leo D., and Olga P. Geoffrion. 1983. *Computers and reading instruction*. Reading, Mass: Addison-Wesley Publishing Co.

Gibson, E. J., and H. Levin. 1975. *The psychology of reading*. Cambridge, Mass.: MIT Press.

Goodman, Kenneth S. 1967. Reading: a psycholinguistic guessing game. *Journal of the Reading Specialist* 4:126–135.

———. 1969. Analysis of oral reading miscues: applied psycholinguistics. *Reading Research Quarterly* 5,1:9–30.

———. 1970. Psycholinguistic universals in the reading process. *Journal of Typographic Research* 4:103–110.

———. 1981. Miscue analysis and future research directions. In *Linguistics and literacy Series 1: Learning to read in different languages,* S. Hudelston (Ed.), ix-xiii. Arlington, Va.: Center for Applied Linguistics.

Goodman, Kenneth S., and Yetta Goodman. 1983. Reading and writing relationship: pragmatic functions. *Language Arts* 60(5):590–599.

Goodman, Yetta M. 1975. Reading strategy lessons: expanding reading effectiveness. In *Help for the reading teacher: new directions in research,* W. Page (Ed.), Urbana, Ill.: National Council of Teachers of English and ERIC.

Goodman, Yetta M. and Carolyn Burke. 1980. *Reading Strategies: Focus on Comprehension.* New York: Holt, Rinehart and Winston.

Gordon, Belita. 1983. A guide to postsecondary reading tests. *Reading World* (10):45–53.

Gorman, Thomas P. 1979. Teaching reading at the advanced level. In *Teaching English as a second or foreign language,* M. Celce-Murcia and Lois McIntosh (Eds.), Rowley, Mass.: Newbury House.

Gough, P. B. 1972. One second of reading. In *Language by eye and by ear,* J. F. Cavanaugh and I. G. Mattingly (Eds.), 331–358. Cambridge, Mass.: MIT Press.

Grabe, William. 1985. Reassessing the term 'interactive'. Paper presented at the 19th Annual TESOL Convention, New York, April, 1985.

Grabe, W., and Robert B. Kaplan. 1986. Science, technology, language, and information: implications for language and language-in-education planning. To appear in *International Journal of the Sociology of Language.*

Graves, Michael; Cheryl Cook; and Michael Laberge. 1983. Effects of previewing difficult short stories on low ability junior high school students' comprehension, recall, and attitudes. *Reading Research Quarterly* 18(3):262–276.

Grellet, Francoise. 1981. *Developing reading skills: a practical guide to reading comprehension exercises.* New York: Cambridge University Press.

Griffin, Suzanne, and John Dennis. 1979. *Reflections.* Rowley, Mass.: Newbury House.

Grinols, Anne Bradstreet. 1984. The potential of computer-assisted instruction in college reading programs. In *Microcomputers and basic skills in college,* Geoffrey Akst (Ed.). New York: Instructional Resources Center, Office of Academic Affairs, The City University of New York.

Guthrie, John. 1981a. How to recognize a reading comprehension program: an afterward. In *Comprehension and teaching: research,* John Guthrie (Ed.), Newark, Del.: International Reading Association.

———. 1981b. Reading in New Zealand: achievement and volume. *Reading Research Quarterly* 17(1):6–17.

Guthrie, John (Ed.). 1981c. *Comprehension and teaching: research.* Newark, Del.: International Reading Association.

Haber, Lyn, and Ralph Norman Haber. 1981. Perceptual processes in reading: an analysis-by-synthesis model. In *Neuropsychological and cognitive processes in reading,* Francis Pirozzoli and Merlin Wittrock (Eds.). New York: Academic Press.

Halliday, M., and R. Hasan. 1976. *Cohesion in English.* New York: Longman.

Hamp-Lyons, Elizabeth. 1982. *Advanced reading and writing, Communication and culture, Discourse in action, Insights, Reader's choice, Reading English for academic study, Skillful reading.* Reviewed in *TESOL Quarterly* 16(2):253–262.

Harris, Albert J., and Edward R. Sipay. 1980. *How to increase reading ability,* 7th ed. New York: Longman.

———. 1985. *How to increase reading ability,* 8th ed. New York: Longman.

Harris, David P. 1966. *Reading improvement exercises for students of English as a second language.* Englewood Cliffs, N.J.: Prentice Hall.

Harrison, Brian. 1978. *The danger light.* Rowley, Mass.: Newbury House.

Hatch, E. 1979. Reading in a second language. In *Teaching English as a second or foreign language,* M. Celce-Murcia and Lois McIntosh (Eds.). Rowley, Mass.: Newbury House.

Haynes, Margot. 1984. Patterns and perils in second language reading. In *On TESOL '83,* J. Handscombe, R. Orem, and B. Taylor (Eds.). Washington, D.C.:TESOL.

Heaton, J. 1975. *Writing English language tests.* New York: Longman.

Higgins, John. 1983. Grammarland: a non-directive use of the computer in language learning. Paper presented at 17th Annual TESOL Convention, Toronto, March, 1983.

———. 1984. Reading and risk-taking: a role for the computer. *ELT Journal* 38(3):192–198.

Higgins, John, and Tim Johns. 1984. *Computers in Language Learning.* Reading, Mass.: Addison-Wesley Publishing Co.

Hill, J. K. 1981. Effective reading in a foreign language: an experimental reading course in English for overseas students. *English Language Teaching Journal* 35(3): 270–281.

Hoffman, J., and W. Rutherford. 1984. Effective reading programs: a critical review of outline studies. *Reading Research Quarterly* 20(1):79–92.

Hosenfeld, C. 1984. Case studies of ninth grade readers. In *Reading in a foreign language.* J. C. Alderson and A. H. Urquhart (Eds), 231–244. New York: Longman.

Hosenfeld, C. et al. 1981. Second language reading: a curricular sequence for teaching reading strategies. *Foreign Language Annals* 14:415–422.

Hudelston, Sarah (Ed.). 1981. *Learning to read in different languages. Linguistics and Literacy, Series 1.* Arlington, Va.: Center For Applied Linguistics.

Hudson, T. 1982. The effects of induced schemata on the "shortcircuit" in L2 reading: non-decoding factors in L2 reading performance. *Language Learning* 32(1):1–31.

Ibrahim, Salwa. 1979. Advanced reading: teaching patterns of writing in the social sciences. In *Reading in a second language*, R. Mackay, B. Barkman, and R. R. Jordan (Eds.), 187–198. Rowley, Mass.: Newbury House.

Ilyin, Donna; C. Doherty; L. Lee; and L. Leny. 1981. *ELSA: English language skills assessment in a reading context*. Rowley, Mass.: Newbury House.

Jamieson, Joan, and Carol Chapelle. 1984. Prospects in computer assisted language lessons. *CATESOL Occasional Papers* 10(Fall, 1984):17–34.

Jenkins, J., and D. Pany. 1980. Teaching reading comprehension in the middle grades. In *Theoretical issues in reading comprehension*, R. Spiro, B. Bruce and W. Brewer (Eds.). Hillsdale, N.J.: Lawrence Erlbaum Associates, Publishers, 555–573.

Johns, A. 1981. Necessary English: a faculty survey. *TESOL Quarterly* 15(1):51–57.

Johnson, R. K. 1982. Questioning some assumptions about cloze testing. In *Language testing*, J. B. Heaton (Ed.), 59–72. London: Modern English Publications.

Johnson, Patricia. 1981. Effects on reading comprehension of a language complexity and cultural background of a text. *TESOL Quarterly* 15(1):169–181.

———. 1982. Effects on reading comprehension of building background knowledge. *TESOL Quarterly* 16(4):503–516.

Johnston, Peter. 1981. Implications of basic research for the assessment of reading comprehension. (Technical report No. 206). Urbana-Champaign: University of Illinois, Center for the Study of Reading, May.

———. 1984. Assessment in reading. In *Handbook of reading research*, Pearson, P. David (Ed.), 147–182. New York: Longman.

Jones, M. B., and E. C. Pikulski. 1974. Cloze for the classroom. *Journal of Reading* 17(6):432–438.

Judson, Horace. 1972. *The techniques of reading*, 3rd ed. New York: Harcourt Brace Jovanovich.

Kaplan, Robert B. 1982. Information science and ESP. Paper presented at the 16th Annual TESOL Convention, Honolulu, May, 1982.

———. 1983. Language and Science policies of new nations (Editorial). *Science*, 221:4614. (Sept. 2, 1983).

———. 1984. Reading and writing: assumptions and presuppositions. *The American Language Journal* 2(2):39–48.

Kenning, M. J., and M-M. Kenning. 1983. *An introduction to computer assisted language teaching*. Oxford: Oxford University Press.

Klare, George. 1984. Readability. In *Handbook of reading research*, P. D. Pearson (Ed.), 681–744. New York: Longman.

Klein-Braley, C. 1983. A cloze is a cloze is a question. In *Issues in language testing research*, John Oller (Ed.), 218–228. Rowley, Mass.: Newbury House.

Krashen, Stephen D. 1982. *Principles and practice in second language acquisition*. New York: Pergamon.

———. 1984. *Writing: research, theory and application*. New York: Pergamon.

Krashen, Stephen, and Tracy Terrell. 1983. *The natural approach*. San Francisco: Alemany Press.

Kucer, Stephen. 1983. Personal communication. October.

Kulik, James A.; Kulik, Chen-Lin C.; and Cohen Peter A. 1980. Effectiveness of computer-based college teaching: a metaanalysis of findings. *Review of Educational Research*, 50(4):525–544.

Leach, Geoffrey, and Andrew Beale. 1984. State of the art: computers in English language research. *Language Teaching* 17(3):216–229.

Lesgold, Alan M., and Charles A. Perfetti. 1981a. Interactive processes in reading: Where do we stand? In *Interactive processes in reading*, Alan Lesgold and Charles A. Perfetti (Eds.). Hillsdale, N.J.: Lawrence Erlbaum Associates, Publishers.

Lesgold, Alan M., and Charles A. Perfetti (Eds.). 1981b. *Interactive processes in reading*. Hillsdale, N.J.: Lawrence Erlbaum Associates, Publishers.

Lesiak, Judi, and Sharon Bradley-Johnson. 1983. *Reading assessment for placement and programming*. Springfield, Ill.: Charles C. Thomas Publisher.

Levenstan, E.; R. N. R.; and S. Blum-Kulka. 1984. Discourse analysis and the testing of reading comprehension by cloze techniques. In *Reading for professional purposes*, A. K. Pugh and J. M. Ulijn (Eds.), 202–212. Exeter, N. H.: Heinemann Educational Books.

Lewin, Beverly. 1984. Reading between the lines. *ECT Journal* 38(2):121–126.

Lewis, Richard. 1973. *Reading for adults*. London: Longman.

Loritz, Donald J. 1983. Artificial intelligence and computer assisted ESL instruction. Paper presented at 17th Annual TESOL Convention, Toronto, March, 1983.

———. 1984. Artificial intelligence and L2 courseware. Paper presented in Panel on CAI & Second Language Learning at 1983 Second Language Research Forum, Los Angeles, February, 1984.

Mackay, Ronald. 1979. Teaching the information-gathering skills. In *Reading in a second language*, R. Mackay, B. Barkman, and R. R. Jordan (Eds.), 79–90. Rowley, Mass.: Newbury House.

Mackay, R.; B. Barkman; and R. R. Jordan (Eds.). 1979. *Reading in a second language*. Rowley, Mass.: Newbury House.

Madsen, Harold. 1983. *Techniques in testing*. New York: Oxford University Press.

Mahon, Denise. 1981. Increasing reading rate without anxiety. J. Haskell (Ed.) *Focus on the Learner, The Collected Papers of the Eighth Annual Convention of Illinois TESOL / BE*, Spring, 1981.

Markosian, Lawrence Z. and Ager, Tryg A. 1983. Applications of parsing theory to computer-assisted instruction. In *SYSTEM, Special Issue: Computer-Assisted Language Instruction*, David H. Wyatt (Ed.), 11(1):3–11.

Markstein, Linda, and Louise Hirasawa (Eds.). 1981. *Developing reading skills: intermediate*. Rowley, Mass.: Newbury House.

———. 1982. *Expanding reading skills: intermediate*. Rowley, Mass.: Newbury House.

―――. 1983a. *Developing reading skills: advanced,* 2nd ed. Rowley, Mass.: Newbury House.

―――. 1983b. *Expanding reading skills: advanced,* 2nd ed. Rowley, Mass.: Newbury House.

Martin, Anne. 1980. Proficiency of university-level advanced ESL students in processing hierarchical information in context. Doctoral dissertation, University of Southern California.

McClelland, J., and D. Rumelhart. 1981. An interactive-activation model of the effect of context in perception. Part I: An account of basic findings. *Psychological Review* 88:375–407.

McKeown, M. G.; J. L. Beck; R. C. Omanson; and C. A. Perfetti. The effects of long-term vocabulary instruction on reading comprehension: a replication. *Journal of Reading Behavior,* 1983.

McPortland, Pamela. 1983. *Americana: a basic reader.* New York: Harcourt Brace Jovanovich.

Merrill, M. David. 1980. Learner control in computer based learning. *Computers & Education* 4:77–95.

―――. 1983. Component display theory. In *Instructional design theories and models: an overview of their current status,* by Charles M. Reigeluth (Ed.). Hillsdale, N.J.: Lawrence Erlbaum Associates, Publishers.

―――. 1984a. What is learner control. In *Instructional development: the state of the art* by Ronald K. Bass and Charles R. Dills (Eds.). Dubuque: Kendall/Hunt Publishers.

―――. 1984b. Don't bother me with instructional design; I'm too busy programming. Paper presented in Panel on CAI & Second Language Learning at 1983 Second Language Research Forum, Los Angeles, February, 1984.

Miller, Lyle L. 1984. *Increasing reading efficiency.* 5th ed. New York: Holt, Rinehart and Winston.

Miller, Wanda M., and Sharon Steeber. 1985a. *Reading faster and understanding more,* Book 1. 2nd ed. Boston: Little, Brown and Company.

―――. 1985b. *Reading faster and understanding more,* Book 2. 2nd ed. Boston: Little, Brown and Company.

Miller, Wanda M.; Sharon Steeber; and Doris Flood Ladd. 1981. *Reading faster and understanding more,* Book 3. Boston: Little, Brown and Company.

Mitchell, D. C. 1982. *The process of reading.* New York: John Wiley and Sons.

Morrison, Donald M. 1984. GAPPER: a microcomputer-based learning game. *System* 12(2):169–180.

Multi-read II: A multi level reading kit. Chicago: Science Research Associates.

Nagy, W.; P. Herman; and R. C. Anderson. 1985. Learning words from context. *Reading Research Quarterly* 20(2):233–253.

Navas, Deborah. 1985. Is it fiction? *Popular Computing* 4(5):182.

Nuttall, Christine. 1982. *Teaching reading skills in a foreign language*. London: Heinemann.

Obah, Thelma. 1983. Prior knowledge and the quest for new knowledge: the third world dilemma. *Journal of Reading* 27(2):129–132.

Oller, John. 1979. *Language tests at school*. New York: Longman.

Ostler, S. 1980. A survey of academic needs for advanced ESL. *TESOL Quarterly* 14(4):489–502.

Papert, Seymour. 1980. *Mindstorms: children, computers, and powerful ideas*. New York: Basic Books, Inc.

Parker, D. H. 1959. *SRA reading laboratories*. Chicago: Science Research Associates.

Pearson, P. David. 1984a. Direct explicit teaching of comprehension. In *Comprehension instruction: perspectives and suggestions*, G. Duffy, L. Roehler and J. Mason (Eds.), 223–233. New York: Longman.

Pearson, P. David (Ed.), 1984b. *Handbook of reading research*. New York: Longman.

Perfetti, Charles A. 1985. *Reading ability*. New York: Oxford Press.

Perfetti, Charles A., and Steven Roth. 1981. Some of the interactive processes in reading and their role in reading skill. In *Interactive Processes in Reading*, Alan M. Lesgold and Charles Perfetti (Eds.). Hillsdale, N.J.: Lawrence Erlbaum Associates, Publishers.

Perkins, K., and K. Pharis. 1980. TOEFL scores in relation to standardized reading tests. In *Research in language testing*, J. W. Oller, Jr., and K. Perkins (Eds.), 142–146. Rowley, Mass.: Newbury House.

Pikulski, John, and Timothy Shanahan (Eds.). 1982. *Approaches to the informal evaluation of reading*. Newark, Del.: International Reading Association.

Pimsleur, Paul, and Donald Berger. 1974. *Encounters*. New York: Harcourt Brace Jovanovich.

Pirozzoli, Francis, and Merlin Wittrock (Eds.). 1981. *Neuropsychological and cognitive processes in reading*. New York: Academic Press.

Rakes, Thomas; Joyce Choate; and Gayle Waller. 1983. *Individual evaluation procedures in reading*. Englewood Cliffs, N.J.: Prentice-Hall.

Rayner, K. 1978. Eye movements in reading and information processing. *Psychological Bulletin* 85(3):618–660.

———. 1981. Eye movements and the perceptual span in reading. In *Neuropsychological and cognitive processes in reading*. F. Pirozzoli and M. Wittrock (Eds.). New York: Academic Press.

Reading attainment system 2. Danbury, Conn.: Grolier Educational Corporation.

Reading attainment system 3. Danbury, Conn.: Grolier Educational Corporation.

Reading for understanding junior. Chicago: Science Research Associates.

Research lab. Chicago: Science Research Associates.

Reigeluth, Charles. M. 1979. Ticcit to the future: advances in instructional theory for CAI. *Journal of Computer-Based Instruction* 6(2):40–46.

Reigeluth, Charles M. (Ed.). 1983. *Instructional design theories and models: an overview of their current status.* Hillsdale, N.J.: Lawrence Erlbaum Associates, Publishers.

Richards, J. 1983. Listening comprehension: approach, design, procedure. *TESOL Quarterly* 17(2):219–240.

———. 1984. Language curriculum development. *RELC Journal* 15(1):1–29.

Richards, J., and T. Rodgers. 1982. Method: approach, design and procedure. *TESOL Quarterly* 16(2):153–168.

Rigg, Pat. 1977. The miscue-ESL project. In *On TESOL '77,* H. Douglas Brown *et al* (Eds.), 109–117. Washington, D.C.: TESOL.

Rivers, W., and M. Temperley. 1978. *A practical guide to the teaching of English as a second or foreign language.* New York: Oxford University Press.

Robertson, D. 1983. English language use, needs, and proficiency among foreign students at the University of Illinois at Urbana/Champaign. PhD. dissertation University of Illinois at Urbana/Champaign.

Robinson, Francis P. 1962. *Effective reading.* New York: Harper and Brothers.

Romiszowski, A. J. 1984. *Designing instructional systems: decision making in course planning and curriculum design.* New York: Nichols Publishing.

Rudd, J. C. 1969. A new approach to reading efficiency. *English Language Teaching* 23(3):231–237.

Rumelhart, David E. 1977. Toward an interactive model of reading. In *Attention and performance.* Vol. 1. Stanislaw Dornic (Ed.), 573–603. New York: Academic Press.

———. 1980. Schemata: The building blocks of cognition. In *Theoretical issues in reading comprehension,* Rand J. Spiro, Betram C. Bruce, and William E. Brewer (Eds.). Hillsdale, New Jersey: Lawrence Erlbaum Associates, Publishers.

———. 1984. Understanding understanding. In *Understanding reading comprehension: cognition, language, and the structure of prose,* J. Flood (Ed.), 1–20. Newark, Del.: International Reading Association.

Samuels, S. Jay. 1981. Characteristics of exemplary reading programs. In *Comprehension and teaching: research reviews,* John Guthrie (Ed.), 255–273. Newark, Del.: International Reading Association.

Samuels. S. Jay, and P. Eisenberg. 1981. A framework for understanding the reading process. In *Neuropsychological and cognitive processes in reading,* F. Pirozzolo and M. Wittrock (Eds.). New York: Academic Press.

Samuels, S. Jay and M. Kamil. 1984. Models of the reading process. In *Handbook of reading research,* Pearson, P. David (Ed.), 185–224. New York: Longman.

Saville-Troike, M. 1973. Reading and the audio-lingual method. In *Reading in a second language: hypotheses, organization, and practice,* R. Mackay, B. Barkman, and R. R. Jordan (Eds.). Rowley, Mass.: Newbury House.

Schell, Leo M. (Ed.). 1981. Diagnostic and criterion referenced tests: review and evaluation. Newark, Del.: International Reading Association.

Schripsema, Robert J. 1985. CLOZE CALL and TEXT WRITE: a reading skills development package utilizing computer assisted language learning. Unpublished paper. University of Southern California.

Schuberth, R. E.; K. T. Spoehr; and D. M. Lane. 1981. Effects of stimulus and contextual information on the lexical decision process. *Memory and cognition.* 9:68–77.

Schulz, Monte. 1985. Review of "The Hitchhiker's guide to the Galaxy." *Popular Computing* 4(5):160–162.

Seliger, Herbert W. 1972. Improving reading speed and comprehension in English as a second language. *English Language Teaching* 27(1):48–55.

Shanahan, T. 1983. A response to Henks and Cziko. *Reading Research Quarterly* 18(3):366–367.

Shanahan, T.; M. Kamil; and A. Tobin. 1982. Cloze as a measure of intersentential comprehension. *Reading Research Quarterly* 17(2):229–255.

Singer, H. 1981a. Teaching the acquisition phase of reading development: an historical perspective. In *Perception of print*, O. Tzeng and H. Singer (Eds.). Hillsdale, N. J.: Lawrence Erlbaum, Associates, Publishers.

———. 1981b. Instruction in reading acquisition. In *Perception of print*, O. Tzeng, and H. Singer (Eds.), 291–311. Hillsdale, N.J.: Lawrence Erlbaum Associates, Publishers.

Smith, Frank. 1971. *Understanding reading*, 1st ed. New York: Holt, Rinehart and Winston.

———. 1973. *Psycholinguistics and reading.* New York: Holt, Rinehart and Winston.

———. 1975. *Comprehension and learning.* New York: Holt, Rinehart and Winston.

———. 1978. *Understanding reading: a psycholinguistic analysis of reading and learning to read*, 2nd ed. New York: Holt, Rinehart and Winston.

———. 1982. *Understanding reading: a psycholinguistic analysis of reading and learning to read.* 3rd ed. New York: Holt, Rinehart and Winston.

———. 1984. The promise and threat of microcomputers for language learning. In *On TESOL 83,* J. Handscombe, R. Orem, and B. Taylor (Eds.), 1–18. Washington, D.C.: TESOL.

Snelbecker, Glenn E. 1974. *Learning theory, instructional theory, and psychoeducational design.* New York: McGraw-Hill.

Spargo, Edward and Glenn R. Williston. 1980. *Timed readings: Fifty 400-word passages with questions for building reading speed.* Books 1–10. Providence, R.I.: Jamestown Publishers.

Spoehr, Kathryn T., and Richard E. Schuberth. 1981. Processing words in context. In *Perception of print: Reading research in experimental psychology,* Ovid J. L. Tzeng and Harry Singer (Eds.). Hillsdale, N.J.: Lawrence Erlbaum Associates, Publishers.

Stanovich, Keith E. 1980. Toward an interactive-compensatory model of individual differences in the development of reading fluency. *Reading research quarterly* 16(1):32–71.

Stanovich, Keith. 1981a. Attentional and automatic context effects. In *Interactive processes in reading*, A. Lesgold and C. Perfetti (Eds.), 241–267. Hillsdale, N.J.: Lawrence Erlbaum Associates, Publishers.

———. 1981b. Letter to the editor. *Reading Research Quarterly* 17(1):157–159.

Stevenson, D. 1982. All of the above: On problems in the testing of FL reading. *System* 9(3):267–273.

Stevick, Earl W. 1963. *A workbook in language teaching.* New York, Nashville: Abingdon Press.

———. 1976. *Memory, meaning, and method.* Rowley, Mass.: Newbury House.

———. 1980. *Teaching languages: A way and ways.* Rowley, Mass.: Newbury House.

———. 1982. *Teaching and learning languages.* Cambridge: Cambridge University Press.

Stotsky, Sandra. 1983. Research on reading/writing relationships: a synthesis and suggested directions. *Language Arts* 60(5):627–642.

Strei, Gerry. 1983. Format for the evaluation of courseware used in computer-assisted language instruction. *CALICO Journal* 1(3):7–9, 16.

Stubbs, Michael. 1983. *Discourse analysis: the sociolinguistic analysis of natural language.* Chicago: The University of Chicago Press.

Taylor, Carolyn. 1985. Schema theory, expectations and authenticity in listening comprehension materials. Paper presented at TESOL convention, New York, April, 1985.

Taylor, I., and M. Taylor. 1983. *The psychology of reading.* New York: Academic Press.

Tennyson, Robert D. 1981–82. Interactive effect of cognitive learning theory with computer attributes in the design of computer-assisted instruction. *Journal of Educational Technology Systems,* 10(2):175–186.

Thonis, Eleanor. 1970. *Teaching reading to non-English speakers.* New York: Collier and Macmillan International.

———. 1983. Reading instruction for language minority students. In *Schooling and language minority students: a theoretical framework.* Los Angeles: Evaluation, Dissemination and Assessment Center, California State University, Los Angeles.

Tzeng, Ovid, and Daisy Hung. 1981. Linguistic determinism: a written language perspective. In *Perception of print*, O. Tzeng and H. Singer (Eds.), 237–255. Hillsdale, N.J.: Lawrence Erlbaum Associates, Publishers.

Underwood, John H. 1984. *Linguistics, computers and the language teacher.* Rowley, Mass.: Newbury House.

van Dijk, T., and W. Kintsch. 1983. *Strategies of discourse comprehension.* New York: Academic Press.

van Naerssen, Margaret. 1985. Relaxed reading in ESP. *TESOL Newsletter.* 19:2(1;6).

Vorhaus, Renee. 1984. Strategies for reading in a second language. *Journal of Reading* 27(5):412–416.

Waldrop, M. Mitchell. 1984. The necessity of knowledge. *Science* 223(March 23, 1984):1279-1282.

Walker, Decker F. and Robert D. Hess. 1984. *Instructional software: principles and perspectives for design and* Belmont, Calif.: Wadsworth Publishing Company.

Wanat, S. 1977. Introduction. In *Issues in evaluating reading. Papers in Applied Linguistics,* Series I, S. Wanat (Ed.), v-xi. Arlington, Va: Center for Applied Linguistics.

Watt, Dan. 1984. Update on LOGO: new versions of LOGO abound. *Popular Computing Guide to Computers in Education,* Fall, 1984:66-69.

Weaver, Constance. 1980. *Psycholinguistics and reading: from process to practice.* Cambridge, Mass.: Winthrop.

West, Michael (Ed.). 1953. *General service list of English words.* London: Longman.

Widdowson, Henry. 1978. *Teaching language as communication,* 88-91. Oxford: Oxford University Press.

―――. 1979. The process and purpose of reading. In *Explorations in applied linguistics,* Henry Widdowson (Ed.), 171-183. New York: Oxford University Press.

―――. 1983. *Learning purpose and language use.* New York: Oxford University Press.

―――. 1984. Reading and communication. In *Reading in a foreign language.* J. C. Alderson and A. H. Urquhart (Eds.), 213-226. New York: Longman.

Winograd, Terry. 1984. Computer software for working with language. *Scientific American* 251(3):130-45.

Wittrock, Merlin. 1981. Reading comprehension. In *Neuropsychological and cognitive processes in reading,* F. J. Pirozzoli and M. Wittrock (Eds.), 229-259. New York: Academic Press.

Wood, Nancy. 1984. *Improving reading.* New York: Holt, Rinehart and Winston.

Wyatt, David H. 1983. Computer-assisted language instruction: present state and future prospects. In *System, Special Issue: Computer-Assisted Language Instruction.* David H. Wyatt (Ed.), 11(1):3-11.

―――. 1984. Computer-assisted teaching and testing of reading and listening. *Foreign Language Annals* 17:393-419.

Yamamoto, Mitsu. 1977. *Bridges to fear.* Rowley, Mass.: Newbury House.

Yorio C. A. 1971. Some sources of reading problems in foreign language learners. *Language Learning,* 21(1):107-115.

Yorkey, Richard C. 1970. *Study skills for students of English as a second language.* New York: McGraw-Hill.

―――. 1982. *Study skills for students of English as a second language.* 2nd ed. New York: McGraw-Hill Book Company.

Zukowski/Faust, Jean; Susan S. Johnson; and Clark S. Atkinson. 1983. *Between the Lines.* New York: Holt, Rinehart and Winston.

Zukowski/Faust, Jean; Susan S. Johnson; Clark S. Atkinson; and Elizabeth Templin. 1982. *In Context.* New York: Holt, Rinehart and Winston.

Index

Index

academic success, 37-38, 51, 72, 161

achievement tests (see tests)

activities (see reading rate building
    activities and prereading activities)

Adams, M., 62

Adams, W. R., 57, 59, 70

Addams, S., 205

administrator
  role of, 26, 35, 43-45, 48, 55-56, 162,
  170

adventure games, 205, 208

AI (see artificial intelligence), 203, 207

Alderson, C., 30, 32, 169, 181

alphabetic systems (see orthographic
    systems)

Al Rufai, M. H., 30

analytic tests (see tests)

Anderson, H., 35

Anderson, J., 72

Anderson, R., 9, 32

antonyms, 70, 170

anxiety, 79, 99, 102

application skills, 39, 41

approach, 26-27, 33, 35

Aronson, D., 211

artificial intelligence (AI), 183

Asimov, I., 35

atmosphere, anxiety free, 99

Ausubel, D., 196

authentic reading materials (see texts,
    natural/authentic), 137

author's stance, 39

automaticity, 7, 44, 56

Bachman, L., 169

background knowledge information,
    30, 34-35, 36, 39, 55, 62, 140, 149,
    165-167

Baker, R. L., 194

Baltra, A., 185

bar graphs, 110-111

Barkman, B., 13, 23

Barrus, K., 78, 102

Bateson, G., 35

Baudoin, E. M., 109

Baum, J., 184

Beale, A., 185

Beck, I., 32, 211

Berliner, D., 48, 87

Berman, R., 32, 37

Bettelheim, B., 127

blackout (cloze) exercises, 85-87

Blanton, W. E., *et al*, 166-167

Blau, S., 33

Blohm, P. J., 196, 200, 209

Bloom, B., 198

book reports, 65-66, 71

boredom, 78

bottom-up (see reading model, reading
    skills)

Bradley, V. N., 184

Bradley-Johnson, S., 168, 181

branching, 184, 198, 207

Briggs, L., 211

Brown, B., 78, 102

Brown, G., 32, 35, 48, 159

Brown, J. D., 181

Brown, P. J., 41

building success into reading program,
    51, 99

Burns, P., 168

Credits

Pp. 91-92, "Notes from the Sea" adapted from "Bottle Overboard" by Gordon Gaskill (*Reader's Digest*, May 1959), taken from *Reader's Digest Reading* © 1959, 1963 by the Reader's Digest Association, Inc. Reprinted with permission; p. 129, Sutherland et al, *English Alfa, Book 4*, page 22. Copyright © 1981 by Houghton Mifflin Company. Reprinted by permission of Houghton Mifflin Company; pp. 130-131, courtesy of Addison-Wesley Publishing Company; pp. 132-133, Stevick, Earl W., *A Workbook in Language Teaching* and Abingdon Press; p. 135 (photo) Reprinted by permission of *Nature* 2-16-84, cover photo. Copyright © 1984 Macmillan Journals Limited; pp. 135-136, Copyright 1984 Time Inc. All rights reserved. Reprinted by permission from *Time*.; p. 141, Hulsizer and Lazarus, *The World of Physics* © 1972, 1977 Addison-Wesley Publishing Company. Reprinted with permission.; pp. 150-152, © 1984 *Los Angeles Times*. Reprinted by permission. pp. 172-173, Dishner, Ernest and John Readence, "Group Informal Reading Inventory," *Reading World* October, 1977, pp. 42-43 and permission of the College Reading Association; p. 174, Rakes, Thomas, Joyce Choate and Gayle Waller, *Individual Evaluation Procedures in Reading* © 1983. Adapted by permission of Prentice-Hall, Inc., Englewood Cliffs, NJ.

About the Authors

Sharon Allerson is an Assistant Lecturer at the American Language Institute at USC. Previously, she taught EFL in Morocco and Mexico, and ESL at Ohio University and Southern Illinois University, where she was Reading Coordinator. She is currently a doctoral candidate in Curriculum and Instruction at USC. Her research interests include reading instruction/assessment, curriculum design, materials development and cross-cultural communication.

Susan Young Dever is an Instructional Design Specialist with the Humanities Audio Visual Center, USC. She has worked intensively in foreign language instructional media design and production and has taught ESL/EFL at the university, adult, and secondary levels in Nigeria, Mexico, and the United States. She has an M.A. in Applied Linguistics and is a doctoral candidate in Instructional Technology.

Fraida Dubin is Associate Professor of English as a Second Language/Education at USC. She has been a classroom teacher, teacher trainer, and administrator in India, Greece, Iran, Israel, Canada, Botswana, and Hungary. Among her publications, she is co-author of three second language reading skills texts: *Reading by All Means, Three Easy Pieces,* and *Reading on Purpose.*

David E. Eskey is Director of the American Language Institute and Associate Professor of Education at USC. He has also taught at Carnegie-Mellon University, the University of Pittsburgh, the American University of Beirut in Lebanon, and Thammasat University in Thailand. He has published in various journals on the subjects of ESL methodology, course design, and, especially, the teaching of second language reading.

William Grabe is an Assistant Professor in the ESL MA program at Northern Arizona University. He has taught ESL/EFL over the last 12 years

247

in Morocco, China, and various parts of the United States. His research interests include written discourse analysis, language policy, literacy, and the application of linguistic theory to teaching practice.

Linda Jensen is a Lecturer at the American Language Institute, USC, and at Santa Monica College. Previously, she was a Fulbright Lecturer in Italy involved in teacher-training. She has also taught ESL at San Francisco State University, and has taught EFL in Portugal. Her areas of interest are reading theory and teaching reading and composition.

Denise Mahon has taught reading to native and non-native speakers of English at San Francisco State University, and has trained teachers in reading at Southern Illinois University and the Shanghai Foreign Languages Institute, where she was a Fulbright Lecturer. Now at the University of California, Berkeley, she has published a variety of articles on education.

Fredricka Stoller is an Instructor in the English Department at Northern Arizona University. She has also taught ESL at the American Language Institute, USC, and Harvard University, and EFL in Barcelona, Spain. Her primary interests include reading theory and instruction, curriculum and materials, and cross-cultural communication.